Islamic movements in Egypt, Pakistan and Iran

Islamic movements in Egypt, Pakistan and Iran

AN ANNOTATED BIBLIOGRAPHY

Asaf Hussain

Mansell Publishing Limited

ISBN   0 7201 1648 1

Mansell Publishing Limited, 6 All Saints Street, London N1 9RL

First Published 1983

Distributed in the United States and Canada by The H. W. Wilson Company, 950 University Avenue, Bronx, New York 10452.

© Asaf Hussain 1983

British Library Cataloguing in Publication Data

Hussain, Asaf
    Islamic movements in Egypt, Pakistan and Iran.
    1. Muslims in Egypt—History—Bibliography
    2. Muslims in Pakistan—History—Bibliography
    3. Muslims in Iran—History—Bibliography
    4. Egypt—History—Bibliography
    5. Pakistan—History—Bibliography
    6. Iran—History—Bibliography
    I. Title
    016′.297′0962   DT77

ISBN 0-7201-1648-1

Printed in Great Britain

Dedicated with love
to
Farkhanda Rashid
and
Ahmad Rashid

Contents

Preface

Perhaps no other political event in the late 1970s has attracted such world wide attention as the Islamic Revolution in Iran. Scholars from various countries, particularly from those in the West, have endeavoured to justify the revolution in terms of their favourite theories. My interest in this unique event was prompted by a special interest in political revolutions and a personal interest in the political role of Islam in Muslim societies. While working at the Islamic Foundation in Leicester which had been established by members of another Islamic movement, the *Jamaat-i-Islami*, I gave a seminar on the Islamic Revolution in Iran and began working on a book on the same subject. As I became increasingly aware of the amount of ignorance, misunderstanding and deliberate distortion that was present in analyses of the Islamic Revolution, the decision to prepare this bibliography also matured.

In order to make the bibliography a comprehensive research tool on Islamic movements, I have selected two other powerful movements that have, in their own rights, blazened the path of Islam since the beginning of this century. These are the *Ikhwan al-Muslimun* in Egypt and the *Jamaat-i-Islami* in Pakistan.

In the preparation of this work a very large number of books and journals have been consulted in many libraries both in the United Kingdom and Pakistan. A special trip was taken to Iran in February 1982, to consult published materials for this bibliography, and to conduct interviews for another book on Iran. Most of the materials available were in the Persian language and the items in English were in journals such as *Echo of Islam*, *Message of Revolution*, *Mahjubah* and the *Islamic Republic Party Weekly Magazine*, etc. These articles were often repetitive, and only those

ix

items relevant to the subject matter were selected. A few books published in English have also been included.

I am grateful to my colleagues at the Islamic Foundation as well as at the Quaid-i-Azam University for encouraging me in this venture. I must also acknowledge with thanks the help of Mrs. Hollingworth and my wife Freda in typing and re-typing many parts of this book with patience.

Asaf Hussain
Visiting Professor
Department of International Relations
Quaid-i-Azam University
Islamabad

Introduction

Islam has been used as a political instrument by Muslim rulers over the centuries. The Arab, Ottoman, Persian and Moghul empires were created in the name of Islam and yet they cannot be referred to as Islamic empires as the dominating factor was the king and not the Qur'an. The ideological foundations of these empires were weak and as such they easily disintegrated in the face of corrupting forces that attacked them both from within and from without. Many of the rulers of these empires had nothing to fight for except their own vested interests. Their contribution, if any, was a negative one, in that they sought to confine Islam within the walls of the beautiful mosques they had constructed in their empires.

The political scene in the twentieth-century Muslim world is no different. The Muslim ruling classes have sought to safeguard their power and privileges through the influence of colonialism, neo-colonialism and imperialism. Some countries in the Middle East such as Saudi Arabia, Egypt and the late Shah's Iran had become client states of US imperialism while some others came under the sphere of influence of Russian imperialism. Despite internal political corruption and the decadence that plagues the Muslim world together with the superpower hegemony that keeps it divided, there remains one force that is free in spite of its misuse, and that is the force of Islam. Someone, somewhere, has always risen up with the banner of Islam and started an Islamic movement that has sought to bring about Islamic change in Muslim and non-Muslim countries. The dynamism of such movements is derived from the message of the Qur'an and not from alien ideologies such as nationalism, communism, or socialism, which have become prevalent in Muslim countries since the beginning of this century. This book deals with some of the Islamic movements that have arisen in the twentieth century.

Not many people are aware of the existence of such Islamic movements in Muslim countries and there is a dearth of studies on them. The rulers of many Muslim countries themselves do not support Islamic movements as they percieve them as some kind of sinister, conspiring, fanatical or anti-state groups. These movements pose a threat to the power positions of the political elites of the Muslim world whose vested interests, autocratic rule and secular regimes attempt to forestall any checks on their power and ambitions. Prominent members of many Islamic movements have been imprisoned, tortured, publicly executed or hanged in jails. The most common course of action taken by the ruling elite has been to ban such movements. In the face of such political oppression, Islamic movements have often had to operate from exile in another country or from the underground within the same country.

Muslim rulers who do not try to politically legitimize their regimes through Islam, live in fear of its revolutionary potential. They attempt to attain political stability by leaning on one superpower or another and use them as crutches to safeguard their vested interests. The Pahlavis thus imported thousands of American personnel to streamline their army and secret police force (SAVAK) in order to control the people. The United States spent about $25,000,000 on the personal security of President Sadat to maintain him in office. The Saudis have been so perturbed by the Islamic revolution in Iran and the internal uprising in 1979 that they have sought US assurances for protection.

The superpowers are also wary of Islamic movements because of the threat they pose to imperialism and their ideologies of capitalism or communism. In the last century some colonial governments were actively engaged in fighting Islamic movements in countries like Algeria and Sudan. More recently, the United States has learnt a difficult lesson from the Iranian movement. Consequently Jansen, in his article 'International Islam' (*The Economist*, 3 January 1980) has correctly observed that:

Today Islam and the modern western world confront and challenge each other. No other major religion poses such a challenge to the west. Not Christianity, which is part of the western world and which has been eaten up from within by the acids of modernity. Not Hinduism and Buddhism, because their radiation to the west has been and is on a high, ethereal plane. And not Judaism, which is too small and tribal a faith. No guru, no swami, no lama, no rabbi has had any impact on the west comparable to that exerted by the Caliph, the Mahdi and the Ayatollah, or by that stereotype haunting the wesern imagination, the 'Mullah' leading 'the Jihad'. This is because Islam has confronted the west militarily off and on for 1,500 years, and the present is an 'on' period.

With such an attitude one of the first things that the Americans did after the Islamic revolution in Iran was to order their security agencies to conduct research studies on what has been labelled as fundamentalist Islam. With all the scholarship at their disposal it is still debatable if they will succeed in understanding Islam. By attempting to analyse Islam through modernization theories or Marxist perspectives, western scholarship limits itself and fails to realise the revolutionary potential of Islam.

Islamic movements cannot be compared to other nationalist political movements because they do not seek power and position as an end in themselves but rather as a means of attaining the objective of totally transforming Muslim polities along Islamic lines. Such movements mobilize the masses to wage a *Jihad* (struggle) against the rulers of the country and try to transform it into an Islamic society with a politico-economic system based on principles derived from the Qur'an. There is serious internal tension in almost every Muslim country between the rulers who use Islam as a means of subjugating or pacifying the masses and the Islamic movements for whom it is imperative to attain the Islamic end. There are no compromises, alliances or coalitions that can deter an Islamic movement from its objectives and principles. Often such tensions result in conflict between the two forces. Such conflicts have raged in the world of Islam since its inception and will, in all probability, continue to do so in the future.

This bibliography has restricted itself to three Islamic movements which have been selected because they are well known and their impact has been felt across transnational boundaries. The Iranian movement can be said to have had a global impact. A knowledge of any two of these movements (the Iranian one being essential) would be adequate to equip the reader with a thorough understanding of the study of any other Islamic movements in the world. It is also one very important method of finding out what Islam is really about. The label 'fundamentalist Islam' is apt in the sense that the fundamental belief system of Islam does not separate religion from politics and is thus opposed to any syncretism of it or the orientalist interpretations of it. It cannot be confined to mosques and regulated through state control as has happened in many Muslim countries, because in Islam the relationship of man to God is regulated by and is dependent upon the relationship of man to man.

For the reader who does not have the opportunity to consult all the sources mentioned in the bibliography, the annotations should provide adequate information on the sources. An attempt has been made to bring out in each annotation the essential points of the article or book and in many cases the viewpoints of the authors have been given in their own words. Thus, although this bibliography does not claim to have included all sources, the items included should provide the reader with sound insight into these Islamic movements.

The selection of items included was based on three criteria: (1) that an item should contribute to the general knowledge about the Islamic movement; (2) the item should throw light on some issue or problem confronted or resolved by the Islamic movement; and, (3) the items should project analyses of Islamic movements from different perspectives (modernization theory, Marxist, Islamic, etc.). A good research tool should include all aspects necessary for the study of a particular subject.

As stated earlier, not many people are familiar with the role of Islamic movements in Egypt, Pakistan or Iran. As such, a brief introduction precedes the annotated bibliography of each Islamic movement. This includes a brief biography of the founder of the movement, its ideology, its political activities and the current status of the movement.

The items listed in the biography have been taken from journals and books, but not newspapers. Greater emphasis has been placed upon the scholarly quality of the analyses rather than on journalistic exposes or propaganda materials. In addition, the bibliography has only focused on materials published in the English language due to limitations of space. There is often a variation in the English spelling of Islamic names. For example, the Qur'an is also spelt as Koran, Mawdudi as Maudoodi, Khomeini as Khumayni, etc. These have been left as spelt by the various authors and are not spelling mistakes.

It is hoped that what is being presented in this annotated bibliography will serve as a useful research tool for scholars and will contribute towards a better appreciation and understanding of Islam. The conclusions to be drawn from the materials are left to the readers.

The Islamic Movement
in Egypt

The Islamic movement in Egypt

The beginning of the twentieth century saw the emergence of the first powerful Islamic movement in the Muslim world, that which emanated from Egypt. Earlier, the influence of men such as al-Afghani and Mohammad Abdou from the al-Azhar in Cairo had awakened the Muslims to a new consciousness of the suppression of their Islamic identity while tied to the yoke of colonialism. But in giving it political expression and political direction through Islam, the credit can only go to one man, Hassan al-Banna.

Hassan al-Banna was born in 1906 in the province of Buhrya in Egypt. His father was an Imam and he was brought up with a strict religious training. His early religious development was considerably influenced by his school teacher, Shaykh Mohammad Zahran. By the age of twelve, while still at school, he became involved with the work of various religious societies that helped in the development of his skills and organizational abilities.

From an early age al-Banna was interested in Sufism and was a member of the *Dhikr* circle as well as the Hasafiyyah Sufi orders. In 1923 he went to Cairo to train at the Dar al-Ulum. The city had a profound influence on young Hassan's mind, particularly when he saw the un-Islamic practices that were rampant in the capital.

The Murshid-e-Aam

In 1927, at the age of twenty-one, Hassan al-Banna graduated from the Dar al-Ulum and took up a teaching post in the State school system. He was active in working for Islam during his teaching career but he was not content with it. He longed for collective action in the service of Islam.

3

In 1928 he founded the *Ikhwan* (the Muslim Brotherhood) together with six friends from Ismailiya. He became known as the *Murshid-e-Aam* (The supreme guide) and until his death continued to strengthen the foundations of the *Ikhwan*. In 1932, he moved its headquarters to Cairo where its membership increased and included a cross-section of Egyptian society, ranging from civil servants, students, urban labourers to peasants. As membership of the *Ikhwan* increased, organizational expansion was supervised by al-Banna. Membership of the *Ikhwan* was arranged in a hierarchal order in which roles and responsibilites were skillfully allocated. As the Brothers devoted their time and energy with an ardent fervour to the task the *Ikhwan* began to attract the attention of the masses.

Al-Banna's whole life had been devoted to the service of Islam and his objective was very clear; to implement an Islamic order in Egypt. While he had made himself very popular among the masses he had also made many enemies. Al-Banna's charisma and commitment to Islam was such that it endeared him to the masses which in turn made those in power feel insecure, and he was eventually assassinated by the secret police in broad day-light on 12 February 1949. Such was the fear of a revolt of the masses that his funeral procession was escorted by tanks and armoured cars, and the Prime Minister of the day stopped saying his Friday prayers in public for fear of his life. What then were the ideas of Hassan al-Banna which made ruling elite feel so insecure? A brief exposition of his ideas in his words will explain the Islamic ideology of the man.

Hassan al-Banna's Political Thought

Hassan al-Banna came from a family of modest means and had seen not only the poverty of his fellow Muslims but had also experienced British colonial rule in the city where he grew up. For al-Banna 'the civilisation of the West, which was brilliant by virtue of its scientific perfection for a long time, and which subjugated the whole world with the products of this science to its states and nations, is now bankrupt and in decline. Its foundations are crumbling, and its institutions and guiding principles are falling apart. Its political foundations are being destroyed by dictatorship: and its economic foundations are being swept by crises.'[1]

Al-Banna, however, was not only critical of the West: the state of the Third World of which he was a product was no better, for nations were like individuals who had their strengths and weaknesses, youth and old age, and who could be afflicted with ailments as well. Al-Banna's diagnosis of the nations was very perceptive for in his words

the disease afflicting these Eastern nations assumes a variety of aspects and has many symptoms. It has done harm to every expression of their lives, for they have been assailed on the political side by imperialist aggression on the part of their enemies, and by factionalism, rivalry, division and disunity on the part of their sons. They have been assailed on the economic side by the propagation of usurious practices

4

throughout all their social classes, and the exploitation of their resources and natural treasures by foreign companies. They have been
afflicted on the intellectual side by anarchy, defection and heresy
which destroy their religious beliefs and overthrow the ideals within
their sons' breasts. They have been assailed on the sociological side by
licentiousness of manners and mores, and through the sloughing off of
the restraints of the humanitarian virtues they inherited from their
glorious, fortunate ancestors; while through imitation of the West, the
viper's venom creeps insidiously into their affairs, poisoning their blood
and sullying the purity of their well-being. They have been assailed
through the workings of a positive law which does not restrain the
criminal, chastise the assailant, or repel the unjust; nor does it even for
one day take the place of the divinely revealed laws which the Creator
of creation, the Master of the Kingdom, and the Lord of souls and
their Originator, has set down. They have been assailed also through
anarchy in their policy of education and training, which stands in the
way effectively guiding their present generations, the men of their
future and those who will be responsible for bringing about their
resurgence. They have been assailed on the spiritual side by a death-
dealing despair, a murderous apathy, a shameful cowardice, an ignoble
humility, an all pervading impotence, a niggardliness and an egocen-
tricity which prevents people from making any effort, preclude self-
sacrifice, and thrust the nation from the ranks of earnest strivers into
those of triflers and gamesters. What hope is there for a nation against
which all these factors, in their strongest manifestations and most
extreme forms, have been conjoined for the assault ... But God and
the believers will not tolerate this. Brother this is the diagnosis which
the Brotherhood make of the ailments of this Umma, and this is what
they are doing in order to cure it of them and to restore it is lost health
and strength.[2]

Al-Banna could have easily turned a blind eye to the disease he
perceived in the Umma had he not had any alternative. But Islam was
his source of strength and that made him part ways with the decadent
generation which he observed in his country. A beginning had to be
made for

the creation of nations, the education of peoples, the realisation of
hopes, and the defence of principles demand of their nation which tries
to achieve them—or, at any rate, of the group which is proselytising
for them—a mighty spiritual strength which may be manifested in
numerous ways: a strong will which no weakness can penetrate; a
steady loyalty unassailable by fickleness or treachery, a noble spirit of
self sacrifice, unaffected by greed or avarice, a knowledge of the principle, a faith in it, and a proper assessment of its value which is immune
to error in its regard ... Every people that has lost these four qualities
or ... whose leaders and proselytisers for reform have lost them, is a

wretched, frivolous people which neither comes to any good nor realises any hope.[3]

Such a group which would lead the Islamic movement would try to convince all types of Muslims and mobilise them. Some of them may be believers who have faith in the mission of the group, but others such as the waverer (anyone to whom truth remains unclear), the opportunist (who does not wish to lend his aid except after finding out how much he will get back as profit) and the prejudiced (who had misgivings about the group)—all have to be made aware of the cause of Islam. The group which leads the Islamic movement must therefore establish its credibility with the masses. In this matter al-Banna writes that the people should

> know that we love them more than ourselves, and that it is pleasing to us to be offered up as a sacrifice for their greatness, if we must make such a sacrifice, and to pay the price for their glory, their nobility, their religion, and their hopes, if we possess the requisite wealth. One thing alone has persuaded us to take this position in their regard—the fellow feeling which seizes our hearts, masters our emotions, keeps us from sleep, and brings us to tears. It is difficult, it is indeed very difficult, to see how our people are presently beleaguered, and then to resign ourselves to humility, or accept a submissive role, or abandon ourselves to despair. For when we work for mankind in God's way, we work harder for ourselves, we are for you and no one else, beloved, nor shall we ever be against you, even for a day.[4]

Al-Banna did not consider himself superior but with his total commitment to the Umma the difference was in the understanding of Islam for 'though we are all in accord in our faith . . . among them it is aneasthetised faith, dormant within their souls, one to which they do not wish to submit and according to whose dictates they do not wish to act whereas it is a burning, blazing, intense faith fully awakened in the souls of the Muslim Brotherhood'.[5] What was this understanding of the Islam which in the masses was considered an anaeasthetized faith? Al-Banna elucidates this by pointing out that the

> term Islamic . . . has a meaning broader than the narrow definition understood by people generally. We believe that Islam is an all embracing concept which regulates every aspect of life, adjudicating on everyone its concerns and prescribing for it a solid and rigorous order. It does not stand helpless before life's problems, nor the steps one must take to improve mankind. Some people mistakenly understand by Islam something restricted to certain types of religious observances or spiritual exercises, and confine themselves and their understanding to these narrow areas determined by their limited grasp. But we understand Islam . . . as regulating the affairs of men in this world and the next. We do not make this claim out of presumption; nor do we enlarge upon it on the basis of our own preconception, rather it is based solely

on our understanding of the Book of God and the biographies of the first Muslims. If the reader wishes to understand the mission of the Muslim Brotherhood in the sense broader than the mere word Islamic, let him take up his Quran and rid himself of whimsy and prejudgment. Then he will get to understand what the Quran is about, and we will see right there the mission of the Muslim Brotherhood.[6]

With such an understanding of Islam the mission of every Islamic movement becomes political.

Al-Banna believed that it was impossible to obtain the consensus of all Muslims on minor points of conflict among themselves but the main goal was to unite the Muslims and the 'Muslim Brotherhood know that there is a sociological aspect which is of the utmost importance for the continued existence of this faith. How fine it would be, if the efforts of the Muslim proselytisers were directed towards organizing people around the idea of fighting these dangerous issues which threaten the faith at its very root.'[7]

Hassan al-Banna practised what he preached and his life was a struggle against the rulers of his times for he believed that *Jihad* was a 'religious duty on every Muslim, categorically and rigorously from which there is neither evasion nor escape.'[8] The influence of Hassan al-Banna's ideas and his islamic movement spread through the Muslim world and other movements such as the *Jamaat* were inspired by it. Al-Banna's struggle in Egypt did not go in vain because it has continued and still continues to inspire young Egyptians in the latter half of the twentieth century.

The Movement

The zeal and fervour with which the *Ikhwan* carried out its mission entrenched it in urban and rural areas and its strongest support base was among the masses. When the *Ikhwan* moved its headquarters from Ismailiya to Cairo, old and young people flocked to the Mosques, to hear the members speak. Wherever there were people, even in the coffee houses and clubs, *Ikhwan* members spoke about Islam and inspired the people. Such attentive audiences, however, were indicative not only of the *Ikhwan*'s popularity but also of its rapid growth. Within 20 years the membership totalled two million people and the movement had established 2,000 branches all over Egypt. Membership consisted of people who were committed to the service of Islam and were ready to sacrifice everything they had for it.

During World War II, the *Ikhwan* wanted Egypt to stay neutral and not involve itself and sacrifice its young men for the wars of the West. But when the homeland of the Muslim was threatened, the *Ikhwan* joined the struggle. Its Mujahideen fought in the Palestinian war in 1948 and its courage surpassed that of the Egyptian army. It even helped an Egyptian garrison when it was besieged. The Egyptian army, frustrated and humiliated at the outcome of the Palestinian war, was tormented with intrigues and plots which culminated in the coup d'état of 1952. But the government of the day was disturbed more by the performance of the *Ikhwan* and thought that it was going to lead a revolution. In order to safeguard its position the Egyptian monarchy banned the movement in November 1948. Thousands of its members were arrested and from then onwards the story of trials of the *Ikhwan* membership can be written in blood. A year later, Hassan al-Banna was assassinated, and only in 1951 did the *Ikhwan* after a legal battle in the Egyptian supreme court, succeed in getting the ban lifted.

Before his death, al-Banna had already established some links with the army. The latter did not have any grassroot influence and needed support from the movement. These links continued and the *Ikhwan* played a prominent role in the army's successful overthrow of the monarchy in 1952. The *Ikhwan* soon started exerting pressure on Nasser's regime to implement the Islamic order and uplift itself from the morass of indignity and subjugation to the vested interests of imperialism. But Nasser's personal ambition began to dominate the revolution. The colonial trained military had developed a secular outlook and was reluctant to implement the *Ikhwan's* Islamic prescriptions.

After the new regime's overtures to buy off the *Ikhwan* failed, relations between the two began to deteriorate. In 1953, when the regime formed its own party, the only opponent who could challenge its power was the *Ikhwan*. The regime then started planning the downfall of the *Ikhwan*. An assassination attempt on Nasser's life provided the cue and in 1954 a thousand members of the *Ikhwan* were arrested, beaten up, tortured, and imprisoned. Some of its key leaders were executed. By 1964 the *Ikhwan* had regained its strength and in 1965 another purge was unleashed on it. This time some 20,000 members were arrested, including some prominent *Ikhwan* women. A new wave of torture and executions followed and the *Ikhwan* was banned.

The organization of the *Ikhwan* had a centralized pyramidal structure with a network of regional, district and local organizations. The most significant aspect of the movement was its military arm known as the *Firaq al-Jawwala* (the rover troops). These men were given active military training and operated as family cells of five to seven members in cities and towns. They joined other organizations and institutions and were activated only when needed for *Jihad*.

The Ideologue of the Ikhwan

In order to ensure survival, any successful movement must be capable of attracting men who can forge ahead with new ideas despite the setbacks suffered by it. Where this does not happen, or the movement attracts men of mediocre ability to its leadership, the power of the movement is diminished if not terminated. The *Ikhwan* was lucky in this respect for it had attracted determined men who were totally committed to Islam. After Hassan al-Banna's assassination in 1949 the leadership of the *Ikhwan* was in the hands of competent men like Hassan al-Hodeibi who was elected as the *Murshid-e-Aam* of the movement. Another prominent figure Abdul Kader Audah, became the secretary of the movement. However, one of the most important members of the movement at that time was Sayyid Qutb (1906–66) who can be considered as the ideologue of the *Ikhwan*. His writings, next to Hassan al-Banna's, had a widespread influence on the minds of the people and is considered essential reading for any study of the *Ikhwan*.

Sayyid Qutb was born in 1906 in the Assiut district of Egypt. His parents were very religious and Qutb received his early religious training from them. Later when the family moved to Halwan—a satellite town of Cairo—Qutb's education started at Tajhizia Darul Uloom, a secondary school in Cairo. After completing his education here he joined Cairo University in 1929 from where he obtained the Bachelor of Arts degree in Education in 1933. After some time he was appointed inspector of Schools in the Ministry of Education from where he proceeded to study the modern system of education and training. His visit to the USA and his observation of a totally materialist civilization had a profound influence on him.

After his return he turned towards the *Ikhwan* and in 1945 joined the movement. His writings soon started to make an impact and by 1952 he was in charge of the *Ikhwan's* Department of Propagation of the Message and a member of the working committee of the *Ikhwan*. In 1954 he became the Chief Editor of the *Ikhwan* journal *Al-Ikhwan al-Muslimoon*. By this time Qutb's political activities had not only drawn him into the political arena but also into conflict with the military regime of Colonel Nasser. He opposed the Anglo-Egyptian Pact entered into by Nasser with the British in July 1954. The military reacted by banning the *Ikhwan* paper in September 1954. As the movement was further drawn into conflict with the military regime, the latter began to fear that its influence on the masses would corrode its own chances of remaining in power. A deadly conflict between the *Ikhwan* and the military was therefore inevitable.

This did not take long and the government, accusing the members of the *Ikhwan* of hatching conspiracies against it, arrested its leaders and thousands of its followers and sympathisers. Sayyid Qutb was among them and in July 1955 he was sentenced to 15 years imprisonment. Some of his most important works like *Fi Zilal al-Quran* (*Under the shade of Quran*)—a commentary—was completed under conditions of extreme pain and suffering in prison. In 1964 on the request of the President of Iraq (Abdus Salam Arif) Nasser ordered his release. But the regime felt very uncomfortable with his release and after a year Qutb was again arrested on charges of conspiring to overthrow the government. His last book *Ma Alim Fil Tareeq* (*Milestones*) was considered as inciting the people to revolution and a military tribunal sentenced him to death. Along with two other companions, one of them being Abdul Kader

Audah, he was hanged on 29 August 1966. The death of Qutb was a great blow to the *Ikhwan* but his writings have continued to be published in many languages and its tremendous influence on the minds of the young people facilitates recruitment to the leadership of the Islamic movement in Egypt.

Syed Qutb had made a thorough study of human societies and found that the only society whose foundations rested on the principles of justice was the Islamic society. The other society was the *Jahiliyyah* society. *Jahiliyyah* was a state of ignorance of divine guidance for mankind; thus any society was considered as 'a *Jahili* society which does not dedicate itself to God alone, in its belief and ideas, in its observances of worship, and in its legal regulations'.[9]

According to this definition, there are many kinds of *Jahili* societies in the world today. Firstly, there was the communist society, which due to its atheistic doctrines, denied the existence of God. Secondly, there were the idolatrous societies which worshipped idols of gods and goddesses such as those that exist in India, Africa, etc. Thirdly, the Jewish and Christian societies are afflicted with *Jahiliyyah* because they have distorted their original beliefs and scriptures and have ascribed the attributes of God to other beings such as in the doctrines of Trinity and in regarding Jesus as the son of God. Lastly, all Muslim societies are *Jahili* societies and this is not because they worship anyone other than God but 'because their way of life is not based on submission to God alone ... some openly declare their secularism and negate all relationships with the religion, some others pay respects to the religion only with their mouths, but in their social life they have completely abandoned it'.[10]

All such societies are a result of man's exploitation of his fellow men. From the very beginnings of human history, man's freedom has been determined by limits prescribed by other men so that they can dominate them. This is not restricted to the domination of one man over another but of ideologies, nations and civilizations over another. The examples of colonialism in the past centuries and of neo-colonialism and imperialism in today's world are apparent.

Islam is a religion which advocates 'a universal declaration of the freedom of man from servitude to other men and from servitude to his own desires'.[11] Thus Islam opposes not only man's domination over other men but man's own desires which know no limit and lays the foundations of the *Jahiliyyah* civilization for although the outward manifestations of *Jahiliyyah* 'may be different during different epochs, yet its roots are the same. Its roots are in human desires, which do not let people come out of their ignorance and self-importance, or in the interests of some persons or some classes or some nations or some races, whose interests prevail over the demand for justice, truth and goodness'.[12] But curbing human desires is necessary for Islam 'did not come to support people's desires, which are expressed in their concepts, institutions, modes of living and habits and traditions, whether they were prevalent at the advent of Islam

10

or are prevalent now both in the East and the West. Islam does not sanction the rule of selfish desires'.[13] In other words human beings are not left to feed their own desires in any directions they want and rule over people according to their whims and fancies. Human history is a glaring example of how great empires have vanished when its ruling elite degenerated and became decadent.

Furthermore, the people who live a *Jahiliyyah* life are powerful. They have to be if they have to live by domination and exploitation over others. As such *Jahiliyyah* society has its own powerful mechanism to spread its tentacles and influence all over the world. In fact, the 'whole environment, peoples beliefs and ideas, habits and art, rules and laws— is *Jahiliyyah*, even to the extent that what we consider to be Islamic culture, Islamic sources, Islamic philosophy and Islamic thought are all constructs of *Jahiliyyah*'.[14] The *Jahiliyyah* world is therefore powerful, strong and well organized. It cannot be demolished merely by theoretical arguments to counteract its progress. This will not even scratch its surface. The aim therefore should be to abolish the existing system and to replace it with a new system which establishes God's sovereignty over the universe. Thus in order to combat the *Jahiliyyah* system the 'new system should also come into the battlefield as an organized movement and a viable group. It should come into the battlefield with a determination that its strategy, its social organization and the relationship between its individuals should be firmer and more powerful than the existing *Jahili* system'.[15]

The fight against the *Jahiliyyah* system should continue at two levels: the individual and the collective. At the individual level one should purge from within oneself all the influences of *Jahiliyyah*. In Qutb's words

> our primary purpose is to know what way of life is demanded of us by the Quran, the total view of the universe which the Quran wants us to have, what is the nature of our knowledge of God, taught to us by the Quran, the kind of morals and manners which are enjoined by it, and the kind of legal and constitutional system it asks us to establish in the world. We must free ourselves from the clutches of *Jahili* society, *Jahili* concepts, *Jahili* traditions and *Jahili* leadership. Our mission is not to compromise with the practices of *Jahili* society, nor can we be loyal to it. *Jahili* society because of its *Jahili* characteristics is not worthy to be compromised with. Our aim is first to change ourselves so that we may later change society. Our foremost objective is to change the practice of this society'.[16]

At the collective level on the other hand the fight against *Jahili* system must continue through the Islamic movement.

Such a struggle with the *Jahiliyyah* is legitimated in Islam through the *Jihad*. Islam is 'a declaration of the freedom of man from servitude to other men'[17] and as such it recognizes that conflict is essential in human interaction for the *Dar ul-Islam* (home of Islam) is the place where the

11

Islamic state is established with the implementation of the *Shariah*. The rest of the world is *Dar ul-Harb* (home of hostility) with which Muslims can have only two relations: either to have peace with it on the basis of a contractual agreement or be at war with it.[18]

To facilitate *Jihad*, Islam also prescribes a methodology for such a struggle. In the first place, being a practical religion, it acts as a movement and 'treats people as they actually are and uses resources which are in accordance with practical conditions' such as preaching and persuasion for reform ideas and beliefs etc. Secondly, as a practical movement it 'progresses stage by stage, and at every stage it provides resources according to the practical needs of the situation and prepares the ground for the next one'.[19] What it wants 'is to abolish those oppressive political systems under which people are prevented from expressing their freedom to choose whatever beliefs they want, and after that it gives them complete freedom to decide whether they accept Islam or not'.[20] In other words, it does not combat practical situations with abstract theories and ideas for *Jihad* can be both offensive and defensive. Thirdly, any 'new resources or methods which it uses during its progressive movement', do not take it away from its fundamental principles and aims'.[21] In other words, once the goal is clear to the Muslim that of 'submission to one God and rejection of lordship of other men', a new method of achieving its goal can be utilized at every stage. Fourthly after dismantling the *Jahiliyyah* system, Islam does not leave it in a vacuum, but offers a solution by implementing the *Shariah*.

The two essential processes of the *Jihad* methodology is through preaching and the movement. The political power of the *Jahiliyyah* is subtle and rests on a complex of 'interrelated ideological, racial, class, social and economic support',[22] and as such 'preaching and the movement—united, confront the human situation with all the necessary methods. For the achievement of the freedom of man on earth—of all mankind throughout the earth—it is necessary that these two methods should work side by side.'[23] But before one can aim for the transformation of all mankind, waging an Islamic *Jihad* is necessary 'wherever an Islamic community exists' for 'it has a God-given right to step forward and take control of the political authority, so that it may establish the Divine system on earth, while it leaves the matter of belief to individual conscience. When God restrained Muslims from *Jihad* for a certain period, it was a question of strategy rather than of principle; this was a matter pertaining to the requirements of the movement and not to belief'.[24] For Sayyid Qutb then *Jihad* was the sword arm of Islam for overcoming the *Jahili* society and its political system.

The Present Status of the Movement

Although the *Ikhwan* was purged by the Nasser regime it could not be annihilated in spite of the torture, imprisonments and executions. By the end of the June 1967 war, hundreds of *Ikhwan* members were released from Nasser's detention camps. They regrouped quickly and started strengthening their organization.

When Nasser died Sadat succeeded him. Under his regime the *Ikhwan* has again consolidated its position and its comeback has been phenomenal. Sadat had his own reasons for not persecuting the *Ikhwan* in the earlier days because he wanted to use it for erasing Nasser's charisma. He therefore started a process of de-Nasserization and declared Nasser's rule as 'the reign of materialism and atheism'.[25] Sadat was just as anti-*Ikhwan* as Nasser had been. He had directed the press campaign against the *Ikhwan* in 1954 himself,[26] and was a member of the 'People's Tribunal' which had condemned to death many of the Muslim Brothers for their alleged attempt on Nasser's life on 26 October 1954. Over the years he had not become Islamic but sought the *Ikhwan's* support to legitimate his rule and his parties to combat the left wing opposition and pro-Nasser groups.

By 1972, tremendous pressure was placed on him by the *Ikhwan* for the Islamization of Egypt on the imposition of Sharia penalties in cases of adultery, theft, assault, drinking of alcohol. Also Islamic legislation was proposed in many areas such as the constitution, Zakat, mass media, public transportation, schooling, segregation of sexes, etc. There were differences among the members of the *Ikhwan* regarding the manner of its application. One group argued that the above proposed legislation passed through the parliament would be sufficient to Islamize Egypt. The other was of the opinion that it would be too superficial for the government was not really Islamic and therefore its implementation would be half-hearted.[27] While the Brothers debated this among themselves the government adopted a cautious attitude towards it and delayed processing such Islamic legislation. In 1976, the Brothers were allowed to bring out their journal *al-Da'wah* and the monthly *al-Itisam* through which their political opinions were expressed. As Sadat's policies tilted towards the American sphere of influence he initiated talks with Israel which finally resulted in the Camp David agreement. The *Ikhwan* was very critical of Sadat's peace policies.[28]

The *Ikhwan's* critical attitude towards Sadat's policies increased the regime's hostility towards it. Sadat is reported to have formed a Committee which was known as the 'Committee for resisting politicization of religion or religionization of politics' whose aim was to monitor the movements of the members of the Muslim Brotherhood and to prevent the spread of their ideas to others.[29]

Much more than the *Ikhwan* Sadat was afraid of the mushrooming Islamic groups that had arisen during the 1970s. They were all inspired by the *Ikhwan* and some took an even more militant line than the *Ikhwan* itself. Ten years ago Egyptian university's student union elections were influenced by leftist groups but today the influence of Islamic groups (*al-Jamaat al-Islamiyyah*) prevades in all of them. Many young women have taken to wearing the veil of their own accord and have joined

Islamic groups and parties like *Jamaat al-Takfir wa al-Hijrah* (the group that charges society with unbelief and advocates withdrawal from it). This group started in the early 1970s and in July 1977 the government charged it with the kidnapping of Shaykh Husayn al-Dhahabi (former Minister of Waqf) who was later found dead. The group's confrontation with the government forces led to the killing of a number of security officers and more than 400 arrests of men and women belonging to the organization were made. Some were charged with the kidnapping and executed on 19 March 1976 while others were given long prison sentences.

Another group, the *Shahab Muhammad* (Muhammad's Youth), led by Salih Abdallah Sariyyah was started in the early 1970s and it too came into conflict with the government forces in 1974 when it attacked the Military Technical College in Cairo for obtaining weapons, vehicles, etc. Sariyyah and his associates were charged and executed on 10 November 1976 and others were imprisoned. The remaining members of this defunct group joined another *al-Jihad* (the Holy War) and they too were prosecuted by a military court in November 1977. Members of another group, the *Hizb al-Tahrir al-Islamia* (Islamic Liberation Party) were also charged with offences against the state in February 1975 and imprisoned. Other groups such as *Jund Allah* (Allah's Army) and the *Jamaat al-Samawi* have also been hunted and purged.

The rising tide of Islam however, could not be suppressed and conflict between the regime and Islamic groups escalated in 1981 when university campuses all over the country erupted with Islamic fervour. A crowd of some 200,000 members of the *Jamaat-i-Islamiyyah* circulated anti-government leaflets in Cairo's Abidin Square. Another 100,000 members offered their prayers in front of the Presidential palace during the month of Ramadhan. About 400 Muslims from the Salaheddin Mosque rioted and clashed with the police, while another 1000 persons from the Shaykh Kishk's Mosque had to be dispersed with tear gas.

The final confrontation and showdown took place when thousands of members of the *Ikhwan* and other Islamic groups were arrested, the *Ikhwan's* publication *al-Dawa* and other newspapers were banned and the editorial staff of *al-Dawa* and its main spokesman Omar Telmassani were imprisoned. Prominent Muslim preachers like Shaykh Kishk were also arrested for their criticism of the Sadat regime. The government took control of 40,000 privately owned mosques in Egypt. All preachers were required to register with the State and no Friday sermon could be given without prior clearance from the Ministry of Waqfs (Religious Affairs) or the Al-Azhar Centre in Cairo.[30] One observer aptly remarked that the 'Egyptian government pursued its drive to break the political power of Islam'.[31]

Sadat wanted to become the regional gendarme and as such 'offered the United States not merely friendship and co-operation but complete subservience to its purposes as he perceived them' but Egypt is linked by 'indissoluble ties of history, religion, culture and language, and, in consequence, the idea that Sadat, the self-made pariah of the Arab world, can now play the role of regional gendarme is in the long run absurd.'[32] Like his predecessor, Sadat had been one of the greatest enemies of the Islamic movement in Egypt. His association with the *Ikhwan* had started in the early 1940s and he had apparently befriended them only to betray later, during Nasser's and his own reign of terror. His assassination on 6 October 1981 by some soldiers and officers sympathetic to Islam was in a way retribution for his deeds. The struggle of the Islamic movement was once again passing through its severest test.

References

1. C. Wendell, trans. *Five Tracts of Hassan al-Banna.* Calif.: University of California Press, 1978, p. 106.
2. Ibid., pp. 61–62.
3. Ibid., p. 85.
4. Ibid., pp. 40–41.
5. Ibid., p. 44.
6. Ibid., p. 47.
7. Ibid., p. 60.
8. Ibid., p. 133.
9. S. Qutb, *Milestones.* Kuwait: International Islamic Federation of Student Organisations, 1978, p. 148.
10. Ibid., p. 154.
11. Ibid., p. 103.
12. Ibid., p. 247.
13. Ibid., p. 240.
14. Ibid., p. 32.
15. Ibid., p. 83.
16. Ibid., pp. 33–34.
17. Ibid., p. 109.
18. Ibid., p. 221.
19. Ibid., p. 99.
20. Ibid., p. 100.
21. Ibid., p. 101.
22. Ibid., p. 106.
23. Ibid., p. 106.
24. Ibid., p. 139.
25. Sadat speech 28 September 1977. *al-Jumhuriyyah*, 29 September, 1977.
26. See *al-Jumhuriyyah*, 6, 9, 11, 14, 16 September 1954.
27. Yusuf al-Qardawi, *Al-Hall al-Islam.* Beirut: Muassasat al-Risalah, 1974, pp. 183–93.
28. *al-Dawah*, November 1977, pp. 50–51. December 1977, pp. 50–51. February 1978, pp. 2–3. March 1978, pp. 42–43. April 1978, pp. 16–17, and 26–27. May 1978, pp. 14–15 and 20–21. July 1978, pp. 2–3. October 1978, pp. 2–3.
29. *Al-Akhbar*, (Kuwait) 28 April 1979. This is a weekly news bulletin of the International Islamic Federation of Students Organizations.
30. J. MacManus, 'The threat to Sadat from Islam', *The Guardian* (London) 4

September 1981. Also P. Finnegan, 'Sadat stores up trouble with his crackdown', *The Guardian*, 6 September 1981.

31. J. MacManus, 'Sadat curbs Islam's power by taking over 40,000 mosques', *The Guardian*, 8 September 1981.

32. D. Hirst, 'The enigma of the Egypt of Sadat', *The Guardian*, 11 September 1981.

1 ABDEL-MALEK, Anouar, *Egypt: military society: the army regime, the left and social change under Nasser.* New York: Vintage Books, 1968.

Brief mention of the *Ikhwan* is made throughout the book. It is considered as a clandestine and subversive organization which, it is alleged, was responsible for a number of murders. A list is provided of those who were assassinated. The government's action in purging the *Ikhwan* is considered justified on the above grounds.

2 ABUBAKAR, M. A., 'Sayyid Kutb: a study of his critical ideas'. Edinburgh: University of Edinburgh, 1978. Unpublished M.A. thesis.

The author gives a detailed biography of this formidable exponent of the *Ikhwan* who was executed for his political activities in 1966. The author contests the opinion that Kutb joined the *Ikhwan* as a result of hearing some of Hassan al-Banna's speeches. He contends that Kutb gave his active support to the *Ikhwan* when 'he witnessed the ecstasy of the American general public at the assassination of Hassan al-Banna' (p. 52). The book concludes with a bibliography of the works of Sayyid Kutb.

3 AGBETOLA, A. S., 'Sayyid Qutb on the social crime: stealing'. *Islamic Studies*, Vol. XX, No. 2, Summer 1981. Pp. 87–95.

Following a brief review of Qutb's life and writings the paper discusses his writings on the crime of stealing.

4 AGHA, A. Dacud, 'Military elites, military-led social movements and the social structures in developing countries: a comparative study of Egypt and Syria'. Berkeley: University of California, Department of Sociology, 1970. Unpublished Ph.D. dissertation, pp. 207–217.

The author finds that Islamic revivalism started in Egypt as a response to economic, political domination by the West which led to disintegration of the value systems of Islam. A brief biography of Hassan al-Banna is given and the *Ikhwan*'s rise to power is discussed. The *Ikhwan*'s support basis in the Egyptian population is also located among the impoverished masses on the one hand and the urban petty bourgeoisie on the other. The *Ikhwan*'s downfall is dated from 1954 when it clashed with Egypt's military regime. The *Ikhwan*'s activities in Syria are also described.

5 AJAMI, Fouad, *The Arab predicament: Arab political thought and practice since 1967.* Cambridge: Cambridge University Press, 1981.

The author gives an incisive analysis of Arab political thought and also discusses trends in 'Radical Fundamentalism' of Islam where he discusses *Al Naksa wa al Ghazwa al Fikri (The setback and cultural*

17

invasion) by Muhammad Jalal Kishk—an author with Muslim Brotherhood affinities. Regarding the *Ikhwan* the author asserts that 'Muslim fundamentalism may never carry the day in Egypt Perhaps the society has gone beyond the puritanism of the fundamentalists and reached the point of no return' but he contends that 'importance of Muslim fundamentalism is not measured best in terms of its capacity to capture political power. Its power may lie in its ability to destabilise a regime, to help bring it down by denying it the religious cover that remains an important source of political power' (p. 119).

6   ALI, Abd al-Rahim, 'The Islamic Revolution: its impact on the Islamic Movement', in K. Siddiqui, *et al*, *The Islamic revolution: achievements, obstacles and goals*. London: The Muslim Institute, 1980. Pp. 37–43.

This is a comparative study of three Islamic movements: the *Ikhwan*, *Jamaat-i-Islami* and the Islamic movement in Iran. For those interested in the study of the *Ikhwan*, it is an interesting article. The author states that there were three major principles common to all three which distinguished them from other forces in the Muslim world: that Islam was a comprehensive way of life and not simply a set of rituals; that Muslim unity transcends national boundaries; that some form of organized work must be undertaken in order to achieve the objective of establishing Islam as a way of life.

The author then poses the question as to why the Iranian Islamic revolution succeeded where others like the *Ikhwan* failed. He finds that the chances for the success of the *Ikhwan* were limited because it had no firm tradition to build upon, unlike the Iranian Ulama leadership since the beginning of this century. Furthermore, while the *Ikhwan* emphasised *tarbiya* (education of the individual), in Iran the emphasis was on *Jihad*, which included educational and intellectual challenges. The public was being prepared for it by the Iranian Ulama while the educated were being prepared by revolutionary intellectuals like Ali Shariati. This was lacking in the case of the *Ikhwan*.

In order to bring about the revolution, the *Ikhwan* although it started as a popular, non-élitist and open movement, was forced to become closed and operate in secrecy under Nasser, while the Iranians through the Ulama had grass-root influence over the masses. Any movement which follows along the lines adopted by the Iranians therefore has more chance of being successful than others. [*see also* 426]

7   ALTMAN, Israel, 'Islamic movements in Egypt'. *The Jerusalem Quarterly*, No. 10, Winter, 1979. Pp. 87–105.

An informative article describing the ideology and activities of the

Ikhwan al-Muslimun from its inception through to the Sadat period. In the latter period, the leadership and activities of other Islamic groups labelled by the author as 'Mahdist' groups are also described. These in particular refer to the *Jamaat al-Takfir wa-l-Hijrah* (the group which changes society with unbelief and advocates withdrawal from it), the *Hizb al-Tahrir al-Islami* (Islamic Liberation Party), *Jund Allah* (God's Army) and the *Shabab Muhammad* (Muhammad's Youth). The latter was led by Dr. Salih Abdallah Sariyyah who was executed on 10 November 1976. Regarding the *Ikhwan*, the author observes that the 'Muslim Brothers have thus far maintained a mode of coexistence with the Sadat regime. They have not openly and directly challenged it ... even though the regimes policies frequently ran counter to their positions ... the Brothers' coexistence with the regime, whether by choice or by reason of their relative weakness, in fact contributed to the appearance of the Mahdist groups and probably led them to revive some of the most radical aspects of Islamic fundamentalism' (p. 104).

8   [ANONYMOUS], *Persecution of Akhwan al-Muslimoon: the story of oppression in Egypt*. Karachi: Anjuman Press, n.d. 52 p.

Gives a brief history of the *Ikhwan* and reports the atrocities committed by the Nasser regime in purging its members.

9   ANSARI, Zafar Ishaq, 'Contemporary Islam and nationalism: a case study of Egypt'. *Die Welt des Islam*, 7, 1961. Pp. 3–38.

An excellent analysis of Islamic thought of the *Ikhwan*. The focus is mainly on the Islamic thinking of al-Banna in relation to nationality, fatherland and nationalism.

10   ARMAJANI, Yahya, *Middle East: past and present*. Englewood Cliffs, NJ: Prentice-Hall Inc., 1970. Pp. 287–290.

Brief introduction to the *Ikhwan*, its organization and ideology and its strategy of communicating ideas to adults, women and youths. Some statistics are given about the number of its branches, being 500 in 1939 and 2,000 in 1953, and its membership rising from 500,000 in 1939 to 2,000,000 in 1953.

11   ATIYEH, George N., 'Middle East ideologies', in W. E. Hazen, *et al*, (ed.), *Middle Eastern subcultures*. Lexington, Mass.: D. C. Heath & Co., 1975. Pp. 47–68.

In this paper the author advocates that the ideologies prevalent in the Arab world which claimed to have solutions for the ills of society were of three types: religious, political and technical. Of the first category, the *Ikhwan* is offered as an example. A brief account then explains various dimensions of its ideology, its influence in the various segments of Egyptian society and its involvement in politics.

Also its enemies have been identified as the Communists and th secular Muslim intellectuals. Currently, it is considered that th movement does not exist in an organized form, but in splinte groups which espouse the *Ikhwan*'s ideology.

12 AUDAH, Abdul Qader, *Islam between ignorant followers and incapabl scholars*. Kuwait: International Islamic Federation of Student Or ganisations, 1977.

An important work on Islamic jurisprudence by a prominent mem ber of the *Ikhwan* who was executed by the Nasser regime. Lik other exponents of *Ikhwan*'s ideology (Qutb, Ramadan) this boo is recommended for reading.

13 AYUBI, Nazih N. M., 'The political revival of Islam: the case c Egypt'. *International Journal of Middle Eastern Studies*, Vol. 12, No. 4 1980. P. 481–499.

After discussing the international significance of Islam and th political role of religion, the author poses the question: why ar many people in Muslim societies in a state of discontent and wha exactly do they want? He answers the questions by stating tha Muslims like other peoples from the non-Muslim Third Worl have similar needs and 'it would be erroneous to continue t attribute every change (or for that matter lack of change) in Mus lim societies to Islam. Most Middle Easterners are Muslims an their political struggle may therefore take an Islamic form or a least acquire an Islamic flavour' (p. 484).

The focus of the paper then shifts to Egypt where the autho discusses the Islamic groups like the *Ikhwan* and the neo-funda mentalists. He arrives at the conclusion that the resurgence of Islan may not be due to 'purely Islamic reasons' stated above.

14 BADEAU, John S., 'A role in search of a hero: A brief study of th Egyptian Revolution'. *Middle East Journal*, 9, No. 4, Autumn, 1955 Pp. 373–385.

Brief discussion as to why free elections could not be permitted b the military elite in Egypt after 1952. They feared that the *Ikhwa* would gain power. Subsequent events led to the removal of Colone Muhanna, a sympathiser of the *Ikhwan* and conflict with the mili tary.

15 BAHADUR, K., *The Jamaat-i-Islami of Pakistan: political thought an political action*. New Delhi: Chetana Publications, 1977.

A brief comparison is made of the *Jamaat* with the *Ikhwan*. Th author contends that there is no evidence to support that an linkages existed between the two prior to partition of the subcon tinent. Both the movements held similar views as regards 'pure and 'undiluted' Islam in their programmes as well as in claiming that Islam was comprehensive and a complete way of life. The differences between the two movements emanated from the different environments, class character and political conditions of the two countries.

16 BAKER, Raymond W., *Egypt's uncertain revolution under Nasser and Sadat*. Cambridge, Mass.: Harvard University Press, 1978.

Brief explanation is given of the *Ikhwan*'s sensitivity to all forms of imperialism. It was against 'external imperialism' by which the country was physically occupied by a foreign power, 'domestic imperialism' in which individuals or groups collaborated with the occupiers and 'cultural imperialism' by which the mind was indoctrinated by Western teachings.

17 AL-BANNA, Hassan, *What is our message?* Lahore: Islamic Publications Ltd., 1974.

This book is a translation of one of Hassan al-Banna's works by A. A. Bilyameeni. It puts forward the ideology of the *Ikhwan*.

18 BAYYUMI, Muhammad Ahmad, 'The Islamic ethic of social justice and the spirit of modernisation: an application of Weber's thesis to the relationship between religious values and social change in modern Egypt. Unpublished Ph.D. dissertation. Temple University, 1976.

The Weberian framework is applied to the study of the *Ikhwan* and Nasser's regime. The aim of the author is five-fold:

1. To analyse the dynamic role of charismatic leaders, such as al-Banna and Abd al-Nasir, and the emergence of their movements as effective forces for social change.

2 To apply the 'general vision', which took the form of studying the Muslim Brethren's attempts to mobilize Islamic values to effect modernization of both individual and societal levels.

3 To apply the 'narrow vision' in the form of examining how religious values of the pre-socialist period led to socio-economic development and the rise of socialism, and to demonstrate that the role of the Brethren movement in the rise of Islamic Socialism in Egypt was similar to that played by Protestantism in the rise of modern capitalism.

4 To demonstrate, in order to trace the direction of religious values during the course of social change, the historical and ideational relationships between the Brethren and revolutionary leaders in which regard the effect of religious values upon the structure of Abd al-Nasir's ideology was given special consideration and analysis.

5 Finally, to compare two models of modernization: that of the

Brethren, which aimed at the mobilization of Islamic values and motivation of the individual toward the creation of an Islamic system, and that of Abd al-Nasir, which was based on the universal Islamic values and the rationalization and creation of a charismatic, powerful state.

19   BEERI, Eliezer, *Army officers in Arab politics and society*. New York: Praeger, 1970.

Brief mention of the relationship of Sadat and the *Ikhwan*. Also how the Nasser regime perceived it as a threat to its own goals is touched upon.

20   BELLO, Ilysa Ade, 'The society of the Muslim Brethren: an ideological study'. *Al Ittihad*, Vol. 17, No. 3, July–September, 1980. Pp. 45–56.

This paper focuses on the ideology of the *Ikhwan* as expressed through the writings of Hassan al-Banna and Sayyid Qutb.

21   BERGER, Morroe, *Military elite and social change: Egypt since Napoleon*. Princeton University: Center for International Studies, 1960.

Difference between the views of the military élite and the *Ikhwan* and the role of the military in using the *Ikhwan* for its own ends, has been explained.

22   BERQUE, Jacques, *Egypt imperialism and revolution*. London: Faber and Faber, 1972.

The author considers that the *Ikhwan* 'was in relation to Islam what the Wafd was in relation to democracy: a diminished reflection' (p. 664). It had the power to raise and mobilize the people to action, but it was not easy to base 'policy on scripture' (p. 664).

23   BILL, James A., 'The military and modernisation in the Middle East'. *Comparative Politics*, Vol. 2, No. 1, October, 1969. Pp. 41–62.

Brief mention of the purging of the Egyptian army officers who were sympathetic to the *Ikhwan*.

24   BILL, James A. and Carl Leiden, *Politics in the Middle East*. Boston: Little, Brown, 1979.

Brief discussion of the *Ikhwan* and its use of force against the Prime Ministers of Egypt. Furthermore, after Hassan al-Banna's death, the author thinks that the organization was 'rent by discord' (p. 61).

25   BINDER, Leonard, *The ideological revolution in the Middle East*. New York: John Wiley and Sons, 1964.

The author considers that the fundamentalist doctrines put forward by the Wahhabis of Saudi Arabia, the Sanusis of Libya, the *Ikhwan* of Egypt, the *Ikhwan al-Islamiyya* of Iraq, the *Fidayan-i-Islam* of Iran, the *Jamaat-i-Islami* of Pakistan and the *Masjumi* of Indonesia were all the same but differed in their internal structures, external support basis and their targets for attack. The *Ikhwan* and the *Fidayan* were opposed to Westernized regimes. For the *Ikhwan* nationalism was good if it meant freedom from 'Western influence', 'a love of country', 'regaining independence', etc., but it was evil if it divided the community, because the community for 'Hassan al-Banna was a community of belief (aqidah)' (p. 137).

26 BORTHWICK, Bruce M., *Comparative politics of the Middle East: an introduction*. Englewood Cliffs, N.J: Prentice-Hall Inc., 1980.

In a chapter on ideological change, the author discusses the *Ikhwan* movement. A brief biography of al-Banna, the ideology of the *Ikhwan* and its repression by Nasser is given. In the end it is compared with the Iranian movement which is considered to have had similar impulses, drives and values. Furthermore, Islam is considered to remain a 'powerful ideological system, moulding the culture that undergirds the structures of the society and polity' (p. 72) in the Middle East.

27 BUSOOL, Assad N., 'The development of Taha Husayn's Islamic Thought'. *The Muslim World*, Vol. LXVII, No. 4, October, 1978.

Shows the attitudes of Egyptian intellectuals like Taha Husayn and al-Aqqad towards the *Ikhwan*.

28 CRAGG, Kenneth, *Islamic surveys: counsels in contemporary Islam*. Edinburgh: Edinburgh University Press, 1965. Pp. 110–124.

A full chapter is devoted to the *Jamaat-i-Islami* and the *Ikhwan*. Regarding the latter, a life history of Hassan al-Banna is given and the aims and objectives of the movement. Al-Banna's three principles are given, of forming an Islamic community, legislating matters concerning human life according to the Sharia, and establishing a brotherhood among nations and castes. Six other concerns of the *Ikhwan* are also given. First, that the Qur'an must be interpreted rationally; secondly, that unity is essential among Muslims; thirdly, there must be economic equality, opportunity and removal of all forms of exploitation, etc.; fourthly, that society should be responsible for removal of poverty, illiteracy and disease; fifth and sixth propositions deal with raising of national pride in Islam.

29 CRECELIUS, Daniel, 'The course of secularisation in modern Egypt', in M.D. Smith (ed.), *Religion and political modernisation*. New Haven: Yale University Press, 1974. Pp. 67–94.

The paper traces the development of secularism in Egypt and

briefly mentions how religion posed a dangerous political problem for the Free Officers after the coup, particularly through the popularity of the *Ikhwan* among the masses.

30   DAWISHA, A. I., *Egypt in the Arab World: the elements of foreign policy*. London: The Macmillan Press, 1976.

Brief mention of the *Ikhwan*, its strength and opposition to the Nasser regime and the relationship of Islam to politics.

31   DEKMEJIAN, R. Hrair, *Egypt under Nasser: a study in political dynamics*. London: University of London Press, 1972.

Brief references are given of the *Ikhwan*, its ideology and popularity among the masses. Also some details have been given about its influence among the Free Officers group in the Egyptian army.

32   DELANOUE, G., 'Al-Ikhwan al-Muslimun', in B. Lewis and V. L. Menage, *et al*, (eds), *The encyclopaedia of Islam*. Leiden: E. J. Brill, 1971.

Presents an historical account of the *Ikhwan*. It divides its period of activities into three phases. The first phase, 1928–36, was dominated by social and religious activities. During the second phase, 1936–52, the organization became involved in political activities. The third phase began after 1952, during which time the organization was involved in conflict and suffered from its defeat by the authorities. Further, focus is also placed on the doctrine of the *Ikhwan* in which they considered 'Islam to be an order (nizam) without equal, because it was revealed by God, which has a vocation to organize all aspects of human life' (p. 1069). Two objectives of the organization have been identified. First, the main objective of the struggle was to free it from foreign domination. Secondly, the objective was to 'create an authentically Muslim state' (p. 1079). The article concludes with a brief bibliography of the works on the *Ikhwan*.

33   ENAYAT, Hamid, 'Islam and socialism in Egypt' *Middle Eastern Studies*, Vol. 4, No. 2, January, 1968. Pp. 141–172.

As the title suggests, the author discusses Islam and Socialism in Egypt. The Nasser regime's accommodating attitude towards al-Azhar in order to thwart the *Ikhwan*'s power has been mentioned. Furthermore, a detailed discussion of Mustafa as-Sibai's (leader of the Syrian branch of the *Ikhwan*) book, 'Ishtrakiyat al-Islam' (Socialism of Islam), has been given. The fact that a member of the *Ikhwan* should discuss socialism is not considered surprising, 'since ideas of social justice and reform, which are identified by some of the Brethren with the whole of socialism, have always constituted one of their fundamental beliefs' (p. 159).

34 FARIS, N. A., 'Modern religious movements among the Arabs and their relation to and influence upon the development of thought, society and politics'. *The Islamic Literature*, Vol. VIII No. 7, July, 1956. Pp. 5–14.

The author focuses on the various religious movements in the Arab world including the *Ikhwan*. He contends that political, economic, intellectual and cultural penetration by the West has given rise to these movements and hopes that more research will be done by investigators to throw more light on its nature, characteristic features and the 'extent of its vitality and the extent to which these masses have been and are being influenced by various reform movements and by modern culture and civilisation' (p. 14).

35 FLOWER, R., *Napoleon to Nasser: the story of modern Egypt*. London: London Editions Limited, 1976.

There are brief comments on the *Ikhwan* which is described as 'a religious movement to vivify Islam, had now openly become a fanatical organization propounding a heady sort of mysticism and the more extreme forms of Koranic doctrines' (p. 163). Its message, the author states was 'one of revenge and hope: a palliative for action rather than a revolutionary force' and the Free Officers after gauging its strength had 'come to the conclusion that for all its grandiloquent appeal to hate ridden extremes of the population, the Moslem Brotherhood was in reality a relatively harmless safety valve for the burgeoning discontent which was once more sweeping through the nation' (p. 163).

36 GIBB, H. A. R., 'The heritage of Islam in the modern world (II).' *International Journal of Middle East Studies*, Vol. 1, 1970. Pp. 221–237.

In the second instalment of a three part article the author focuses on the social order of Islam. In this discussion the rise of the *Ikhwan* is also analyzed as being a movement which springs from the ranks of the people to put forward a programme of social order based upon the principles of Islam. But the author sees this as a 'fumbling and rather pathetic attempt' (p. 229) to integrate Islamic values into a modern state. From this analysis the author argues 'the fundamental question raises its head. Just how valid are those ideals in the modern world? Has the failure of the Muslim Brotherhood and the rise of Arab Socialism pointed a way towards a final renunciation of the heritage of classical Islam in modern Middle Eastern society?' (p. 229). He concludes that 'it is by no means inconceivable that such a movement, hitherto suspect in the eyes of national governments, may one day gain instead their support and encouragement. If the governmental institutions of the Middle East continue to follow the present trend towards authoritarian or oligarchic regimes, the time may well come when such governments, finding themselves deprived of external support, will feel the need to seek again the active support of their own masses. And that support, if it is to be real, giving firm popular backing, will have to be bought at a price. The Muslim Brotherhood, as organised by the schoolmaster Hasan al-Banna, may have passed into history— but its history remains to show, beyond doubt, what the price will be' (p. 230).

37 GILSENAN, M., *Saint and Sufi in modern Egypt*. Oxford: Clarendon Press, 1973.

The author mentions the rise of the 'powerful organisation of the Muslim Brotherhood' (p. 203) and that the *Ikhwan*'s ideology was popular among the lower middle and middle classes because its interpretation of Islam was relevant to the present context. He cautions the readers that the successes of the *Ikhwan* 'should warn us therefore against assuming that the currents of secularization run as deep as examination of formal institutions might lead us to suppose; or that the normative and value changes to which attention has been drawn proceeded at equal pace among the different social strata. It should warn us also against the too-ready assumption that the decline of the Sufi Orders indicated a diminution in the significance of religion as a motive force in action' (p. 204).

38 GOLDSCHMIDT, Arthur, Jr., *A concise history of the Middle East*. Boulder, Colorado: Westview Press, 1979.

Brief mention of the rise of the *Ikhwan* as a reaction to the Westernized reforms imposed on Egypt by its foreign rulers.

39 HADDAD, Y., 'The Arab-Israeli wars, Nasserism and the affirmation of Islamic identity, in J. L. Esposito, ed. *Islam and development: religion and sociopolitical change*. New York: Syracuse University Press, 1980. Pp. 107–121.

The article points out that the rise of 'Islamic consciousness is in no small part the result of Arab-Israeli wars of 1967 and 1973. It is also the result of political and military realities, realignments and perceptions of these confrontations as well as the end of the Nasser regime and its policies' (p. 107). The Nasser regime in particular had 'nationalised' the al-Azhar to legitimate its policies and silenced the *Ikhwan* through executions. But the Islamic identity, in spite of it all has still reaffirmed itself.

40 HALPERN, Manfred, *The politics of social change in the Middle East and North Africa*. Princeton, N.J.: Princeton University Press, 1963. Pp. 137–154.

The author labels the *Ikhwan* as a 'neo-Islamic totalitarian movement' which rejected reformation to 'purify Islam from the accretions of its decadence' (p. 138). It appealed to the peasants, students, Ulama, workers, white collar workers and the lower middle classes who felt exploited by the elite and their monopoly of power and wealth. The *Ikhwan*, it is alleged, in its bid for power made temporary alliances with the Palace in 1946, Wafd Party in 1950 and General Nagib in 1954. The *Ikhwan* was considered to have two parts to its organization: one which was visible as a 'hierarchy of groups' which was composed of 'families' and 'clans', which integrated members into the organization ideologically as well as being helpful with their personal problems. The second part was invisible and organized as a 'secret apparatus' with the capability for political violence (p. 145). In the end the *Ikhwan*'s programme, fate and potential is described. The conclusion derived from the analysis is that such 'totalitarian movements—whether Islamic or post-Islamic—will probably continue to sprout in the Middle East until their roots can no longer find inviting soil' (p. 154).

41   HAMIDI, Khalil, 'The movement of al-Ikhwan-ul-Muslimun'. *Muslim News International*, Vol. 5, No. 4, October, 1966.

Brief report of the *Ikhwan* and its activities during the early period of military rule and its conflict with it in 1954.

42   HARRIS, Christine P., *Nationalism and revolution in Egypt: the role of the Muslim Brotherhood*. The Hague: Mouton & Co., 1964.

The book focuses on the study of the *Ikhwan*. After describing the colonial and Islamic context of Egypt, the *Ikhwan* is considered to have been the outcome of 'various political, social and spiritual tensions' (p. 14). Al-Banna's life and the *Ikhwan*'s teaching are given in one chapter. The others narrate its history during the period 1928–1952. Finally, the *Ikhwan*'s 'challenge' to the 'leaders of the revolution' and the loss of its 'bid for power' are discussed in separate chapters. [*See also* 64].

43   HASSAN, S. Badrul, *Syed Qutb Shaheed*. Karachi: International Islamic Publishers, 1980.

An introduction to the life and works of a prominent member of the *Ikhwan*. His book *Ma'alim Fil Tareeq* (*Milestones*) which led to his trial and subsequent execution by the Nasser regime is also discussed.

44   HAVENS, Murray C. and others, *The politics of assassination*. Englewood Cliffs, NJ: Prentice-Hall Inc., 1970.

A whole chapter is devoted to the assassination of Hassan al-Banna of Egypt. The chapter focuses on the conditions in Egypt which gave rise to the movement, the life of al-Banna, the conspiracy to kill him and the organization and struggles of the *Ikhwan* after the assassination of its leader.

45 HEYWORTH-DUNNE, J., *Religious and political trends in Modern Egypt*. Washington, DC: McGregor & Werner Inc., 1950.

This book focuses mainly on the rise of the *Ikhwan* before the military revolution. After a brief historical background of Egypt, it gives the biography of Hassan al-Banna and the rise of the *Ikhwan* and its transformation from a religious to a political movement. It then compares the *Ikhwan* with various groups (e.g. *Misr al-Fatat*), institutions (e.g. *al-Azhar*) and also follows its political relations with the Wafd. The rest of the book is devoted to the exposition of al-Banna's social and political doctrines.

46 HOPKINS, Harry, *Egypt the crucible: the unfinished revolution of the Arab World*. London: Secker and Warburg, 1969.

Brief mention of the *Ikhwan* alliance with the Communists to launch a 'common attack on the regime's pro-Western proclivities exemplified by its negotiations for a settlement with Britain' (p. 147).

47 HOURANI, Albert, *Arabic thought in the liberal age 1798–1939*. London: Oxford University Press, 1970. Pp. 359–360.

The writer makes a brief mention that the ideology of the Egyptian military regime in its early period did not go unchallenged. The prime political force to challenge them was the *Ikhwan*. A brief discussion of the political and economic ideas of Hassan al-Banna is given, with the observation that his political ideas were more lucid than his economic ideas, although it stressed Islamic ideas of social justice and its repudiation of the unequal distribution of wealth in society.

48 HUDSON, Michael C., *Arab politics: the search for legitimacy*. New Haven: Yale University Press, 1977.

Brief mention of the *Ikhwan*, about its banning in 1954 and that it has not been eliminated. In the mid-seventies it has emerged again and has monitored some revolts against the Sadat regime.

49 HUMPHREYS, R. Stephen, 'Islam and political values in Saudi Arabia, Egypt and Syria'. *Middle East Journal*, Vol. 30, 1979. Pp. 1–19.

The general theme of the paper is of modernist values and fundamentalist Islam. Brief mention of how the works of two prominent members of the *Ikhwan*, Sayyid Qutb and Mustafa Sibai, were fundamentalist in tone but modernist in content and have influenced the official ideologies of Arab Socialism.

50 HUSAINI, Ishak Musa, *The Muslim Brethren: the greatest of modern Islamic movements.* Beirut, Lebanon: Khayat College Book Co-operative, 1956.

An exhaustive study of the *Ikhwan* from the original sources. It deals in its first part with the life of al-Banna and his leadership of the organization. The second part focuses more intensively on the leadership of the organization under Hudaybi. The problems which the latter had to face are also analysed and the *Ikhwan*'s relationship with the army and its purge have also been covered in considerable detail.

51 HUSSEIN, A., 'Islam and Marxism: the absurd polarisation of contemporary Egyptian politics', in *Review of Middle East Studies 2.* London: Ithaca Press, 1976. Pp. 71–83.

The development of ideology in Egypt has been traced from the beginning of the nineteenth century. After World War II, two new ideological developments can be detected: the *Ikhwan* movement and the Communists movement. Since the latter could not relate to the Islamic history of the country, the strength of the former increased, creating polarization of the two extremes, Islam and Marxism. During the fifties, this led to the emergence of the new ideology of socialism which was espoused by Nasser.

In the present context, the author perceives three sub-groups following the development of the *Ikhwan*. The first merely repeats old dogmas. The second has emerged with the doctrines of Islamic socialism following Mustafa al-Sibai's interpretation. The third group argues that the Qur'an and Sunnah lays down general directions that are not incompatible with scientific achievements, social sciences or even Marxism.

52 IBRAHIM, Saad Eddin, 'Anatomy of Egypt's militant Islamic groups: methodological note and preliminary findings'. *International Journal of Middle East Studies*, Vol. 12, No. 4, 1981. Pp. 423–453.

The author has made a detailed comparative analysis of two militant Islamic groups, the *Jamaat al-Fanniyya al-Askariyya* (Technical Military Academy Group) and the *al-Takfir w'al-Hijra* (Repentance and Holy flight). Furthermore these movements were influenced by the idea of Hassan al-Banna, Sayed Qutb, Mawdudi and Shariati. The author defines Islamic militancy as an 'actual violent group behaviour committed collectively against the state or other actors in the name of Islam' (p. 427). Their perception of Egyptian society was not similar for according to the Military Academy group the political system is corrupt but the society at large may be riddled with problems but need not be blamed. According to the Repentance and Holy Flight group a corrupt society breeds a corrupt political system and vice versa. The author concludes that 'two sets of factors will decide the future of Egypt's Islamic militancy. The first set has to do with the ability of the present regime or another secular alternative to address itself to the issues ... (independence, social equity and a credible vision for the future that enlists the commitment of the educated youth). The second set has to do with other regional models ... However the most salient regional effect on the future growth of Islamic militancy in Egypt and elsewhere is likely to come from the Iranian Revolution' (p. 499).

53   JAMEELAH, Maryam, *Islam in theory and practice*. Lahore: Matbaat-ul-Maktab-al-Ilmiyyah, 1973.

Gives a brief biography of al-Banna and a history of the *Ikhwan*. Quotations of al-Banna are also given.

54   JANSEN, G. H., *Militant Islam*. London: Pan Books Ltd., 1979.

Brief biography of Hassan al-Banna is given, along with the *Ikhwan's* history during the Nasser regime. Its widespread power in Egypt is acknowledged.

55   JONES, J. M. B., 'Hasan al-Banna' in H. A. R. Gibb and J. H. Kramers, *et al*, (eds). *Encyclopaedia of Islam*, Vol. 1. Leiden: E. J. Brill, 1967.

Brief biography of al-Banna which focuses more on the earlier part of his life.

56   KAPLINSKY, Z., 'The Muslim Brotherhood'. *Middle East Affairs*, Vol. 5 (12), December, 1954. Pp. 377–385.

This paper gives considerable detail on various aspects of the *Ikhwan*. First, it focuses on its organization and the use of all systems to penetrate other structures of Egypt. Secondly, its ideology is analysed. Thirdly, its relationship with the Wafd party is assessed, and lastly, events leading to the conflict with the Nasser regime are discussed. It is considered that the rifts within the *Ikhwan* weakened it, but on the whole have not robbed it of its mass appeal. Kaplinsky forecasts that it may emerge again in the years to come.

57   KARPAT, Kemal H., *Political and social thought in the contemporary Middle East*. New York: Praeger, 1968.

In a three-page introduction, Karpat narrates the biography of Hassan al-Banna, the history of the *Ikhwan*, its goals and its help in the success of July 1952 military coup d'état. Also its rapprochement with the military regime later and the subsequent events are mentioned. Some reasons for the *Ikhwan*'s failure are also given, followed by a selection of al-Banna's writings.

58   KHADDURI, Majid, *Political trends in the Arab World: the role of ideas and ideals in politics.* Baltimore: The Johns Hopkins Press, 1972.

Throws light on various aspects of the *Ikhwan*: a brief life history of Hassan al-Banna is given; the *Ikhwan*'s social, economic and political ideology is explained in some detail; the shift in the trends of thinking of the *Ikhwan* is shown during al-Banna's lifetime and after his assassination in 1949, and that of its new leader. Lastly, it points out the issues which caused internal schism and dissensions within the *Ikhwan* that ultimately led to its weakening.

59   KHALID, Walid and Yusuf Ibish (eds), *Arab political documents, 1965.* Beirut: American University of Beirut, 1966. Pp. 413–456.

Gives extracts from the 'Report by the Legislative Committee of the United Arab Republic National Assembly on the Republican Law regarding the Muslim Brotherhood'. This report projects the regime's view of *Ikhwan*.

60   KHALIDI, W., 'Political trends in the fertile crescent', in W. Z. Laqueur (ed.) *The Middle East in transition.* London: Routledge and Kegan Paul, 1958. Pp. 121–128.

Brief mention is made of the two powerful forces which are exerting powerful influences on Arab nationalism and the Arab officer class. On the extreme right is the *Ikhwan* and on the extreme left are the Communists. The *Ikhwan* is considered to have been weakened in Egypt, but is strong in Syria, Jordan, Lebanon and Iraq. It is considered to be anti-Communist and anti-Western politics, but not anti-West. It is also observed that the *Ikhwan* is carefully following the course of events in Egypt and waiting for a chance to regroup its forces.

61   KOURY, Enver M., *The patterns of mass movements in Arab revolutionary progressive states.* The Hague: Mouton & Co., 1970.

This study deals with five 'revolutionary-progressive states': Algeria, Tunisia, Syria, Iraq and Egypt. In its discussion of the latter, it focuses on the *Ikhwan* as a reactionary movement against the status quo in Egypt. Its struggle, therefore, against the military was inevitable. It resulted in defeat due to three reasons: first, Naguib's dismissal removed the sympathiser of the *Ikhwan* from the Revolutionary Command Council; secondly, Nasser counteracted it by starting the Liberation Rally; and thirdly, internal dissensions within the *Ikhwan* weakened its leadership. The author, however, predicts that 'as long as the present unwanted status quo prevails in the Arab society, it is likely that the Muslim Brotherhood will continue to be a spiritualising force in the realm of politics' (p. 54).

62 LAFFIN, John, *The dagger of Islam*. London: Sphere Books Ltd., 1979.

Brief mention of the *Ikhwan* is made in a comparative context, along with other Islamic movements.

63 LAQUEUR, W. Z., *Communism and nationalism in the Middle East*. London: Routledge and Kegan Paul, 1957.

In Chapter 18 the author discusses the origins, organization, ideology and political activities of the *Ikhwan*. He believes that the *Ikhwan* was in close collaboration with the Egyptian communists. An agreement had been reached in July 1954 between Muhammad Abdul Munim Tamam, the communist representative and the *Ikhwan* to have a common platform on two points: a) the cessation of negotiations with Britain and the renewal of the armed fight, and b) the abolition of military law and all laws opposed to freedom (p. 241). This 'change in attitude of the Brotherhood towards communists and vice versa, from extreme hostility in 1945–46 to close co-operation in 1953–54 should be seen against the background of common opposition to western influences and the attempt of the junta to westernize (or rather modernize) the country. No ideological affinity was needed to cement that common front' (p. 242). In conclusion the author observes that 'the *Ikhwan* were incapable of ruling the country, but they were powerful enough to sabotage effective rule for years' (p. 247).

64 LENCZOWSKI, George (ed), *The political awakening in the Middle East*. Englewood Cliffs, NJ: Prentice-Hall Inc., 1970.

Contains two articles on the *Ikhwan* reprinted from previously published works. One is from C. P. Harris' *Nationalism and revolution in Egypt* (1964) [*see also* 42], and the other from Sayed Qutb's *Social justice in Islam* (1953), entitled 'The Brotherhood's political theory'.

65 LEWIS, B., *The Middle East and the West*. New York: Harper and Row Publishers, 1966.

A brief account of the *Ikhwan*'s political activities is given, and is considered to have played 'an important and stormy role in Egyptian politics' (p. 111). When the *Ikhwan* was severely purged in 1954 after making an attempt on Nasser's life, the University of Al-Azhar issued a statement on 17 November, 1954 accusing the Brotherhood of having 'crossed the limits fixed by God in revelation between good and evil' (p. 111).

56 LEWY, G., 'Nasserism and Islam: a revolution in search of ideology', in D. E. Smith, (ed.) *Religion and political modernisation*. New Haven: Yale University Press, 1974. Pp. 259–281.

This paper mentions the Islamization of nationalism in Egypt and the contradictions it developed because the Christian minority in Egypt, who, it is asserted, had played a leading role in the development of nationalism, did not like to have religion mixed with it. Nasser's interpretation of Islam also sought to accommodate it with modern Egypt. It was reformist and modernist while the *Ikhwan* sought total transformation of Egypt along Islamic lines. As such obstacles on the course of modernization are created not only by the lack of intellectual incisiveness on the part of the ruling elite but, at least as importantly, by the continuing strength shown by the traditional Islamic ethos among the masses (p. 277).

Thus, even though Nasser had died,
unless the Muslim Brotherhood can regain its influence in the armed forces it seems unlikely that the society can overthrow the regime established by him. The ruling officers, as we have seen, have been quite successful in appropriating the Islamic ethos. Islam, even for westernised intellectuals is part of the national heritage and the regime is careful to nourish this sentiment. The Muslim religion serves as the basis for minimum agreement between the members of the political community and it will continue to serve in this capacity until a new and secular formula can evolve and find acceptance. Meanwhile, a confusion of norms will prevail. The task of nation-building within the framework of Islam will be difficult; for Muslims have never successfully developed a realistic theory of the state (p. 279).

57 LITTLE, Tom, *Egypt*. London: Ernest Benn Ltd., 1958.

The author has analysed in some detail the ideology, organization and involvement of the *Ikhwan* with the political situation in Egypt. He thinks that the *Ikhwan* took a political turn in 1938 because Hassan al-Banna defined it as 'a salafite movement, an orthodox way, an athletic group, a scientific and cultural society, an economic company and a social idea' (p. 154). It developed a terrorist wing because Hassan al-Banna talked of Jihad which, it is alleged, 'clearly marked out a path towards the conquest of power' and with the masses behind him 'loosed them in armed action against their adversaries' (p. 155). The *Ikhwan* developed its contact with the military through Abdul Moneim Abdul Raouf. In the opinion of the author, it was Raouf who later turned against the Revolutionary Command Council when they did not implement Islamic rule in the country and 'eventually organised the plot to assassinate

Nasser' (p. 248). The rest of the account shows how Nasser tried to destroy and dismantle the movement.

68 MALIK, Hafeez, 'Islamic political parties and mass politicisation' *Islam and the Modern Age*, Vol. III, No. 2, May, 1972. Pp. 26–64.

The author distinguishes between two types of political parties: the Islam-oriented parties and the traditional-ideological parties. In the former are included the All India Muslim League and the Masjumi Party of Indonesia, while in the latter category are the *Ikhwan al-Muslimun*, the *Jamaat-i-Islami* of Pakistan and *Nahdatu Ulama* and the *Dar al-Islam* of Indonesia. The focus of the author is mainly on a comparative study of the *Ikhwan* and *Jamaat*. This the author does by using an analytical framework based on Talcot Parson's paradigm, in which the political action is assessed according to adaptation, pattern maintenance, goal attainment and integration of these movements.

69 MARLOWE, John, *Anglo-Egyptian relations 1800–1956*. London Frank Cass Ltd., 1965.

The author believes that the *Ikhwan* turned from a religious to a political organization and as such what began with 'a means to an end' soon became 'an end in itself, practised indiscriminately pointlessly with great skill, self sacrifice and powers of organisation (p. 351). It is attributed with the assassination of the Prime Minister of Egypt (Noqrashy Pasha). Its support was drawn mainly from the frustrated middle and lower classes. Furthermore, he believe that the Communist Party was not so much of a threat as the *Ikhwan*, but at that time 'any attack on the *Ikhwan* during its period of growth into a terrorist movement would probably have been widely stigmatised as an attack on Egyptian nationalism, as an act of tyranny against true patriots, as a deed almost of treason dictated by subservience to a foreign power'. Noqrashy's successor, Abde Hadi, however, set his mind to suppress the movement and the prisons 'were emptied of Zionist suspects and filled with member of the Muslim Brotherhood' and Hassan al-Banna was assassinated The focus on the *Ikhwan* is mainly on its rise to power during the pre-1952 period.

70 MAYFIELD, James B., *Rural politics in Nasser's Egypt: a quest fo legitimacy*. Austin: University of Texas Press, 1971.

A brief account of the *Ikhwan* is given, referring particularly to it ideology and grass-root influence among the Egyptian Fellahin and mention is made of the *Ikhwan*'s social work among the Fella hin. Furthermore, the writer, on the basis of his research, assert that although as an effective organization it does not exist on the surface, its ideology has great appeal in both urban and rural areas

71   MEHDI, S., 'The way ahead for the Ikhwan al-Muslimoon'. Part I, Part II and Part III. *Suara al-Islam*, Vol. 3, Nos. 1–3, and 4–5, January–May, 1977.

In three separate issues of the journal, the main focus of the author is on the failure of the *Ikhwan* to rise up strongly in the Middle East. This state of affairs has been brought about, in the author's opinion, due to compromises with the Saudi regime. The *Ikhwan* must mobilize the people of Saudi Arabia to ask the following questions:

(a) Why is the ruling elite above the Shariah? Why is the gambler Fahd not punished on the basis of Islamic law?

(b) Why is the Shariah ignored and every year millions of riyal invested in US and European capital interests?

(c) Why is the Shariah overlooked and non-Saudi Muslims denied political and social rights?

(d) Why is the Shariah discarded and attempts are made to seek political accommodation with Israel (p. 10).

Part I and Part II have focused on these areas.

In Part III the author evolves a goal and strategy for the success of the *Ikhwan*. The immediate task should be to establish an *Ikhwan* headquarters in exile, to establish a centre to finance revolutionary activity in the Middle East and the immediate reformulation of the workers training programme (pp. 15–16). This is necessary if the following goals are to be achieved: the revolutionary seizure of power and establishment of an Islamic state in the valley of the Nile in the first decade of the twenty-first century; the establishment of a political union between the Islamic republic of the Nile and the Arabian Peninsula, five to ten years later; the liberation and establishment of an Islamic state across the river Jordan in the second decade of the twenty-first century.

72   MITCHELL, Richard P., *The Society of the Muslim Brothers*. London: Oxford University Press, 1969.

A very exhaustive study of the *Ikhwan* compiled from original sources. Part I deals with the history of the *Ikhwan*, in which the life of Hassan al-Banna and the rise of the movement and its interaction with the military regime is discussed in detail. In Part II the organization structure is discussed in terms of its tripartite division into its leadership (*al-murshid al-amm*), guidance council (*maktab al-irshad al-amm*) and the Consultative Assembly (*al-hay'at al-ta'sisiyya*). Other aspects of the organization which are discussed are its administrative structure and communication and indoctrination methods. Part III discusses the ideology of the *Ikhwan* and projects its views on political, economic and social affairs. Part IV gives the conclusion and the place of the *Ikhwan* in Islam's modern history.

It is considered to be the best study done on the *Ikhwan* by a non-Muslim.

73 MORRISON, S. A., 'Arab Nationalism and Islam'. *The Middle East Journal*, Vol. 2, No. 2, April 1948. Pp. 147–159.

A discussion between nationalism and Islam in which the author considers that the 'new enthusiasm for Muslim orthodoxy' through the Young Men's Muslim Association and the Muslim Brotherhood 'whose influence now reaches out from Cairo to most of the intellectual centers of the Arab world, religion and politics are inextricably intertwined. Once nationalism and Islam are identified in men's thoughts there is no hesitation in looking to the state to protect Islam both from supposed betrayal from within and from corrosion from without' (p. 156).

74 NEGUIB, Mohammed, *Egypt's destiny*. London: Victor Gollancz 1955.

Brief references to the *Ikhwan* are made throughout the book. The author, who was the general who carried out the coup d'état in 1952 and was later ousted by Nasser, focuses mainly on the revolution. He mentions that some officers, like Colonel Mehanna, were so strongly committed to the *Ikhwan* that the Free Officers after the revolution could not accept them as members of the executive committee (p. 150). Also Neguib accepts that the most powerful political organization after the Wafd was the *Ikhwan*.

75 NUTTING, Anthony, *Nasser*. London: Constable, 1972.

Brief discussion of the *Ikhwan* and its role before and after the 1952 Revolution. The author considers that the *Ikhwan* assassinated Prime Minister Ahmed Maher due to his subservience to the British. Furthermore, the *Ikhwan*'s relationship with the Nasser regime is also discussed.

76 PERETZ, Don, *The Middle East today*. New York: Holt, Rinehart & Winston, 1978.

Brief introduction to the inception of the *Ikhwan*, its ideology organizational structure and its struggle against Zionism and the monarchy.

77 PERLMUTTER, Amos, *Egypt: the praetorian state*. New Brunswick NJ: Transaction Books, 1974. Pp. 68–80.

The author compares the attitudes of the *Ikhwan* and the Nasserite regime towards various aspects of Egyptian polity, as follows: attitudes towards the West and modernization; attitudes toward Egypt; attitudes towards patriotism and nationalism; attitudes towards Islam; attitudes towards leadership; attitudes towards political parties and organizations.

78 PISCATORI, J. P. and R. K. Ramazani., 'The Middle East', in W. J. Feld and G. Boyd, (eds), *Comparative regional systems.* New York: Pergamon Press, 1980.

The authors have briefly discussed the role of the *Ikhwan* in the Middle East. They contend that although the government has suppressed the activities of the *Ikhwan*, it has still endured although in splintered form such as *al-Tahrir al-Islami* and *al-Tafkir wa al-Hijra.* Furthermore the authors contend that the persistence of such movements like *Ikhwan* exist because modernization in the region is eroding all political, social and economic values. The quest for identity among young Muslims seeks to anchor itself in the most reliable of anchors—Islam. Such concern then 'permeates the region' (p. 277).

79 QUTB, Sayyid, *Islam and universal peace.* Indianapolis, Ind.: American Trust Publications, 1977.

This book gives a brief outline of Sayyid Qutb's life and focuses on the Islamic concept of peace and its relationship to all aspects of human life particularly conscience, home, society and the world.

80 QUTB, Sayyid, *Islam: the religion of the future.* Kuwait: International Islamic Federation of Student Organisations, n.d.

Qutb's exposition that Islam is the best system of all and as such 'the need of humanity for the Islamic way of life now, in contrast to other systems, is no less great in importance than it was in the Holy Prophet's time (p. 125).

81 QUTB, Sayyid, *Milestones.* Kuwait: International Islamic Federation of Student Organisations; Lebanon: The Holy Koran Publishing House, 1978.

An important work by Qutb who lost his life after its publication. The book is essential reading for anyone interested in the revolutionary dimensions of fundamentalist Islamic thinking.

82 QUTB, Sayyid, *This religion of Islam.* Kuwait: International Islamic Federation of Student Organisations, 1977.

Qutb's exposition of various aspects of Islam to convince the weak to become committed to Islam.

83 RAHMAN, Fazlur, 'al-Ikhwan al-Muslimun: a survey of ideas and ideals'. *Bulletin of the Institute of Islamic Studies*, pp. 92–102.

The author has summarized the life and ideas of Hassan al-Banna. The ideas of other *Ikhwan* writers such as Sayyid Qutb and Abd al-Qadir Audah have also been given on certain issues of the political system of Islam.

84   RAMADAN, Said, *Islam and nationalism.* Silver Spring, Maryland: The Crescent Publications, n.d.

Ramadan was a prominent member of the *Ikhwan* as well as the son-in-law of Hassan al-Banna. In this booklet he explains the relationship of Islam and nationalism with regard to Arabism. He poses the questions: if Arab unity has been so much identified with Islam, on what grounds, then, can one conceive of its rebirth without Islam?

85   RAMADAN, Said, *What we stand for.* n.p., n.d. 56p.

Ramadan, an important member of the *Ikhwan*, focuses on the social and economic order, system of government, foreign policy and other aspects of the *Ikhwan*.

86   RODINSON, Maxime, *Marxism and the Muslim World.* London: Zed Publications, 1979.

Interesting perception of the *Ikhwan* is given through the eyes of a Marxist. Considers the *Ikhwan* as 'Fascistic Muslim Nationalism' which was encouraged to develop by the British after World War II. It 'modernised primitive Islam' for the establishment of 'an authoritarian state with socialist implication' (p. 28).

87   ROSENTHAL, F., 'The Muslim Brethren in Egypt'. *The Muslim World*, Vol. 37, October, 1947. Pp. 278–291.

After giving a brief history of the *Ikhwan*, the author has translated a pamphlet of the *Ikhwan* entitled *Rasail al-Ikhwan al-Muslimun: Dawatuna* published in Cairo in 1943 and summarized its contents.

88   RUSTOW, Dankwart A., *Middle Eastern political systems.* Englewood Cliffs, NJ: Prentice-Hall Inc., 1971.

Brief mention of the *Ikhwan*, comparing its extensive support basis among the lower middle classes with the narrow support basis of the Wafd party, through patronage of village headmen and small landowners. The *Ikhwan*'s suppression in 1954 is attributed to an attempt to assassinate Nasser, but it is believed that the organization still leads a clandestine existence.

89   Al-SADAT, Anwar, *In search of identity.* London: Collins, 1978.

Sadat reports his conversation and impression of Hassan al-Banna and the 'perfect organisation of the Muslim Brotherhood' (p. 22). Elsewhere he relates that the 1965 purge of the *Ikhwan* was because the 'authorities were led to believe that the Muslim Brotherhood were plotting to overthrow the government, that is, to mount a counter-revolution. This, however, was purely imaginary. Perhaps the rulers really believed it or they might have wanted to achieve certain objectives of their own in this way. In any case, thousands of victims fell ...' (p. 50).

90   Al-SADAT, Anwar, *Revolt on the Nile.* New York: John Day, 1957.

Interesting account given by Sadat of his meeting with Hassan al-Banna and interaction with the movement. The attitude of the Free Officers towards the *Ikhwan* is summed up with the words: 'in its early days the Muslim Brotherhood seemed a useful ally ... (it) was to become an organisation of unbounded fanaticism' (p. 28). Regarding their alliance with the *Ikhwan*, Sadat observes that the 'ideology of the Brotherhood was essentially different from ours ...' (p. 44).

91   As-SAMMAN, Muhammad Abdullah, 'The principles of Islamic government'. *Die Welt des Islam*, Vol. 5, 1958. Pp. 245–253.

This pamphlet was written by as-Samman, a member of the *Ikhwan* in 1953. It was entitled 'Usus al-hukm fi'l Islam'. The pamphlet has been translated by Sylvia G. Haim, who gives a brief commentary about the thinking of *Ikhwan*. Her commentary on the author states that 'as-Samman's way of thinking is interesting because it is so representative of the political attitudes of the Muslim urban, semi-literate mass. He is impressed by Western techniques and material progress, but he has no use for Western methods of government. There is a craving for new, sweeping revolutionary remedies, a craving fed by the revolt against actual conditions. What makes it more than a mere specimen is the author's insistence on making Islam a politically radical religion' (pp. 245–246).

92   SHARABI, Hisham, 'The transformation of ideology in the Arab World', *Middle East Journal*, Vol. 19, 1965. Pp. 471–486.

The paper shows the transformation of ideology from the complacency of the pre-World War I Muslim generation to the post-World War II generation committed to personal and political action. This is illustrated by the generation of doctrinal political parties whose objective was to capture political power and transform the social order in toto. The two most important doctrinal parties were the Syrian National Party of Antun Saadah and the *Ikhwan* of Hassan al-Banna. The ideas of Afghani (1839–97) and Abduh (1849–1905) were considered to have reached full circle in al-Banna's ideology. His doctrines for political control are discussed, as well as Islamic reformation through which al-Banna wanted to restore Egypt to its supreme glory.

93   SHARABI, Hisham, *Nationalism and revolution in the Arab World.* Princeton, NJ: D. van Nostrand & Co. Inc., 1966. Pp. 108–110.

Excerpt from Hassan al-Banna's 'Risalat al-Mu'tamar al-Khamis ('Message of the Fifth Conference', Cairo, n.d.) is given. Selection focus on the following topics: meaning of Islam; force and revolu tion; the *Ikhwan*; government and national, Arab and Islamic unity

94 SMITH, Donald E., *Religion, politics and social change in the Thir World*. New York: The Free Press, 1971. Pp. 133–139.

This is a source book and offers a brief history of the *Ikhwan* and it conflict with the military regime. Its second excerpt is from th Legislative Committee report of U.A.R. issued in December, 1965 In this report the government's hatred of the *Ikhwan* is evident an ‚is considered as an organization which attempted to gain powe through bloodshed and destruction.

95 SMITH, Wilfred Cantwell, *Islam in modern history*. Princeton, NJ Princeton University Press, 1957.

The *Ikhwan*'s objectives are considered praiseworthy because the endeavour to build a society on the basis of justice and humanit from the 'best values that have been enshrined in the tradition fron the past' (p. 156). However, the author finds two drawbacks witl the movement. First, a 'lamentable lack of a realistic awareness o the actual problems of the modern state or its society, let alon solutions to them' and secondly, it is 'not the failure of the *Ikhwa* as a movement, so much as of the society in which it operates tha society has deteriorated to a point where violence is almost inevi table' (p. 158). There is therefore a constant struggle between mer who want to change the status quo and those who resist change Such a movement in the author's opinion 'must discriminate be tween good and bad factors apparently working together in it upsurge and still to sort themselves out: real religion and neuroti facism, honest idealism and destructive frenzy. It would be wron to deny the former and perhaps dangerous to ignore the potentialit of the latter' (p. 159).

96 STEPHENS, Robert, *Nasser: a political biography*. London: Aller Lane, 1971.

Brief references to the *Ikhwan*, its relationship with the Free Officer and Nasser's personal dislike of their mixing religion with politics

97 STEWART, D., 'Egypt and Islam: continuity and change'. *Neu Middle East*, No. 54, March, 1953. Pp. 29–32.

Brief history of the *Ikhwan* and its political strategy are discussed The *Ikhwan*, it is contended, was reactionary and al-Banna's philo sophy was religious and his final goal was defensive and other worldly. But such a message was difficult to spread in Egyptiar society. Al-Banna could have become an 'Egyptian Gandhi', bu the latter 'operated in a vaster, less challenged, less male-assertive society' (p. 30). Al-Banna, on the other hand, lived in a male-assertive society which can become 'vindictive and violent when dominated'. The struggle of the *Ikhwan* with Nasser was therefore inevitable because Nasser wanted to control and use Islam while the former wanted Islam to dominate.

98 STOAKES, Frank, 'Political forces in the Middle East', in Michael Adams (ed.) *The Middle East: a handbook*. London: Anthony Blond, 1971.

Brief mention is made of the *Ikhwan* as the most powerful movement over the Turkish and Persian groups. Furthermore, the impact of its ideology on the modernizing culture of Egypt is shown by the failure of modern politics to solve the problems of the lower class among whom the *Ikhwan* was very popular.

99 SULEIMAN, Michael W., *Political parties in Lebanon: the challenge of a fragmented political culture*. Ithaca, NY: Cornell University Press, 1967.

Brief mention of the *Ikhwan* is made by observing that it emerged as a reaction to internal (colonial dominance) and external (Western influence) factors. Its social work in the fields of education, health and hospitals, mosques and business is described. In the latter its workers shared profits in business concerns of the *Ikhwan* which projected a kind of Islamic socialism. Lastly, the influence of the Ikhwan in Lebanon's political arena is mentioned, which was mainly led by non-Lebanese leaders like Issan Attar, Tewfic Shawi, Zeid Wazir and Omar Amri. These men were arrested in 1966 to curtail their influence.

100 al TAFAHUM, Abd 'A Cairo debate on Islam and some Christian implications'. *The Muslim World*, Vol. 44, Nos 3–4, July–October 1954. Pp. 236–52.

The author discusses Sayyid Qutb's book *Al-Adalah al-Ijtima-iyyah fi-l-Islam*.

101 VATIKIOTIS, P. J., *The Egyptian army in politics: pattern for new nations?* Westport Conn.: Greenwood Press, 1975.

The author discusses the rise of the *Ikhwan* and its development into a powerful organization. This rise is attributed to its ability to channel 'national religious emotion into serious and meticulous planning' (p. 30). He further observes that although the *Ikhwan* had an autocratic hierarchial structure, it had built a skilful network of information and tasks in which both those placed high up in the hierarchy and those in low positions were given a sense of participation. The *Ikhwan*'s popularity was due to the fact that it had bridged the gap between the traditional leadership, which had become alienated from the political realities which existed around them, and the apathetic masses.

102 VATIKIOTIS, P. J., *Nasser and his generation*. London: Croom Helm Ltd., 1978.

A full chapter is devoted to 'The Society of Muslim Brethren'. In general it focuses on the relationship between the Free Officers and the *Ikhwan*. The author observes that the *Ikhwan* was a native mass movement with a tremendous popularity among the masses. It had formed a special secret organization (*al-Gihaz al-Sirri*) in 1946, whose daring exploits in the Palestine war in 1948 and sabotage of the British, impressed most sectors of Egyptians except the government. Egyptian army officers too were impressed by it and this may have attracted them to form relations with the *Ikhwan* during the period 1946–52. In 1950–51, when Nasser realized that the monarchy could be overthrown by a military coup d'état he 'also recognized the dangers of a successful mass religio-political movement on the loose' (p. 95). He therefore exploited them. During the Free Officers conspiracy the *Ikhwan* helped by secreting arms for them. But after coming to power, when they fell out over the Anglo-Egyptian evacuation agreement, Nasser 'used this knowledge and old association to discredit them' (p. 95). He did not want to compete for the loyalty of the masses with such a rival.

103 VATIKIOTIS, P. J., 'Recent developments in Islam', in P. W. Thayer, *Tensions in the Middle East*. Baltimore: Md., The Johns Hopkins Press, 1958. Pp. 165–190.

In his survey of Islam in the Middle East, the author mentions the existence of Islamic Movements which act as mass organizations catering to the social, economic, educational and political grievances of the people. Such movements by 'avoiding the creation of an intellectual gap between them and the public, have had greater success in the recent past. The Muslim Brotherhood is a good example . . . is still a formidable religious political force in the Arab World' (p. 176).

104 VIGNEAU, Jean, 'The ideology of the Egyptian revolution', in W. Z. Laqueur (ed.) *The Middle East in transition*. London: Routledge and Kegan Paul Ltd., 1958. Pp. 129–144.

Brief mention of the *Ikhwan*'s opposition to the Anglo-Egyptian Agreement of 27 July, 1954. It is also attributed with the unsuccessful attempt on 26 October 1954 to assassinate Nasser, following which the *Ikhwan* was banned and its leaders tried and executed. It is observed that with the dissolution of the *Ikhwan*, Nasser's regime removed its greatest obstacle and has since been more or less free from crisis.

105 WAKIN, Edward, *A lonely minority: the modern story of Egypt's Copts.* New York: William Morrow & Co., 1963.

Mentions a secret organization which the Copts had formed to hit back, through violence, against its enemies. It was known as the Umma Coptya (Society of the Coptic Nation).

106 WATERFIELD, Gordon, *Egypt*. London: Thames and Hudson, 1967.

Brief biography of Hassan al-Banna and the rise of the *Ikhwan*. Its retaliation against the British, involvement with the military regime and its purges in 1954 and 1966 are briefly discussed.

107 WENDELL, Charles, *Five tracts of Hassan al-Banna (1960-1969)*. Berkeley, Calif.: University of California Press, 1978.

Five tracts selected from the *Mujmu'at Rasa'il al-Imam al-Shahid Hassan al-Banna* have been translated from the Arabic. The tracts are entitled 'Between yesterday and today', 'Our mission', 'To what do we summon mankind', 'Towards the light' and 'On Jihad'.

The tracts have been selected for an audience of the 'interested student' and would help them if they are specializing in social and political history of Islam and area studies of the region. The author in the beginning gives a general introduction of al-Banna's life and his *Ikhwan*. The author postulates that al-Banna's goal was to establish a world state modelled after the Al-Khulafa al-Rashidun. His movement, however, attracted mainly the 'city proletariat' and the 'lower middle class' from the urban areas. From his discussion, the author concludes that 'Hassan's view of Islam is the product of crisis and the result of the cross-cultural interplay between Europe and the Islamic domain that had begun in the 18th century' (p. 7).

108 WINDER, R. B., 'Islam as the state religion: a Muslim Brotherhood view in Syria'. *The Muslim World*, Vol. 44, Nos. 3-4, July-October 1954. Pp. 215-226.

The Syrian branch was started by Shaykh Mustafa al-Sibai and a document by him entitled 'The establishment of Islam as a state religion of Syria' is published in this article. This reflects the *Ikhwan* thinking.

The Islamic movement
in Pakistan

The Islamic movement
in Pakistan

In the history of the Indo-Pakistan subcontinent there have been many Islamic reformers. Among them one of the exponents of Islam was Maulana Abul A'la Mawdudi. Mawdudi (1903–1979) was born at Aurangzeb (Deccan). His early Islamic socialization began in his family which for generations had been deeply committed to Islam. His formal schooling was completed at the Madarassa Fawqaniyah but his undergraduate studies at *Dar al Ulum* (Hyderabad) were disrupted due to death in the family and his own illness. This did not deter Mawdudi from the pursuit of knowledge and he taught himself Arabic, Persian, English and Urdu.

Mawdudi took to journalism and was appointed as editor of the journal *Taj*, published from Jubalpore (Madhya Pradesh) in 1920. Later he moved to Delhi and became editor of a Muslim newspaper from 1921 to 1923 and later served as editor of *al-Jamiyat* (1925–1928). Both of these were affiliated with the *Jamiyat-i-Ulama-Hind*. About this time he also became involved with the Khilafat Movement and the *Tahrik-i-Hyat*, an anti-British movement. Differences of opinion with the aims and strategies of the *al-Jamiyat* made him resign in 1928, whereupon he returned to Hyderabad. In 1933 he assumed the editorship of *Tarjuman al-Quran*, a monthly journal which remained his main vehicle for the dissemination of his ideas to the Muslim world.

The Ameer

Mawdudi was invited to the Punjab by the Islamic philosopher Iqbal. He moved to Pathankot (East Punjab) and from there he launched the *Jamaat-i-Islami* in 1941. He became the Ameer of the *Jamaat* and under his leadership the *Jamaat* became one of the leading Islamic movements of the twentieth century in the Muslim world. He travelled to many countries (Egypt, Syria, Jordan, Saudi Arabia, Kuwait, Turkey, England, U.S.A. and Canada) to spread his ideas but had to resign his leadership in 1972 due to ill health.

Mawdudi's academic output has been enormous. In the formation of his political ideas he was influenced by Ibn Khaldun, Shah Waliullah, Abul Kalam Azad, Mohammad Iqbal and Hassan al-Banna.[1] He wrote over 120 books and pamphlets and has over a 1000 speeches and press statements to his credit. He was a bold critic of any un-Islamic practices prevailing among Muslim societies and his movement attempted to bring change through political control. For holding such views he was often imprisoned in Pakistan and in 1953 he was even sentenced to death on a charge of sedition. The sentence was later commuted because of pressure from leaders of the Muslim world.

His first major work entitled *Al-Jihad fi al-Islam* won him acclaim from his contemporaries. His magnum opus was, however, the *Tafhim al-Quran*, a *Tafsir* (exegises) of the Qur'an which took 30 years to complete. He also worked on compiling a four volume biography of the Prophet Mohammad. Most of Mawdudi's work has been translated into other languages (English, Turkish, Persian, Hindi, German, French, Swahili, Tamil Bengali, etc.) and as such his influence is extensive in the Muslim and non-Muslim world.

Mawdudi's Political Thought

For Mawdudi, the 'distinguishing mark of the Islamic state is its complete freedom from all traces of nationalism and its influences. It is a state built exclusively on principles.'[2] Four conditions were necessary for such a state to exist:

1. Affirmation of the sovereignty of Allah.
2. Acceptance by the government of the limitation that it would exercise its powers and discharge its functions within the bounds laid down by Allah.
3. A decision that all existing laws which were contrary to the *Shariah* would be repealed, and that
4. all new laws would be in accordance with the teachings of Islam.[3]

Such a state however, does not exist anywhere because man's rule over man has created ignoble governments that allow all kinds of evil practices and corruption to flourish in the political system. For

a man of ordinary sense can understand this point that where people are quite free to commit adultery, no amount of sermons can put a stop to this. But if after getting hold of the power of government adultery is stopped by force, people will themselves give up this illicit course and take to the licit one. It will be impossible to succeed if you want to stop by means of sermons the evils of drinking, gambling, usury, bribery, obscene shows, indecent dress, unethical education and such other things... So this is an obvious matter requiring no great thinking that no scheme of reform for the people can be implemented without acquiring control of the government machinery. Whoever really wants to root out mischief and chaos from God's earth and is genuinely anxious to ameliorate the conditions of God's creation, it is useless for him to work as a mere preacher. He should stand up to finish the government run on wrong principles, snatch power from wrongdoers and establish a government based on correct principles and following a proper system.[4]

So if the Muslims believe that 'the answer to these questions is only this that the earth, the human beings and all these materials have been created by God alone, then it means that the land belongs to God, the wealth belongs to God and the people also belong to God. When this is the situation, how can anybody become their claimant so as to run His writ in the land of God? How can it be considered correct to govern God's subject by any other law except that of God or by a law made by the subjects themselves?'[5] But to change the status quo of secular Muslim states to the Islamic state is not easy because a threat to the vested interests of the elite would lead to conflict. For this reason an Islamic revolution is necessary which 'can be brought about only when a mass movement is initiated based on the theories and conceptions of the Qur'an and the example and practice of Mohammad (Peace be upon him) which would, by a powerful struggle, effect a wholesale change in the intellectual, moral, psychological and cultural foundations of social life'.[6]

Who can then take up the task of leading the Islamic revolution? Such a task

requires a group of workers who are fearful of God and implicitly follow the law of God without consideration of gain or loss, no matter where they come from, whether from this community which is now called Muslim or from outside. A handful of such men are more valuable for this purpose than the huge crowd... Islam does not stand in need of a treasure of copper coins which passes for gold mohurs. Before examining the stamp on the coins, Islam seeks to find out whether or not pure gold lies beneath. One such coin is more valuable to Islam than a whole heap of spurious gold coins. Then, again the leadership which God requires for the glory of His name is the type of leadership which should not budge an inch from the principles which Islam seeks to uphold no matter what the outcome may be, whether all the Muslims perish by hunger or go down before the sword.[7]

Expanding further on this calibre of leadership, Mawdudi spells out the criteria of how such gold mohurian leadership can be discovered. This will be found when in this struggle its torch bearers should furnish proof of their moral strength and sincerity by facing adversities, braving dangers and by offering in money and lives. They must go through all forms of trial and emerge like pure gold which everyone may declare unalloyed after having it tested. During their struggle they should by word and deed exemplify in their conduct and bearing, that particular ideology which they claim to represent. In everything they say or do, it should be apparent to all who came into contact with them that the ideological state which these selfless, truthful and God-fearing men of pure character and sacrificing spirit are inviting the world must certainly be guarantee of social justice and world peace. Through such struggle all those elements in society whose nature is not entirely devoid of truth and justice will be attracted to the movement. The influence of people of low mentality and those who resort to mean tricks will disappear t a palpable degree in the face of a lofty movement like this. A revolution will take place in the mentality of the masses and the collective life of humanity will cry out for a state system like this.[8]

Mawdudi's method for bringing about an Islamic change in society was reformist in character and it was to be directed by the select few who could claim themselves to be true Muslims.

The Movement

The *Jamaat-i-Islami* was founded to guide the Muslims towards the path of God as given in the Qur'an and Sunna. Abul A'la Mawdudi was quick to perceive the deteriorating socio-political conditions of the Muslims the world over. In the subcontinent the Khilafat movement had failed, while in the Middle East the Arabs and Turks were fighting each other. The whole Muslim world lay under the direct or indirect hold of colonialism and Western ideas such as 'nationalism' had turned Muslims against Muslims.

The *Jamaat* therefore sought to remedy these ills through the unification of Muslims, and focused on the individuals committed to Islam leading to the ultimate creation of the Islamic state. For the *Jamaat* the opportunity to do so presented itself when Pakistan was created. From the very beginning it exerted pressure for framing the constitution along Islamic lines. The ruling elite felt very insecure when challenged by the *Jamaat* and charged Mawdudi with not supporting the Pakistan movement. In a confrontation with the government in 1953 the *Jamaat* was accused of instigating sectarian riots and several of its members were persecuted. The *Jamaat* continued steadfastly in its constitutional battle against the government for its secularized ideas and rule. The latter, on the other hand, kept the *Jamaat* at bay, sometimes by banning the movement and at other times, incarcerating its members in prison.

The *Jamaat* policy, as stated earlier, stood for gradual change and transformation of the post-colonial state. For such a protracted struggle it needed individuals with a total commitment to Islam. The *Jamaat*'s organizational structure was such that recruitment into its higher ranks was not a matter of right but was subject to selection through the Islamic merits of each case. Great emphasis was placed on the development of personal character so that its members would be incorruptible, honest and bold and could practice what they preached. In the second category were persons who were not governed by the *Jamaat* but were accepted as *Muttafiqun* (sympathisers). Such persons were considered as being potentially valuable for the *Jamaat*. The third category included the ordinary membership which consisted of the majority of *Karkuns* (workers) who operated at grass root levels. Despite this structure, the *Jamaat* had a weak support basis among the masses. Its hold extended mainly to the lower middle class intelligentsia of Pakistan.

The highest decision making body of the *Jamaat* was the Central Executive Council (*Markazi Majlis-i-Shura*) which had a membership of fifty. The members were elected for a three year period and were responsible for policy making. From this *Majlis* the Ameer nominated a Working Committee of twelve members as well as a Secretary General who were responsible for overlooking the work of its various departments of finance, workers training, social services, labour welfare, adult education, translations, public relations, parliamentary affairs, etc. There were also a number of committees that looked after the work of the departments and these were on economic, agrarian, educational, labour and political problems, international and parliamentary affairs, law and legislation.[9]

In competition with other political parties the *Jamaat* has had to formulate a manifesto for seeking the support of the electorate. Its programmes have sought to cover, within an Islamic framework, all aspects of human lives that could ultimately evolve into an Islamic society. In the economic field it wanted to eradicate the capitalist system by breaking up the concentration of wealth in a few hands, forbidding all forms of interest, speculation, gambling, hoarding, etc. On the rural side, it sought to provide peasants with land sufficient for their basic needs. It also laid down various rules and regulations for the provision of social welfare and social insurance for orphans, the poor and the unemployed. It wanted to infuse the education system with moral training so that a theistic concept of life could permeate every science and art. Its legal system would be based on the *Shariah* that would stop adultery, consumption of alcohol, gambling, prostitution, etc.[10] However, in spite of such a political programme its lack of mass support meant that it would never acquire enough votes to take control of the political system. By 1977, Bhutto had transformed Pakistan into a One Party State under the domination of his socialistic Pakistan Peoples Party. The people were very disillusioned because he had failed to fulfil their expectations. After the rigged 1977 elections, the prospect of suffering under a re-elected Bhutto proved to be too much of a test of endurance for the people, so they began to protest. The *Jamaat*, along with the support of eight other disgruntled

political parties took a leading part in providing leadership and directio
to the newly formed Pakistan National Alliance. Almost every majc
town of Pakistan erupted in political protest against Bhutto's secon
term. In July 1977, the struggle between Bhutto's party and the oppos
tion forces brought the country to the brink of a civil war, which led th
military to carry out its coup d'état. The new regime leaned towards Isla
to legitimize its intervention into the political arena of Pakistan. Th
provided the *Jamaat* with its first opportunity to join the Ziaul Ha
Cabinet. The *Jamaat* remained with the government for almost a yea
during which time it could only suggest cosmetic changes towards th
Islamization of Pakistan.

Present Status of the Movement

The *Jamaat* is the only organization which has kept up a steady pressur
on all governments of Pakistan for bringing about the *Nizam-e-Mustaj*
(the Islamic system). In order to accomplish this it has acted both as a
Islamic movement and a political party. However, its effectiveness ha
been thwarted at every step and it has not been very successful. Th
reason for this is that the Jamaat has had to face many political as well a
structural obstacles.

The two major forces that have created political hinderances in th
Jamaat's course have been the feudal and the secularist groups. Thes
forces have vested interests in the country which aim at maximizing thei
own power. The secularist forces are the bureaucracy and the military
These institutions are the remnants of British colonial power which wer
structured so that they could maintain control over the people. An
move by the people to resist or check their power was not allowed. Th
training and ethos that permeates these organizations is still colonial i
structure. When the bureaucracy was in control of political power (unt
1958), all efforts made by the *Jamaat* were suppressed by them. Th
military regimes that have since ruled Pakistan intermittently have nc
changed their tactics either. Each regime has tried to legitimize its ru
and the last one has given a special importance to Islam. But this i
merely a personal effort by General Ziaul Haq and not an organizationa
change in military socialization towards Islam. Such a policy helps in th
political legitimation of the military regime.

The feudal forces in the country are the *Zamindars* (land lords) an
Pirs (holy men) who dominate in the rural areas. The *Pirs* have larg
followings and landed estates and influence in their region. Both thes
groups were created by the British and had helped the latter in recruitin
men for the British Indian Army. The *Jamaat's* ideology is too radical fo
these forces for it would attempt to change the lord-serf relationship a
well as bring about redress of economic grievances. Both these step
would corrode and undermine the authority of the landlords and *Pir*

A third group that has opposed the *Jamaat* in Pakistan are religiou
parties such as the *Jamaitul-Ulema-i-Pakistan* and the *Jamaitul-Ulama-*

Islam. These religious parties, unlike Islamic movements are struggling to acquire political power only as an end in itself. Their doctrinal interpretations and sectarianism have led to differences with the *Jamaat* and this disunity weakens them all while it strengthens the secularist and feudal forces.

The *Jamaat* has also had to face a fourth problem which emanates from the ethnic social structure of Pakistani society which is divided into ethnic groups such as the Pathans, Punjabis, Sindhis, Baluchis and Muhajirs (refugees from India). The *Jamaat* was started by the latter group and has had great difficulty in penetrating the populace of Sind, Punjab, Baluchistan and the Northwest Frontier Province who consider themselves as 'sons of the soil' and follow their regional leader because of ethnic ties rather than an Islamic affinity.

In the face of such opposition the *Jamaat* still survives in Pakistan. This is so because its organizational structure is unique – its hierarchical order and strict discipline have prevented it from splintering into factions even after the death of its leader. This organizational structure has held together the *Jamaat* even though its leadership leaves much to be desired. No one has equalled or excelled Maulana Mawdudi in either the dynamism of his personality or in the quality and quantity of his Islamic writings.

References

1. Sayed R. Ahmed, *Maulana Mawdudi and the Islamic State.* Lahore: People's Publishing House, 1976, p. 158.
2. S. Abul A'la Mawdudi, *The process of Islamic revolution.* Lahore: Islamic Publications Ltd., 1970.
3. S. Abul A'la Mawdudi, 'Twenty nine years of the Jamaat-e-Islami', *The Criterion*, (Karachi), Vol. 6, No. 1, Jan.–Feb. 1971, p. 29.
4. S. Abul A'la Mawdudi, *Fundamentals of Islam.* Lahore: Islamic Publications Ltd., 1976, p. 246.
5. *Ibid.*, p. 247.
6. S. Abul A'la Mawdudi, *The Process of Islamic revolution*, op. cit., pp. 24–25.
7. *Ibid.*, pp. 28–29.
8. *Ibid.*, pp. 21–23.
9. Sayed R. Ahmed, *op. cit.*, pp. 165–166.
10. For a full text of the *Jamaat's* programme see, 'The Jamaat-e-Islami's Manifesto', *The Criterion* (Karachi), Jan.–Feb. 1970.

109 ABBOT, Freeland, *Islam and Pakistan*. Ithaca, NY: Cornell University Press, 1968.

The main theme is to find out how far the various expressions of Islam have conformed with time. The first chapter is entitled 'Is change possible in Islam?' and the last 'Muslim modernism in Pakistan'. The author is interested in tracing the development and movements of Islam from the eighteenth to the twentieth century. The book also focuses on the activities of the *Jamaat* and Mawdudi's views on various aspects of Islam.

It is an important book for the study of Islam in the subcontinent and Pakistan. The author ends with the note that 'Pakistan has thus far produced few theologians to take their place among the modernists, but their appearance must soon be expected, unless the process of religious change has little in common among religions, or unless the idea of religion itself has no place in the modern world' (p. 231).

110 ABBOT, Freeland, 'The Jamaat-i-Islami of Pakistan'. *The Middle East Journal*, Vol. II, No. 1, Winter, 1957. Pp. 37–51.

An important article focusing on the political activities of the *Jamaat*. The author concludes that as a political party the *Jamaat* has run into contradiction of its doctrines because 'politics requires some opportunism' (p. 50). Furthermore, it has to 'compete with the percolation of new ideas into Pakistan' (p. 50). As for Mawdudi, whatever his critics might think of him 'he does reflect and represent the value of Islam, the spiritual importance of a faith that will not be abandoned, however differently individuals might interpret it. In this lies his strength' (p. 51).

111 ABBOT, Freeland, 'Maulana Mawdudi on Quranic Interpretation'. *The Muslim World*, Vol. XLVII, No. 1, January 1958. Pp. 6–19.

The author posed a number of questions to Mawdudi in June 1955 and received lengthy replies to his questions on Qur'anic interpretation. These have been reproduced in this article. In his introduction the author observes that Mawdudi's appeal within Pakistan is among those 'mullahs who are neither ultra reactionary nor tinged with Westernism. Politically, however, his party has never demonstrated much strength' (p. 6).

112 ABBOT, Freeland, 'Pakistan and the secular state', in D. E. Smith (ed.), *South Asian politics and religion*. Princeton, NJ: Princeton University Press, 1966. Pp. 352–370.

The author discusses the concept of secular and religious state in the Pakistani context and the role of the Ulama, including the *Jamaat*.

113 ABD, A. R., *Sayyed Maududi faces the death sentence*. Lahore: Islamic Publications Limited, 1979.

This is an account of the court proceedings against Mawdudi in which he was sentenced to death in 1953. At the end of the account there is a bibliography of Mawdudi's works as well as a chronological account of his life from his birth in 1903 until 1973.

114 ADAMS, C. J., 'The ideology of Mawlana Mawdudi', in D. E. Smith (ed.) *South Asia politics and religion*. Princeton, NJ: Princeton University Press, 1966. Pp. 371–397.

This is an important article on the *Jamaat-i-Islami*. It focuses on the life of Mawdudi and his 'ideology of Islam' and 'the Islamic state' as envisaged by him. After discussing these areas in considerable detail the author derives some conclusions from his study. He finds three reasons for Mawdudi's appeal to Pakistan. First, Mawdudi spoke in a language which the majority of the Muslims understood and his analysis and solutions to fellow Muslims' problems were approached within the religious framework of Islam. Secondly, the *Jamaat-i-Islami* which he founded was led by men with 'dedication and moral excellence' for 'in a country where cynicism and corruption have been growing problems, these men have quietly and conscientiously lived up to the principles they profess' (p. 380). Thirdly, 'some credit must be given to Mawdudi's logical turn of mind and his ability to construct a connected argument. Behind the exaggerations and oversimplifications necessitated by political polemics, there has been a set of logically structured ideas. One may question that Mawdudi rightly deserves to be called a thinker or an intellectual, in a strict sense, but he has appeared as such to many Pakistanis. They find in him a certainty of his own convictions, the capacity to state these convictions persuasively and to elicit their relevance for the pressing problems of social life' (pp. 380–81). Regarding Mawdudi's ideas, the author believes that he was 'an innovator of a fairly radical type and to be no less responsive, even in his notions about fundamental Islamic matters, to the peculiar historical conditions of the Muslim community in his lifetime than are his modernist opponents. Mawdudi ... is a product of recent Muslim history, and his presentation of Islam is not a photographic duplication of the faith of the Prophet, but, like modernism, a reaction to questions posed by the unique situation of Muslims in the modern world' (p. 394).

Mawdudi, the author believes, influenced by historical circumstances of the times, created a system where none existed in a form in which he was influenced by nineteenth century philosophies 'that has brought about the emergence of ideologies in the 20th century' (p. 395). The author comments that 'Mawdudi is best understood as a representative of one important Muslim reaction to the challenges of the modern world. His efforts ... have been inspired by the need to mount a vigorous defense against destructive inroads from the outside. The method adopted has been to revive what Mawdudi looks upon as the pure and static ideal pattern of the basic sources of Islamic wisdom. In reclaiming that ideal pattern Mawdudi understands himself to be rejecting what is modern, but without his realising it, much that is modern has worked to form his grasp of the ideal and his method of expounding it' (pp. 396–97).

115 AHMAD, Aziz, 'Activism of the Ulama in Pakistan', in Nikki R. Keddie (ed.), *Scholars, saints and sufis: Muslim religious institutions in the Middle East since 1500.* Berkeley, Calif.: University of California Press, 1972. Pp. 257–272.

The political role of various groups led by different Ulama are discussed in this paper. One such group is the *Jamaat-i-Islami* whose objective has been 'Islamisation of the society and the theocratization of the state' (p. 263). Mawdudi, the author contends, 'kept his programmes and organization quite separate from that of the Ulama' (p. 271). But the main adversary of all such Ulama groups was the Westernized upper middle class elite from where the politicians, civil services and military were recruited.

116 AHMAD, Aziz, 'Mawdudi and orthodox fundamentalism in Pakistan'. *The Middle East Journal*, Vol. XXI, Summer, 1967. Pp. 369–380.

After a brief discussion of Mawdudi's career, the author discusses his *Weltanschauung*. When Mawdudi entered the political arena in Pakistan it was to a policy of political manoeuvre, compromise and opportunism. Furthermore, he observes that 'it is an article of faith with Mawdudi that Islamic laws are not antiquated or out of date'. He does not believe in the historical evolution of mankind. But he does believe, like the traditionalists, in historical continuity in the sense that the Islamic community and the society based on the teachings of the Qur'an and the Sunnah of the Prophet have been continuously in existence since 'the very first day of the advent of Islam'. And in the sense that Muslim people living in various parts of the world share a single and identifiable religious and cultural personality, sharing the same 'beliefs, modes of thinking, ethical standards and values, acts of worship and mundane affairs' and a common way of life. The paper is important because it gives an insight not so much into Mawdudi's thinking but into the author's own Western-oriented contentions.

117 AHMAD, Aziz and G. E. von Grunebaum, *Muslim self-statement in India and Pakistan, 1857–1968.* Wiesbaden: Otto Harrassowitz, 1970. Pp. 156–166.

Two selections of Mawdudi's writings translated by Charles C. Adams are presented in this anthology. One is a selection from Mawdudi's *al-Jihad fi 'l-Islam* on 'The necessity of divine government for the elimination of oppression and injustice' and the other is from *Tahrik-i-Islami ki Aklaqi Bunyaden* and is entitled 'The moral foundations of the Islamic Movement'.

118 AHMAD, K., 'Despite partial power, Islamists succeed in laying grounds for an Islamic order'. *Islamic Horizons*, Vol. VII, No. 2, February, 1979. Pp. 5–6.

Professor Ahmad visited the Muslim Students Association (MSA) headquarters in the USA on 12 January 1978 and gave an interview to *Islamic Horizons*, the MSA's news bulletin. The talk is important for it explains why the *Jamaat-i-Islami* joined the Zia government in Pakistan. The title suggests the theme that they joined the government not to acquire power positions but to attempt to lay the grounds for an Islamic order—which hitherto had never been done in Pakistan's political history through its government.

119 AHMAD, K., ed. *Studies in the family law of Islam.* Karachi: Chiragh-e-Rah Publications, 1961.

The Goverment of Pakistan set up a Commission on Marriage and Family Laws in the 1950s. The Commission headed by Justice Mian Abdur Rashid issued a questionnaire to the leading thinkers in Pakistan. This book offers a thorough critique of the Report of the Commission. In Chapter 2 the questionnaire filled in by Mawdudi is printed in full. Chapter 3 contains the full Report of the Commission on Marriage and Family Laws as given by Justice Rashid. Chapter 4 is a critique of the modernist approach to the family laws as depicted in the Commission's report and in Chapter 5 reflections on the Commission's report are given by the editor. The book is an important contribution of the *Jamaat-i-Islam*'s thought on the Marriage and Family Laws.

120 AHMAD, K. and Z. I. Ansari, eds., *Islamic perspectives: studies in honour of Mawlana Sayyid Abul A'la Mawdudi.* Leicester: The Islamic Foundation, 1979.

The book consists of essays written by various scholars. The material is organized into four parts. Part I (Intellectual Perspectives) Part II (Islamic Intellectual Heritage) and Part III (Islamic Society, State and Economy) focus on various aspects of Islam. Part IV (Scholars and Reformers) contains three important studies on Mawdudi. The whole collection is an important contribution to the literature on Islam and on Mawdudi. Some of the prominent Muslim scholars are M. Nejatullah Siddiqi, Ishtiaq Hussain

Qureshi, T. B. Irving, Zafar Ishaq Ansari, Ismail R. Faruqi, A. K. Brohi, Hamid Algar and A. L. Tibawi.

121 AHMAD, K. and Z. I. Ansari, 'Mawlana Sayyid Abul A'la Mawdudi: an introduction to his vision of Islam and Islamic revival', in K. Ahmad, *et al, Islamic perspectives: studies in Honour of Sayyid Abul A'la Mawdudi.* Leicester: The Islamic Foundation, 1979.

An important contribution by a man who knew Mawdudi not as a bureaucrat or defence lawyer, but as his stalwart and close confidant. Much as others try to be 'objective', this essay gives the view by an insider of the Jamaat-i-Islami. The essay is divided into three parts. Part I deals with Mawdudi's life, Part II deals with his Vision of Islam and Part III deals with his Vision of Islamic Revival which covers various aspects, such as 'Vision of History', 'Objectives and Strategy of Islamic Revival', 'Revolution or Reform'. The author believes that 'under the influence of Mawdudi's ideas a considerable amount of activity is visible in different parts of the world' (p. 381).

122 AHMAD, Manzooruddin, 'The political role of the Ulama in the Indo-Pakistan subcontinent'. *Islamic Studies*, Vol. VI, No. 4, December 1967. Pp. 327–354.

The author discusses the political role of the various Islamic groups in Pakistan including the *Jamaat-i-Islami*. Other groups besides the Jamaat are those led by Ghulam Ahmad Parvez and the Mutamar-e-Alam-e-Islam. In conclusion, the author observes that the 'Ulama still constitute a formidable political force in Pakistan. They are fighting their ideological battle mainly on two fronts: (1) against a highly Westernized semi-secularized bureaucracy and (2) against the liberal reformist leadership. Although the Ulama have never held political authority themselves, yet they have always demonstrated remarkable political awareness' (p. 346).

123 AHMAD, Mumtaz, 'Class, power and religion: some aspects of Islamic fundamentalism in Pakistan'. Paper presented at the Conference on Islamic Revival, Center for Middle Eastern Studies, University of Chicago on May 28–31, 1980.

An important paper which focuses on the social basis and limits of Islamic fundamentalism in Pakistan.

124 AHMAD, Mumtaz, 'Perceptions and attitudes of the Ulama to problems and policies of economic development in Pakistan'. Paris: Editions du Centre National de la Recherche Scientifique, 1978.

This is a paper presented at the VI European Conference on Modern South Asian Studies held on 8–13 July 1978. It presents the results of an empirical research conducted on the Ulama in Pakistan. It is important for understanding the attitudes of the contemporary Ulama in Pakistan.

125 AHMAD, R., *Constitutional and political developments in Pakistan 1951-54*, Rawalpindi: Pak-American Commercial Ltd., 1981.

The *Jamaat*'s involvement in politics during the period mentioned above has been briefly discussed.

126 AHMAD, S. A., *Maulana Maududi and the Islamic state*. Lahore: People's Publishing House, 1976.

An important contribution to the study of *Jamaat*. Mawdudi's role as a thinker in the evolution of Islamic political thought and his contribution to contemporary thinking on the role of the state is analyzed. In the evolution of Islamic political thought various medieval thinkers (al-Mawardi, al-Ghazali and Ibn-i-Khaldun) and the trends of the founders of various movements in the eighteenth and nineteenth centuries like Abd al-Wahhab in Central Arabia, Jamaluddin al-Afghani in the Middle East and Shah Waliullah in South Asia are traced as background to Mawdudi's thinking on the Islamic state.

In focusing on Mawdudi, the author first discusses his early life and the influences during the formative years. Such influences on Mawdudi's thinking came from Ibn Khaldun, Shah Waliullah, Abul Kalam Azad, Allama Iqbal and Hassan al-Banna.

Mawdudi's role in the formation of Pakistan is also covered. Mawdudi, it is contended, opposed nationalism and as such the Muslim League, because the latter seemed to him to be concerned only with Muslims of South Asia and not the cause of the Islamic revolution embracing the whole muslim world.

The part played by Mawdudi in the problems of constitution-making in Pakistan is significant because the author contends that it seemed to bring changes in Mawdudi's thinking and his writings began to cover a vast range of subjects. Many aspects of his thoughts on theocracy, democracy, Islamic state, Jihad, economic structure of the Islamic state and the position of non-Muslims and women are discussed.

127 AMIN, M., 'Jamaat-e-Islami: Pakistan'. Lahore: University of Punjab, 1958. Unpublished MA thesis.

Focuses on the activities of the *Jamaat*, its ideology to usher in a divinely-regulated Islamic order, its recruitment patterns and the elitist nature of the organization.

128 [ANONYMOUS], 'Irreparable loss to the Islamic Ummah—the

demise of the Islamic luminary, Maulana Sayyid Abul Ala Maududi'. *Al-Islam*, December–January, 1979–80. Pp. 10–11.

A two-page summary of Mawdudi's life, publications and achievements.

129 [ANONYMOUS], 'Jamaat-e-Islami's manifesto'. *The Criterion*,
Vol. 5, No. 1, January–February 1970. Pp. 70–77.

This manifesto was accepted by the *Jamaat*'s Central Executive
Body on 20 December 1969 and is a revealing document of the
political framework of the *Jamaat*.

130 [ANONYMOUS], *Political parties: their policies and programmes*. Lahore: Ferozsons Ltd., 1971.

Gives the programmes of all parties including the *Jamaat* for the
elections held later that year under the Yahya regime.

131 [ANONYMOUS] 'Sayid Abul A'la Mawdudi (1903–1979), *Rabitat al-Alam al-Islami*, Vol. 6, No. 12, October 1979. Pp. 6–7.

A short appreciation of Mawdudi's life which was first printed in
Dawn (Karachi) and later reprinted in the journal mentioned
above.

132 [ANONYMOUS], 'Sayyid Mawdudi: convictions, courage and
foresight'. *Islamic Horizons*, Vol. VIII, Nos. 10–11, October–November, 1979.

Brief extracts from Mawdudi's writings and brief chronology published by the editors after his demise.

133 [ANONYMOUS], 'Sayyid Mawdudi, the great Islamic leader
passes away'. *Islamic Horizons*, September 1979. Pp. 1–3.

An editorial appreciation of Mawdudi's achievement published
after his death. After Iqbal and Hassan al-Banna, it considers
Mawdudi as 'the last of the giants, who played a formidable role
in the awakening of Muslims' (p. 1).

134 ANSARI, Zafar I., 'Islamic Movements in the Indo-Pakistan subcontinent: Jamaat-i-Islami, Pakistan'. Paper presented at the International Islamic Conference held in London in April by the
Islamic Council of Europe, 1976.

An important contribution on the literature about the *Jamaat-i-
Islami*. The paper gives an in-depth analysis of the ideology and
programme of the Jamaat. The author observes that future his-
torians cannot ignore the effective role played by the *Jamaat* in
Pakistan's politics and 'it is partly *Jamaat-i-Islami*'s confidence in
the efficiency of democratic institutions as a means for smooth

transformation of a society, and partly Maulana Mawdudi's personal sense of horror against violence and bloodshed, that the *Jamaati-i-Islami* has confined its activities to peaceful, constitutional methods. It has constantly been subjected to persecution, and was twice even dissolved; still it chose to abide by the law—even an unjust law—and confine its struggle to peaceful methods' (p. 25).

135 AZIZ, K. K., *Party politics in Pakistan 1947–1958*. Islamabad: National Commission on Historical and Cultural Research, 1976.

The author critically discusses party structure, ideology and the role of the *Jamaat* in Pakistan politics. The author shows that Mawdudi in his early years was impressed by Nazi and Fascist parties and disliked democracy but encouraged the idea of a totalitarian Amir (Head of State) to whom could be shown obedience and discipline.

Furthermore, the author asserts that Mawdudi made a threefold classification of the Muslims in Pakistan. The majority (90 per cent) comprised the poor and uneducated masses. The remainder was more or less equally divided into those uncontaminated by Western influence and those that were. The *Jamaat* was interested only in those who were immune from Western influence.

Finally the author gives some idea of the *Jamaat*'s propaganda machinery, membership regulations and social welfare activities such as maintaining dispensaries, helping flood-stricken victims and operating reading rooms.

136 BAHADUR, Kalim, *The Jamaat-i-Islami of Pakistan: political thought and political action*. New Delhi: Chetana Publications, 1977.

A critical evaluation of the political role of the *Jamaat*. The *Jamaat*'s organizational structure and ideology is discussed and its framework for Islamic economics, Islamic ethics and Islamic social justice. Furthermore the political antecedents of the *Jamaat* are traced to the various Islamic movements in the eighteenth and nineteenth centuries in India. The author also focuses on Mawdudi's life and *Jamaat* political activities in prepartition times and its attitude towards the Pakistan movement. Other chapters deal with its political role under Ayub, Yahya and Bhutto.

In conclusion the author observes that 'Mawdudi and the *Jamaat-i-Islami* can be best understood as representatives of one of the most important Muslim reactions to the challenges thrown by the modern world' (p. 206). It is essential reading for any study of the *Jamaat* to test the contentions of the author.

137 BARKAT, A. M., 'The Islamisation of Pakistani law and Christian theological responsibility'. *Al-Mushir*, Vol. XX, No. 3, Autumn 1978. Pp. 115–118.

The author discusses the whole issue of the Islamization of Pakistani law and its relevance to the political order in Pakistan. He concludes by stating that a critical dimension of the Islamic order must be kept open to engage in dialogue about it otherwise 'if all laws are drawn from the Qur'an and *Sunnah,* then no questions can be raised as to the desirability and validity of these laws. It will be impossible to debate and to question any law, because that would be considered opposition to Islam. That would inhibit public debate and discussion, without which thinking could not take place. The political consequences could be serious for the development of democratic polity, which is built on debate and discussion with regard to all laws and policies. This would also entail a far greater burden and responsibility than hitherto assumed by any previous government. Then government would have the duty to preserve not only political order but also the purity of religious truth. This would require extraordinary qualities of religious conduct and behaviour. It would require that only Muslims be part of the political, legal and social institutions in Pakistan. Where would such persons come from?' (pp. 117–118). The author is obviously putting forward the secularist line of argument that sovereignty belongs to the people and as such laws made by them could be debated by them.

138 BINDER, Leonard, *Religion and politics in Pakistan.* Berkeley, Calif.: University of California Press, 1961.

An important contribution to the study of Islam in Pakistan. The author discusses the various Islamic issues and conflicts between the government's view and the views of the Ulama. Among the latter the author considers the *Jamaat-i-Islami* as the 'only significant fundamentalist organization in Pakistan, and its chief, Maulana Mawdudi ... its principal thinker and spokesman' (p. 75). After giving a brief history of Mawdudi, the author discusses the 'official history of the Jamaat' and Mawdudi's political theory, and role in the creation of Pakistan. The author concludes by writing that 'to the extent that Pakistan will remain prematurely democratic (in the sense that economic development and literacy may be the proper basis of democratic government) to that extent will Islam be stressed rather than actual political issues. To the extent that economic development and literacy increase, to that extent will Islam become more of a real issue in itself' (p. 380).

139 BROHI, A. K., 'Mawlana Abul A'la Mawdudi: the man, the scholar, the reformer', in K. Ahmad, *et al, Islamic perspectives: studies in honour of Sayyid Abul A'la Mawdudi.* Leicester: the Islamic Foundation, 1979.

The author has acted as defence lawyer in many of Mawdudi's political trials and has been deeply influenced by his personality and his writings. The author traces the historical role which Mawdudi played in Pakistan's politics and that the 'one person responsible for mobilizing public opinion in favour of establishing a state which was to reflect the Muslim ideal was none other than Mawdudi' (p. 295). Mawdudi, in the opinion of Brohi, was 'made of the stuff heroes are made from' (p. 304). Brohi's essay written within this perspective is a positive contribution to the literature about Mawdudi.

140 CONN, H. M., 'Socialism in Pakistan: an overview'. *Islamic Studies*, Vol. XV, No. 2, Summer 1976. Pp. 111–121.

Mawdudi's view on Islam as 'a golden mean between capitalism and Marxism' has been given.

141 CRAGG, K., *Counsels in contemporary Islam*. Edinburgh: Edinburgh University Press, 1965. Pp. 120–124.

The author finds many similarities between the *Jamaat-i-Islami* and the *Ikhwan*. Mawdudi, like Hassan al-Banna, started his career as a journalist and did not strictly belong to the Ulama. Also like the *Ikhwan*, Mawdudi insisted that Islam can come to terms with modern life but only by a 'renewal of sound faith and pure discipline'.

The author then briefly summarizes the arguments put forward by Mawdudi in his various books like *Towards understanding Islam, Nationalism and India, Muslims and the present political struggle* and *The process of Islamic revolution*. The appeal of the *Jamaat*, although not as widespread as the *Ikhwan*, was 'mainly to those who, like the founder, had little or no acquaintance with the Western languages and learning, but counted themselves intellectuals and men of prayer. Membership involves a probation and promises of religious and doctrinal loyalty' (p. 124).

Furthermore, despite the compromises the *Jamaat* has had to make, it has contrasted favourably 'with the opportunism of the secular Muslims and the airiness of the liberals' (p. 124) and 'if one is looking for a serious Islam making a sustained effort after loyalty of worship and the sense of God, in the midst of bewilderment and shifting passions and much time-serving, one may find it in the discipleship of al-Banna and Mawdudi' (p. 124).

142 DASKAWIE, M. A. Q., 'Legal aspects of an Islamic order'. *Al-Mushir*, Vol. XX, No. 3, Autumn 1978. Pp. 108–114.

The author points out the legal aspects of the ideal Islamic order and without referring directly to the *Jamaat-i-Islami* alludes to it by writing that 'the conservative elements of our society have been clamouring for the introduction of the total Sharia immediately, as a panacea for the many ills which plague our society. There are others, however, who while agreeing with this demand would like to see first that the other conditions (social, economic and cultural) as provided for in the Sharia are fulfilled as a pre-condition to the introduction or imposition of the Sharia' (p. 114). The goal therefore should be to make Pakistan an ideal Islamic state which would serve as a pattern for other Muslim countries provided the prerequisites for it can be fulfilled.

143 DEKMEJIAN, R. H., 'The Islamic revival in the Middle East and North Africa'. *Current History*, Vol. 78, No. 456, April 1980. Pp. 169–74.

Discusses the revival of Islam with special reference to Libya, Syria, Iraq and Pakistan.

144 DIL, F. S., ' The myth of Islamic resurgence in South Asia'. *Current History*' Vol. 78, No. 456, April 1980. Pp. 165–68, 185–86.

Discusses the resurgence of Islam in Afghanistan, Bangladesh and Pakistan.

145 ESPOSITO, J. L., 'Pakistan: quest for Islamic identity', in J. L. Esposito, (ed.) *Islam and development: religion and sociopolitical change.* New York: Syracuse University Press, 1980. Pp. 139–162.

The article focuses on Pakistan's quest for an Islamic identity in the post-colonial period right through to the Zia-ul Haq regime. It concludes by stating that 'the quest to articulate its Islamic identity has yielded limited results' (p. 157).

146 FARUQI, Ziya-ul-Hasan, *The Deoband school and the demand for Pakistan.* New York: Asia Publishing House, 1963.

The book gives a brief reference to Maulana Mawdudi but its importance lies in giving a good background to the Islamic groups in the subcontinent such as the Deoband and Barelawi schools whose impact has not diminished.

147 FELDMAN, H., *The end and the beginning: Pakistan 1969–1971.* Karachi: Oxford University Press, 1976.

Brief references to the *Jamaat-i-Islami*'s role as an opposition group during the Yahya regime.

148 GAUHAR, A., *Translations from the Quran.* London: Islamic Information Services Ltd., 1977.

The book contains selected translations from Mawdudi's *Tafheemul Quran* which the writer has translated into English. A brief introduction has been added and the writer concludes that 'the spontaneity, warmth and precision of language, which is characteristic of Syed Abul A'la Mawdudi's style, comes from a profound understanding of the Qur'an, the life of the Prophet, and Islamic history. The approach is always objective and the exposition illuminating. No extraneous ideas are introduced and the sole concern of the author is to bring the reader into immediate and intimate contact with the original' (pp. 42–43).

149 GAUHAR, A., 'Mawlana Abul A'la Mawdudi—a personal account', in K. Ahmad, *et al, Islamic perspectives: studies in honour of Sayyid Abul A'la Mawdudi*. Leicester: the Islamic Foundation, 1979. Pp. 265–288.

A bureaucrat's impression of his encounter with Mawdudi and the influence which the latter's work (*Tafhim al-Quran*) had on him.

150 GEIJBELS, M., 'Pakistan, Islamization and the Christian minority'. *Al Mushir*, Vol. XXI, No. 2, Summer 1979. Pp. 31–51.

The author discusses the origin and development of the Islamic state in Pakistan. The struggle of the various groups for the Islamization of Pakistan is traced through the political history of the country right up to Pakistan's National Alliance role which ousted Bhutto from the political arena. Some opposition to the rules for Islamization is shown by the Shia, who by following the Fiqh Jafariyya opposed those laws framed under the Sunni Fiqh in Pakistan.

151 GEIJBELS, M., 'Salient features of an Islamic order'. *Al-Mushir*, Vol. XX, No. 3, Autumn 1978. Pp. 90–98.

The author discusses the various aspects and issues of the implementation of the Islamic order. With relevance to its implementation in Pakistan, he detects three trends, the liberal, moderate and traditional. In this last category he places Mawdudi as belonging to the trend of Islamic thought which considers Islam to be a complete code of life.

152 GHAYUR, M. A., *et al*, 'The Religio-political parties (JUI, JUP, JI): role of the Ulama in Pakistan's politics'. Paper presented at the New England Conference of the Association for Asian Studies held at the University of Connecticut, Storra, Connecticut on 20–21 October, 1979.

The paper considers the Ulama as an elite group in Pakistan with particular reference to the three political parties, *Jamiat-i-Ulama-i-Islam* (JUI), *Jamiat-i-Ulama-i-Pakistan* (JUP) and *Jamaat-i-Islami* (JI).

153 GILANI, Syed Asaf, *Maududi: thought and movement*. Lahore: Matbaat-ul-Maktabal-el-Ilmiyyah, 1978.

This book aims to present Mawdudi from all aspects. Internally his life is presented through his autobiography printed in Chapter 3 and through excerpts of his writings on various aspects of Islam (Chapter 16). How Mawdudi is viewed by others is given in Chapter 8 entitled 'Mawdudi in the eyes of others'. The author's own contribution has been to write an introduction to his thought (Chapter 4), Dawah (Chapter 5), Trials (Chapter 7), Service to Islam (Chapter 10), role as statesman (Chapter 11), introduction to his publications (Chapter 18). Also included is a supplement giving chronological events from 1915 to 1972. The book is therefore an important contribution to the political biography of Mawdudi because so few have been written.

154   Government of the Punjab, Report of the Court of Inquiry constituted under Punjab Act II of 1954 to enquire into the Punjab Disturbances of 1953. Lahore: Government Printing, 1954.

This is a report of the court of inquiry into the rioting which occurred in the Punjab province in March 1953 on the non-compliance of the government to the demands of religious parties to declare the Ahmadis as non-Muslims. Martial Law was declared in the province for the first time and the rioting was brought under control. The report is important because it investigates the viewpoints of the Ulama and the *Jamaat* and gives its own bureaucratic interpretation of *Jamaat* and Islam.

155   HAQ, M., 'Some reflections on Islam and constitution-making in Pakistan 1947–56'. *Islamic Studies*, Vol. V, No. 2, 1966. Pp. 209–220.

Gives the viewpoints of political parties, including the *Jamaat* in constitution-making in Pakistan during the period 1947–1956.

156   HUSSAIN, Asaf, *Elite politics in an ideological state: the case of Pakistan.* Folkestone, Kent: William Dawson & Sons Ltd., 1979.

The author analyzes the political system of Pakistan from an elitist point of view. Six elite groups are identified who play a crucial role or exert political influence on the political system. These groups are the landlords, bureaucrats, military generals, industrialists, professional elites (lawyers, intellectuals, etc.) and the religious elites. The elite group is composed of various types of religious groups like local Maulvis, Ulama and Pirs in the provinces. All these, according to their different interpretations of Islam, subscribe to different political parties such as *Jamiatul-Ulema-i-Pakistan*, *Jamiatul-Ulema-i-Islam* and the *Jamaat-i-Islami*. Among these the most important is the latter and the main focus of the chapter on 'Religious Elites' is on the *Jamaat* and its political role in Pakistan.

157 HUSSAIN, Asaf, 'From nationhood to Umma: the struggle of Islam in Pakistan'. *Asian Thought and Society*, Vol. V, No. 13, April 1980. Pp. 47–57.

The paper focuses on three aspects. First, it explores how Islam played the most important role in the formation of Pakistan. Secondly, how the generation of anti-Islamic forces within the country have ideologically conflicted with the Islamic forces in post-colonial Pakistan. Lastly it examines the future of Islam in Pakistan.

158 JAHAN, Rounaq, *Pakistan: failure in national integration*. New York: Columbia University Press, 1972.

The author considers the *Jamaat* as being mainly a party dominated by the then West Pakistan *Muhajirs* (refugees) and as such it failed to establish grass-root linkages among the indigenous people in East Pakistan (now Bangladesh). It established its support base among the *Muhajirs* 'partly because the Jamaat was the only organization doing social work among them, and partly because the idea of true Islamic community has been very real to the refugees, who sacrificed so much for it' (p. 134). The author focuses mainly on the strength of the *Jamaat* in East Pakistan which was very weak due to reasons other than those given above. It could not mobilize various sectors of Bengali society because they had been penetrated by other political parties such as the *Nizami-i-Islam*. Furthermore, it could not cultivate the students as it did in West Pakistan because they too had been mobilized by leftist and nationalist parties such as the Awami League. The *Jamaat*, in spite of its highly disciplined, cadre party' could not attract much support in Bengali society.

159 JALIL, Yusuf, 'Political aspects of an Islamic order'. *Al-Mushir*, Vol. XX, No. 3, Autumn 1978. Pp. 99–107.

The author points out the political aspects of the Islamic order, but reaches the conclusion that 'as Pakistan is about to introduce the Nizam-i-Islam, one of the questions to be decided is: which form of government the country is going to adopt. To this question the Qur'an and Sunna give, in our opinion, no definite answer' (p. 106). Also he contests the fact whether sovereignty belongs to God and in order to counteract this claim of Mawdudi quotes from F. Rahman who blamed Mawdudi for drawing 'the comic conclusion that sovereignty in Islam, i.e. possessing the real power of legislation, is God, not man ... it is obvious enough that here the idea of political sovereignty has been illegitimately transferred to God' (p. 106). Drawing from this the author concludes that parliamentary democracy is in conformity with the spirit of Islam.

160 JAMEELAH, Maryam, *Who is Mawdudi?* Lahore: Muhammad Yusuf Khan, 1973. 68p.

The author has compressed a lot of information about Mawdudi's life as an introduction to those who want to know something about the man. Extensive quotations are given from Mawdudi's writings and press statements.

161 JONES, Philip E., 'Islam and politics under Ayub and Bhutto: a comparative assessment'. Paper presented to the 7th Wisconsin Conference on South Asia, 3–4 November, 1978. South Asia Center, Wisconsin University.

The author compares the role of Islam under the regimes of Ayub and Bhutto and how these dictators tried to manipulate it. The author notes that 'mass political consciousness came to Muslims in India by way of religion, so too did notions of systemic economic change. In this sense, Islam has been a moderating force. But, it has also been a modernising force, introducing concepts of systematic change, which also point the way to crucial cognitive and ideological transformations' (p. 22).

162 KHAN, A. A., *Jamaat-e-Islami. Pakistan. Introduction Series No. 2.* Dacca: Maktaba Jamaat-e-Islami, n.d. 18p.

Gives a brief history of the *Jamaat*, its technique of work and its political and economic programmes.

163 KHAN, Mohammad Ayub, *Friends not masters: a political autobiography.* New York: Oxford University Press, 1967.

General Ayub Khan ruled Pakistan for almost a decade and in his autobiography his view of the Ulama sheds interesting light on why the military regime was constantly in conflict with them. While writing about the Ulama he singles out Mawdudi and observes that 'this venerable gentleman was appalled by what he saw in Pakistan: an un-Islamic country, un-Islamic government, and an un-Islamic people. How could any genuine Muslim owe allegiance to such a government. So he set about the task of convincing the people of their inadequacies, their failings and their general unworthiness. All this was really a facade. The true intention was to re-establish the supremacy of the Ulama and to reassert the right to lead the community. Since the movement for Pakistan was guided by the enlightened classes under the leadership of a man who was the symbol of Western education, the prestige of the Ulama had been badly damaged. This damage had to be repaired. The political Ulama had two courses open to them: either to re-examine their own position and to revise their attitudes so that the people might be able to gain from their knowledge in dealing with their problems; or to demolish the position of the educated classes in the eyes of God-fearing but uneducated masses. Not unnaturally, they adopted the latter course' (p. 203). Ayub was a Sandhurst-trained general and his attitude was not unnaturally to adopt the former course.

164 LATIFF, M. R. A., 'The way ahead for Jamaat-e-Islami', Part I. *Saura al-Islam*, Vol. 3, Nos. 9–10, September–October, 1977. Pp. 6–9, 17.

The author surveys the role of the *Jamaat* in Pakistan's politics by focusing on its strengths and weaknesses. Its strength lies in its efforts to establish the Islamic way of life, discipline of its members, ability to relate the teachings of Islam to current happenings in society and its ability for conflict-management both at intra-group and intergroup levels. The author therefore summarizes its strengths by writing that 'the Jamaat has given an Islamic analysis of the Pakistani situation. Nobody in Pakistan can put forward the idea that Islam is a religion which can exist alongside liberalism, socialism, nationalism, communism, etc. It is in this sense that we can say that the Islamic revolution is at a more advanced stage in Pakistan than anywhere else in the world today' (p. 17). On the other hand, the author notes that: 'However there is little prospect that an Islamic state can be established in Pakistan within the next decade. Despite the 36 years struggle of the Jamaat it remains a small party with no impact on the life of the 80 percent of the Pakistanis who live in the villages. Even in cities where its influence is greatest, immorality, Westernization and views of all sorts flourish and increase. Its strength derives from its superior organizational ability, its higher level of social analysis and its success in co-ordinating activity in many spheres of society. Its strength does not flow from a fundamental change in the moral orientation of the majority of the Pakistani people. That is why although there is no organized group in Pakistan which can challenge its ideology and the policies that originate from this ideology the Jamaat remains incapable of posing a threat to those in power' (p. 17).

165 McDONOUGH, S., 'Pakistan'. *The Muslim World*, Vol. LVI, No. 4, October 1966. Pp. 262–269.

This whole issue of *The Muslim World* is devoted to a symposium on 'Islam in Politics'. In the section on Pakistan, the author discusses the conflict between religion and politics in Pakistan. The author observes that religious dissent in Pakistan is headed by Mawdudi who like other Pakistanis has grown and changed some of his ideas in the course of Pakistan's sometimes turbulent history, but 'his ideal remains unchanged. This ideal is something like "government by the pure" and the implication is that the "pure" namely, completely trustworthy and incorruptable leaders can be trained and moulded by the right teachers and the right system. An upholder of the belief in such a government by the "pure" has always an advantageous position over any government actually in power. Mawdudi, himself attracts much support because his own integrity is unquestioned, and because he, therefore, seems to many something like a beacon of purity indicating the ideal. His attractiveness perhaps derives more from his personality than from his ideas' (p. 268).

166 McDONOUGH, S., 'Some leading ideas constitutive of Pakistan's nationhood'. *Islamic Studies*, Vol. VII, No. 1, 1968. Pp. 9–31.

Discusses Mawdudi's thought and power in Pakistan. With regard to the latter the author writes that Mawdudi's 'power in the Pakistan context derives from the appeal of writings and from the example of his followers. He has undertaken to create a nucleus of devoted disciples who incarnate his beliefs, who are active in many areas of social service and who are ready to seek political power through democratic channels as long as this is the system open to them' (p. 23). The thoughts of Ghulam Ahmad Parvez are also discussed in the latter part of the paper.

167 MAHMOOD, Safdar, *A political study of Pakistan*. Lahore: Sheikh Muhammad Ashraf, 1978.

In the section on political parties the author discusses the role of the *Jamaat* in Pakistan's politics. It was a highly organized party but due to its restricted membership 'it never tried to grow into a mass organization like other political parties'.

168 MAWDUDI, S. Abul A'la, 'Iqbal and Islam'. *The Universal Message*, Vol. I, No. 8, January 1980. Pp. 5–7.

Mawdudi's assessment of Iqbal, the poet-philosopher of Pakistan. He considers that Iqbal had nothing but 'Islam and its supremacy in his mind' (p. 7).

169 MAWDUDI, S. Abul A'la, *Jihad in Islam*. Kuwait: International Islamic Federation of Student Organizations, 1977.

In this booklet, Mawdudi's speech delivered on Iqbal Day on 13 April 1939 at the Town Hall in Lahore is reprinted. Mawdudi's exposition of the revolutionary concept of Jihad.

170 MAWDUDI, S. Abul A'la, *The moral foundations of the Islamic movement*. Lahore: Islamic Publications Ltd., 1976.

The speech published in this booklet was delivered by the author at Dar-ul Islam near Pathankot (East Punjab) on 21 April 1945.

The author contends that the real goal of religion in this world is to establish the leadership of the righteous.

171 MAWDUDI, S. Abul A'la, *The process of Islamic revolution*. Lahore: Islamic Publications, 1970.

An important work on the process of Islamic revolution which describes the ideological state, the divine Caliphate, the method of Islamic revolution and the technique of Islamic movement. The work advocates a gradual and not a radical move towards the Islamic revolution.

172 MAWDUDI, S. Abul A'la, *A short history of the revivalist movement in Islam*. Lahore: Islamic Publications Ltd., 1963.

The author discusses the conflict between Islam and un-Islam, the nature of Islamic revival, achievements of some great Mujaddids and work of Shah Waliullah of Delhi.

173 MAWDUDI, S. Abul A'la, 'Twenty-nine years of the Jamaat-e-Islami'. *The Criterion*, Vol. 5, No. 6, November–December 1970. Pp. 28–62.

On 26 August 1970, the Foundation Day of the *Jamaat*, Mawdudi delivered a speech in which he recounted the political role of the *Jamaat* over 29 years. It is a very important article which views the *Jamaat* through Mawdudi's eyes.

174 MEHDI, Sibte, 'Jamaat-i-Islami's policy towards the Zia regime'. *Saura al-Islam*, Vol. 4, No. 7, July 1978. Pp. 6–17.

An analytical article on the *Jamaat*'s policy of supporting the military regime of General Zia ul Haque. The author contends that the Jamaat's support for the regime is based on the following factors: (1) the opinion of the *Jamaat* that the Zia regime is able and willing to institutionalize Islamic practices at the collective level in Pakistan; (2) the inability of the *Jamaat* to raise the Islamic consciousness of the people sufficiently on the basis of its own 30 year struggle for the establishment of an Islamic state.

The author concludes that should the *Jamaat* form a coalition with the Zia regime, it should observe certain conditions such as: (1) focus attention on developing a cultural and economic base for the party; (2) agreement with the Zia regime ... for government neutrality in the struggle between the *Jamaat-i-Islami* and those who oppose the construction of an economic and cultural base by the *Jamaat*; (3) the *Jamaat* should not accept more than two ministries; (4) ministers nominated by the *Jamaat-i-Islami* should not be intellectuals, technocrats or experts ... but revolutionary militants like Malik Shafi, Burakullah and Aminuddin Hussaini who are at home in the villages and in the trade unions and who are loved by the masses; (5) the strategy of educating the elite should be abandoned (p. 17).

175   MEHDI, Sibte, 'The way ahead for Jamaat-i-Islami'. *Saura al-Islam*, Vol. 5, No. 1, January, 1979. Pp. 8–16.

The author contends that the *Jamaat* must give up its reformist approach because: (1) such an approach will involve a sacrifice of the Islamic revolutionary identity of the party; (2) sacrifice of the Islamic revolutionary identity must mean a practical renunciation of Maulana Mawdudi's thought on the process of systemic transformation; (3) Maulana Mawdudi's analysis of the need for another method of achieving systemic transformation is fundamentally correct; (4) the present regime is not committed to a fundamental transformation (p. 9).

The author therefore proposes that the way towards bringing an Islamic revolution should be to build the party as a fortress of Islam, give a comprehensive programme for economic base construction, arm the workers, develop an intensive programme of moral, spiritual and religious training, encourage criticism and appraisal, seize power in civil society and neutralize the state's repressive machinery.

176   MEHDI, Sibte, 'The way ahead of the Ikhwan al-Muslimoon'. Part 2. *Suara al-Islam*, Vol. 3, Nos. 2–3, February–March 1977.

Criticism of the *Jamaat*'s Saudi policy by Mawdudi arising out of what Mawdudi wrote that 'Saudi Arabia is the heart of the Muslim world . . . even if all the Muslim countries in the world were steeped in inequity and laxity it would not cause as much harm to the cause of Islam, as it would if, God forbid, Saudi Arabia starts showing these trends . . .'. The author states this policy by pointing out the misconceptions of the Jamaat about the Saudi regime.

177   MINTJES, H., 'Mawlana Mawdudi's last years and the resurgence of fundamentalist Islam'. *Al-Mushir*, Vol. XXII, No. 2, Summer 1980. Pp. 46–73.

An important article which discusses Mawdudi's concern with Islam and Pakistan till the very end of his life. The author makes a distinction between fundamentalism and the Ulama. The former is a movement 'somewhere in between Westernizing modernism and Ulama traditionalism' (p. 53). It does not represent conservative Islam but 'preaches a return to the fundamentals of Islam so as to make the Islamic law (Shariah) a renewed, vital code for all aspects of life which will result in a perfect Islamic socio-political system (p. 53). The Ulama's model is based on medieval Islam while the fundamentalists take it from pristine Islam. Mawdudi therefore cannot be classed with the Ulama but with the fundamentalists. His contribution is therefore lasting but it 'lies more in removing doubts and misgivings about Islam and in stiffening Muslim self-confidence than in offering detailed suggestions for an Islamic order' (p. 72). As for the resurgence of Islam the author contends there are two reasons. In the first place Islam is central to all aspects of human life and therefore it has not allowed itself to become 'privatised and pushed from public life' (p. 55). Secondly, the fundamentalist Islamic resurgence is due to petro-dollars in some Muslim countries.

178 MOGNI, A., 'Islamic renaissance in modern times'. *Radiance*, February 8, 1981. Pp. 3–4, 11.

Islamic renaissance is seen as an outcome of the domination of the East by the West through colonial rule. Some of the leaders of nationalist movements such as Maulana Mohammad Ali and Maulana Abul Kalam Azad were also leaders of Islamic renaissance. However, the Western educated elites opposed all forms of Islamic renaissance. As a result, there arose from among the masses a new breed of leaders such as Maulana Mawdudi who led fundamentalist Islamic movements. The author then briefly discusses the ideology of fundamentalist Islam.

179 MUTAHAR, S. H., 'Abul Ala Maudoodi: sublime in thought and performance. *Rabitat al-Alam al-Islami*, Vol. 6, No. 12, October 1979. Pp. 4–5.

A short appreciation of Mawdudi's life written after his death on 22 September 1979.

180 MUTAHAR, S. H., 'Maudoodi's views on Islamic polity'. *Rabitat al-Alam al-Islami*, Vol. 6, No. 12, October 1979. Pp. 52–56.

The author interviewed Mawdudi in January 1970 and his views on Islamic polity in question-answer form are given.

181 QURESHI, I. H., *Ulama in politics*. Karachi: Maaref Publishers Ltd., 1971.

The author surveys the political activities of the Ulama in the South Asian subcontinent from 1556 to 1947. References are made to Mawdudi as an important Ulama in pre-partition politics and his way of thinking on issues confronting the Muslims is given on various aspects. The idea of Muslims that they were a separate community from the Hindus was often opposed by the latter who, as nationalists, wanted them to belong to the 'Indian nation'. Mawdudi exposed this fallacy through his writings and one of his convincing arguments was that 'the trouble with these persons is that they consider manifestations of civilisation to be culture itself

... In fact culture is that way of thinking, that ideology and those criteria, which determine the choice of a goal from among many which attract a substantial section of humanity. Under the influence of a chosen goal a people adopt one of the different ways of life. Civilisation is another name for a way of life and a culture springs from the (chosen) civilisation' (p. 337).

Mawdudi has often been criticized for his lack of optimism in the creation of Pakistan. The author corrects this misconception by stating that Mawdudi had three alternatives of autonomy, federation and confederation of the Muslim British India, for his aim was to create an Islamic community and not a secular state (p. 370).

While many people may not concur with Mawdudi's views the author believes that his superior knowledge, cold logic and vast knowledge of law and political science made it difficult for others to rebut him. His role in prepartition politics can be assessed from this book and shows him to be a very prominent and politically concerned Ulama during those times.

182 RAHMAN, Fazlur, 'The controversy over the Muslim family laws', in D. E. Smith (ed.), *South Asian politics and religion*. Princeton, NJ: Princeton University Press, 1966. Pp. 414-427.

The whole area of family laws with particular emphasis on polygamy, divorce and inheritance is discussed in the context of the controversy over it in Pakistan. In the conclusion entitled 'Obstacles to Islamic revival', the author makes the following observations. First, that conservative groups in Pakistan are uncompromising and have 'clung tenaciously to relatively external expressions of the faith, expressions which are more or less formal, at the expense of inner growth' (p. 427). Secondly, 'academic life' in 'religious seminaries' has been inferior as compared to Al-Azhar in Egypt and Zaytunah in Tunis. The outcome of this has been the 'quality of our Ulama in general, despite certain exceptional men who have arisen now and again, is generally poorer than that of the Middle Eastern Ulama in point of scholarship' (p. 427). Thirdly, the 'Middle Eastern countries are in more direct and frequent contact with Europe, and this influence has naturally had some effect on the development of the Ulama also' (p. 427) and lastly, men like Shaikh Muhammad Abduh have risen from the ranks of the Ulama and have exerted widespread influence on orthodox developments in the Middle East, while in the subcontinent 'people who have played a prominent role in introducing modernist thinking to Islam have been outside the ranks of the Ulama and, although they have left a tremendous legacy to the Muslim community as a whole, have not been able to influence the custodians of the Shariah to any large extent' (p. 427).

183 RAHMAN, Fazlur, 'Current religious thought in Pakistan'. *Islamic Studies*, Vol. VII, No. 1, March 1968. Pp. 1–7.

The author focuses on the *Jamaat* as one of the strong undercurrents of religious thought in Pakistan. He observes that the *Jamaat* has turned conservative 'even though they had started as a partly liberalising force. This unfortunate development is only partly, not wholly, connected with the external fortunes of Mawdudi and his party in Pakistan since the partition . . .' (p. 4). He then poses the question whether Mawdudi would have functioned as a genuine liberalizing intellectual force 'if he had not come into politics and been in constant conflict with the established authority? . . .' (p. 5).

184 RAHMAN, Fazlur, 'Implementation of the Islamic concept of state in the Pakistani milieu'. *Islamic Studies*, Vol. VI, No. 3, 1967. Pp. 205–224.

The problems arising from the implementation of the Islamic concept of State and the *Jamaat*'s view's on various aspects of it have been discussed.

185 RAHMAN, Fazlur, 'Islam and the new constitution of Pakistan'. *Journal of Asian and African Studies*, Vol. VIII, Nos. 3–4, 1973. Pp. 190–204.

The article focuses mainly on the discussion of the Constitution of 1973 adapted in Pakistan during Bhutto's rule. It also refers back to the most crucial issue in which the author differs from the *Jamaat* by stating that 'so far as Islam is concerned, the most formidable difficulty faced by the constitution-makers of Pakistan at the very outset was the location of the sovereignty in the new state and whether democracy was Islamic or not. Already before the creation of Pakistan . . . Mawdudi had forcefully contended that Islam could not accept modern democracy since in a democracy people are law-makers, whereas in Islam God is the law-giver. Twisting the purely religious sense in which the Qur'an speaks of God as 'sovereign in heaven and earth' into a modern political sense, Mawdudi and, following him, the traditionalist Ulama insisted that the constitution must recognize the sovereignty of Allah. The idea behind this was, of course to accept the sovereignty of the Sharia law. The modernist should have stood firm in the principle of the political sovereignty of the people because otherwise one would have to admit the ludicrous conclusion that in officially atheistic countries God had set up governments in exile! The modernist instead compromised' (p. 199).

186 RAHMAN, Fazlur, 'Some Islamic issues in the Ayyub Khan era', in D. P. Little, *Essays on Islamic civilisation*. Leiden: E. J. Brill, 1976. Pp. 284–302.

Various issues such as family laws, family planning, banking and interest, Zakat, mechanical slaughter of animals, etc., which created political furore during the Ayyub regime are discussed. The Islamic interpretation is given of various religious parties including the *Jamaat*.

187   RICHTER, W. L., 'Pakistan', in M. Ayoob (ed.), *The politics of Islamic reassertion.* London: Croom Helm, 1981. Pp. 141–164.

The article discusses the causes for the downfall of Z. A. Bhutto and the role of the *Islam—pasand* (lovers of Islam) parties, notably the *Jamaat-i-Islami*, the *Jamiat-ul-Ulema-i-Islam* and the *Jamiat-ul-Ulema-i-Pakistan.* The author asserts that General Zia reflects Mawdudi's ideas which are that '(1) the sovereignty of Allah, as defined in the Sharia, should be recognised as the basic law of the land; (2) the state should be ruled by a single man whose tenure of office and power are limited only by his faithfulness to the ideology of the state; (3) the *Amir* (ruler) is to be assisted by a *Shura* (advisory council) composed of men with the educational qualification to make valid applications of the fundamental law of the Quran and the Sunnah; (4) there should be no political parties and no provision for an opposition; (5) non-Muslims may be allowed to reside safely in an Islamic state, but not to hold any policy making decisions; and (6) minorities must vote as separate electorates' (p. 151).

188   RICHTER, W. L., 'The political dynamics of Islamic resurgence in Pakistan'. *Asian Survey*, Vol. XIX, No. 6, June 1979. Pp. 547–57.

The author focuses mainly on the period immediately preceding the downfall of Bhutto and on the military regime which took over. The role of Islam and the Pakistan National Alliance in Pakistan politics is analysed and the author contends that the people of Pakistan, being disillusioned by the loss of Bangladesh and the capitalist and socialist ideologies, reverted back to Islam in which the *Jamaat* as the dominant party in the PNA played a leading role.

189   ROSENTHAL, E. I. J., *Islam in the modern national state.* Cambridge: Cambridge University Press, 1965.

Two of the chapters in the book are entitled 'An Islamic state for Pakistan?' and 'The Islamic republic of Pakistan'. Rosenthal discusses the Islamic solutions proposed for Pakistan by G. A. Parvez and Sayyid Abul A'la Mawdudi. The focus is mainly on the latter's writings and his thoughts and influence on the political system of Pakistan. After an exposition of Mawdudi's ideas regarding the Islamic state, Rosenthal comments 'Objections could be raised against Mawdudi's aims and intentions both from a more liberal, modernist religious point of view and from a laicist and secularist position. His ideas may be medieval, but it is undeniable that there is faith and religious conviction behind his detailed exposition and practical proposals. They are presented by a determined political leader who is imbued with religious zeal and fights in the lecture hall, on the platform, on the radio and in numerous pamphlets and articles in his own monthly *Tarjuman al-Quran* for an Islamic state as the goal of an Islamic renaissance. That he was imprisoned several times, once condemned to death even, is eloquent testimony to the notice the government of Pakistan takes of this clear-headed religious scholar and forceful leader of a political movement in opposition to it and its policy' (pp. 152–153). The *Jamaat*'s importance for Pakistan's politics is summarized in the above remark.

190 SAULAT, Sarwar, *Maulana Mawdudi*. Karachi: International Islamic Publishers, 1979.

One of the very few full-length political biographies of Mawdudi. It contains 14 chapters and two Appendices. Appendix I is useful because it contains a 'Chronology of important events' of Mawdudi's life. Appendix II contains a bibliography which is not fully comprehensive. The book covers the period of Mawdudi's life under General Zia's regime. Other chapters list his writings and give excerpts of his writings as well as an appreciation of his services in the Muslim world.

191 SAYEED, K. B., 'Islam and national integration in Pakistan', in D. E. Smith (ed.), *South Asian politics and religion*. Princeton, NJ: Princeton University Press, 1966. Pp. 399–413.

The article discusses the role of Islam in relation to national unity and sectarian conflict. Written before the creation of Bangladesh the paper surveys the extent to which Islam was considered as an effective bond of unity between East and West Pakistan. The result of a survey indicated that only 46.6 per cent of East Pakistanis considered it as an effective bond as compared to 80.8 per cent in West Pakistan. Among sectarian conflicts the paper considers the conflict between the Ahmadis and Muslims.

The paper also surveys the role of the *Jamaat-i-Islami* on the legislative processes of Pakistan. What laws could a legislature invested with popular sovereignty legislate in a country like Pakistan? The modernists favoured legislation without any constraints while the orthodox maintained that it had to be in accordance with the limits prescribed in the Qur'an and the *Sunnah*. Certain provisions, like the prohibition of alcohol, interest and gambling and laws for criminals, like cutting off the hands and stoning to death for adultery, could not be repealed or modified by the legislature.

These, according to Maulana Mawdudi were 'mandatory legislation'. Then there was the area of 'recommendatory legislation' and also of 'permissible legislation'. In the latter category legislation was permitted 'keeping in view the ever-increasing requirements of every age' (p. 402). But according to Mawdudi, 'the present Western-educated Muslim leaders of Pakistan were not competent to initiate legislation even within the permissible field, because they were neither well versed in Islamic doctrine nor good Muslims' (p. 402).

192   SAYEED, K. B., 'The Jamaat-i-Islami movement in Pakistan'. *Pacific Affairs*, Vol. 30, No. 1, March 1957. Pp. 59–68.

The paper focuses on the *Jamaat* and its ideology. A brief biography of Mawdudi and his method of recruiting members to the *Jamaat* is given. According to the author the membership of the *Jamaat* is very selective for Mawdudi's aim 'is to train leaders and workers and not to increase mere membership. Mawdudi divides the Muslim population of Pakistan as follows: 90 per cent of the Muslims, he says, who are poor and uneducated, are deeply devoted and loyal to Islam, but they are so grossly ignorant of its cardinal doctrines and principles that their love of Islam can be easily exploited by what he calls "religious merchants" and Westernised leaders. Out of the remaining ten per cent probably four or five per cent who have not been contaminated by Western influence and culture are loyal and practising Muslims. It is these Muslims that the *Jamaat* is interested in training as potential leaders and active workers who will spread the gospel of the *Jamaat* among the 90 per cent of Muslims who are being misled and exploited by Westernised leaders. To the remaining category belonged Westernised Muslims who, in his view, are determined to foist by fair means or foul a Western and secular sort of state on Pakistan' (p. 64).

While surveying Mawdudi's economic ideas the author states that 'Mawdudi's economic views are influenced not only by Islam but also by the economic theories of men like Marx, Hobson and Major Douglas, but he makes no acknowledgement to them and one can infer the fact only by reading his views in his pamphlet *The economic problem of man and its Islamic solution*'.

The author's overall conclusion is that 'shorn of some of their modern trappings and the jargon of social sciences, Mawdudi's ideas will seem similar to those of the Ulama's whom he criticizes for being out of date and reactionary. What then explains his fundamental disagreement with the liberal wing of religious and political thought? Perhaps the answer lies in the kind of British liberal education that has been imparted in the British universities and to which Mawdudi has never been exposed'.

193 SAYEED, K. B., 'Mass urban protests as indicators of political change in Pakistan'. *Journal of Commonwealth and Comparative Politics*, Vol. XVII, No. 2, July 1979. Pp. 111–135.

The author throws light on the dynamics of the 1977 Urban Conflict against Bhutto in which the role of the *Jamaat* and Islam are pointed out as an important factor in mass urban political mobilization. He contends that much more than the religious political parties the personality of Prophet Mohammad inspired the masses. He observes that for both religious and practical reasons processions would start from the mosques in Karachi and all the other cities. The slogan which inspired the processionists to face the police lathis or even bullets was the establishment of *Nizam-i-Mustafa*. This was a very powerful symbol because it combined the religion of Islam and the personality of the Prophet Mohammad. Devotion to Islam was there, but the love that the Prophet's personality inspired was for the common man perhaps even more electrifying. This explains why the name of Haji Aftab, a cloth merchant of Lahore, became a legend, for he led the procession against police fire. Some eyewitness accounts have suggested to the author that this encounter was perhaps one of the deadliest blows struck at the Bhutto regime. When the author, in February 1978, toured parts of the walled city of Lahore which had been the battleground of the movement, he was repeatedly told that the movement was not created by any political party or any organization. It was a 'miracle' which could not be explained by reason or logic. People who did not strictly follow Islam nevertheless advanced to face bullets in the name of Nizam-i-Mustafa (p. 130).

194 SIDDIQI, Q. Z., *et al*, 'A bibliography of writings by and about Mawlana Sayyid Abul A'la Mawdudi', in K. Ahmad, *et al* (eds), *Islamic perspectives: studies in honour of Mawlana Sayyid Abul A'la Mawdudi*. Leicester: The Islamic Foundation, 1979. Pp. 3–14.

A comprehensive bibliography which lists 138 items of Mawdudi's writings and also indicates in which languages they have been translated. Part two of the bibliography lists 62 items written about Mawdudi, mainly in English and Urdu.

195 SIDDIQUE, Kaukab, 'In memorium: Sayyid Abul Ala Maudoodi: 1903–1979'. *Islamic Revolution*, Vol. II, No. 8, September 1980. Pp. 20–22.

A brief but good appreciation of the Mawdudi's works such as *Al-Jihad-fil-Islam*, *Tafhim ul-Quran*, and *Khilafat-o-Mulookiat*.

196 SIDDIQUI, Ghayas Uddin, 'An approach to the study of Jamaat-i-Islami in Pakistan'. Seminar Paper, presented at the Muslim Institute, London, 13 November 1976. 12 p.

This is an important paper that gives an incisive analysis of the *Jamaat-i-Islami*. The author argues that the *Jamaat* has proved incapable of providing alternative political leadership in Pakistan because it lacks a clear vision of the future in conceptual terms of leading the Islamic movement. Its internal organization is also faulty because Mawdudi controlled it with an iron hand and the *Jamaat* has been very sensitive to criticism. Before the partition of India Mawdudi was busy organizing it and in the post-colonial period 'he put the Jamaat on a course for which she was neither prepared nor ready and hence the failures' (p. 6). The *Jamaat* attracted mediocre leadership and as such has lacked grassroot influence and has not been able to challenge the westernized power elites such as the military, bureaucracy, feudals, industrialists, etc. Thus 'had Jamaat succeeded in gaining political power, in the absence of a strong conceptual base, she would have either allowed the existing Western institutions to continue, as Jinnah did in 1947, or resorted to oppression to keep herself in power' (p. 8).

197 SIDDIQUI, Kalim, *Beyond the Muslim Nation States*. London: The Open Press Ltd., 1980. 16 p.

In this booklet the author discusses the difference between Western political science and the Islamic perspective of it. He contends that there is the necessity for a new political science since 'in no field of human endeavour is the contemporary Muslim more confused that he is in the field of political science' (p. 1). Furthermore, he observes that the revivalist movements like the *Ikhwan* and the *Jamaat* have failed to reach their goals 'because of inadequacies in their structures, leadership roles and styles and other human factors' (p. 7).

198 SMITH, D. E., *Religion, politics and social change in the Third World*. New York: The Free Press, 1971.

This is a source book and gives excerpts from various documents, reports, books and statements pertaining to religion and politics in the Third World. Excerpts of various aspects of Islam in Pakistan have also been placed under various headings such as 1956 Constitution, Muslim Family Laws in Pakistan, and The Ideological Islamic State. An excerpt from Mawdudi's book *Nationalism and India* has also been given under the heading 'Nationalism is opposed to Islam' (pp. 113–115).

199 SMITH, Wilfred C., *Islam in modern history*. Princeton, NJ: Princeton University Press, 1957.

Writing more than a decade after his *Modern Islam in India* (*see item* 200), the author follows the same trend and is still very critical of Mawdudi. In Chapter 5 of the book entitled 'Pakistan Islamic State' he devotes two pages to Mawdudi and the *Jamaat-i-Islami*'s political role in Pakistan. Commenting on Mawdudi he observes that 'to judge from his own expositions, it would appear that he aims at imposing his system on Pakistan, if he can contrive to get his group into a position of power ... He evinces but scant concern both for the human beings and their individual welfare who would live under his rule, and with the human beings and their potential weaknesses who might help him enforce it. His ideology seems to make little allowance either for the propensity, which men in positions of authority have all too often demonstrated through human history, to distort even the finest of schemes by individual aberration' (p. 235). Again, in spite of his own prejudices, Smith has to confess that 'nevertheless, one must not underestimate the force of what Mawdudi has to say. In a situation of extreme confusion his movement had propounded an intellectually coherent, almost massive case' (p. 235).

200 SMITH, Wilfred C., *Modern Islam in India: a social analysis.* Lahore: Ripon Printing Press, 1947.

The author is very critical of Mawdudi's ideas and considers him 'the most ominous representative of this trend back to religious conservatism' (p. 177) and his thesis is that 'none of this modern European or American democracy, this Bolshevik regimentation, this Fascist apotheosism, this Turkish revolt from Islam' impresses Muslims for 'the only state for Muslims, for that matter for all the world, is the Islamic theocracy' (p. 277). In Smith's opinion Mawdudi is a 'member of the old school of ignorant, intolerant repressive religionists' (p. 180). In spite of this, Smith is forced to acknowledge Mawdudi's ability 'to win the attention and to hold the esteem of an astonishingly large section of the Muslim student body. The religiously minded Muslims in the universities of India in the early forties have considered him to be the outstanding modern interpreter of Islam' (p. 177).

201 SWEETMAN, J. W., 'Viewpoints in Pakistan' I and II. *The Muslim World*, Vol. XLVII, Nos. 2 and 3, April and July 1957, pp. 111–124, 224–238.

In the first of a two part article the author surveys the Islamic view of prominent Muslim scholars in Pakistan. These include Mawdudi, Sulaiman Nadwi, Muhammad Shafi. In the second part of the article the discussion focuses on Islam and Communist thought.

202 WHEELER, R. S., *The politics of Pakistan: a constitutional quest.* Ithaca, NY: Cornell University Press, 1970.

In discussing the politics of Pakistan the role of the *Jamaat* is also analysed in terms of its programme for the creation of an Islamic order, which involves four tasks: (1) 'The purification of Islam of its accretions; (2) The search for righteous and honest people and their training; (3) The reform of the society along Islamic lines; (4) The reform of the government and the national leadership through constitutional means' (p. 228).

The latter two tasks have involved the *Jamaat* in the political arena but 'successive governments in Pakistan have regarded the *Jamaat* as a threat which cannot be adequately met by political means, in view of its authoritarian and allegedly conspiratorial organization and its reliance on divine sanctions to achieve its ends' (p. 254).

203 WILCOX, Wayne A., 'Ideological dilemmas in Pakistan's political culture' in D. E. Smith, (ed.), *South Asian politics and religion*. Princeton, N.J.: Princeton University Press, 1966. Pp. 339–351.

The article discusses the role of Islam in Pakistan's politics before and after the creation of the state in 1947. Pakistani nationalism, the author contends, was beset with a unique problem for it did not contain the general attributes of nationalism such as 'a common language, a common past, a common territory under foreign rule, common customs or common class interests' (p. 347). While the Muslim aristocracy and upper classes were feuding over their own vested interests, the Muslim League politicized Islam as it was the only strong issue and 'by manipulating religious symbols and awakening the peasantry into politics in the name of religion, the Muslim League was able to mobilize the Muslim masses and at the same time undercut the urban-based Muslim coalition parties ... it was possible to bring the lower middle class of the cities into opposition to the aristocracy or the upper classes dominating Muslim politics in a given area' (p. 344).

After the creation of Pakistan, its politics became polarized between groups with different vested interests. This produced a 'crisis in the sense of national unity throughout the country because it did not relate to common elements of participation and belief which were politically important' (p. 351). There were also those to whom Islam was 'worth great human sacrifice. Those who suffered for the new Muslim state, and those who identified with Islam as a cluster of values and directions in human society, wanted Pakistan to embody those values as social realities' (p. 350). This has therefore led to the ideological dilemma confronting Pakistan but one thing is clear and that is 'no popular figure can govern Pakistan without reference to the religious faith which links leaders and masses, and which acts as a foil to provincial and parochial loyalties' (p. 350).

204 YUSUF, M., 'Iqbal and Maudoodi'. *The Universal Message*, Vol. I, No. 8, January 1980. Pp. 8–10.

Mawdudi's correspondence with Iqbal is given. The letters are dated 26 July 1937, 10 August 1937, and 23 April 1938.

205 YUSUF, M., 'Maudoodi: a formative phase'. *Islamic Order*, Vol. I, No. 3, 1979. Pp. 33–43.

The paper throws light on the relationship of Mawdudi with Choudhry Niaz Ali Khan who offered his lands for Waqf purposes.

206 ZIRING, Lawrence, *Pakistan: The enigma of political development*. Folkestone, Kent: Dawson & Sons, 1980.

While discussing the political history of Pakistan the author discusses the political role of the *Jamaat*. The *Jamaat* is considered as 'something of an ideological movement, addressing itself to strict Muslim practices, and in furthering its evangelistic programmes has enlisted the assistance of a small but disciplined cadre, particularly from university youth where it has had its great success' (p. 110).

In the 1977 mass movement against Z. A. Bhutto the author contends that the fundamentalist Islamic orders like the *Jamaat* sensed 'the volatility of a re-emerging Islamic sentiment in the country and they settled for a blistering attack upon Bhutto's anti-Muslim behaviour and proclivities. The loss of East Pakistan had impacted on the intelligentsia more than on the majority of Pakistanis. At first disoriented, then placing their hope in Bhutto and his party, they now began to realize their circumstances and for the first time took stock of the direction in which they were heading ... Bhutto had indicated one way and, in their stupor, they had followed his lead. Having regained their equilibrium, however, and cognisant that Bhutto may not be the answer to their prayers and that the times called for a definite reaction, the intelligentsia returned to the well spring that was their Islamic tradition' (p. 130).

The Islamic movement in Iran

The Islamic movement in Iran

The names of Hassan al-Banna and Maulana Mawdudi are well known in Islamic circles in the Muslim world. However, Ayatollah Khomeini's name, it can safely be asserted, is well known in all parts of the world. Khomeini's fame does not rest on his merely being a prominent religious leader but on his leading a successful Islamic revolution in Iran. This revolution is particularly significant because of its Islamic nature and its global implications because Iran was pivotal to superpower hegemony in the region.

Khomeini's political actions have evoked both negative and positive reactions in various parts of the world. He has been revered or hated by the millions of Muslims in the world. In the West he has been perceived as a Torquemada for religious reasons and feared because of his defiance of Western imperialism. Regardless of the impact of his actions abroad, he did achieve what he set out to in Iran. There was no political leader or force powerful enough within Iran that could have dismantled the monarchy. However, with the support of the Iranian people Khomeini succeeded in doing so where previously others (Mossadeq) had failed. His method of achieving this goal opened up a new way for revolution in the Muslim world because a mass uprising like the one that took place in Iran had not taken place since the beginning of this century. The dynamic force that initiated this revolution and gave it a unique character was Islam. It did not involve a class struggle or a conflict between traditional and modern elite groups, and as such, it made the Muslim world re-evaluate the political potential of Islam. The much discussed resurgent Islam was conceived mainly with the political activation of Islamic doctrines which provided a powerful ideology for the mobilization of people and the overthrowing of un-Islamic regimes. Khomeini's success was a result of several essential components—he had an ideology (Islam), leadership (his own and other religious leaders) and a support base (masses) which neither the Iranian military nor the secular leadership of the Shah could withstand. The main thrust of this discussion will be on Islamic leadership in the revolution.

The Ayatollah.

Khomeini was born at Khomein near Isfahan on 9 April 1900, and came from a very religious family. His early educational training took place in the madrassas of Isfahan, Arak and Qom. In 1927 he started teaching philosophy at Qom. When Reza Shah started to limit the role of the clergy, Khomeini retaliated without fear of the Pahlavis and soon came to the notice of the state authorities. But Khomeini's opposition to the Pahlavi rule was not restricted to vocal articulations for in 1941 he wrote a book *Kashf al-Asrar (Discovery of secrets)* which openly attacked the Pahlavi dynasty and called for an end to imperialist influences in Iran. From the very start of his career Khomeini was fiercely critical of the foreign influences and the corrupt Pahlavi dynasty.

In 1953, when Mossadeq rose to curtail the power of the Shah, Khomeini maintained his distance from the nationalist as well as from the Communist forces under the influence of the Tudeh Party. Between 1953 and 1960 Khomeini was politically active behind the scenes but in spite of his growing reputation among his followers and students as an anti-monarchist, he managed to keep a low political profile. But after Ayatollah Burujirdi (1875-1961) the *Marja-e-Taqlid* (source of emulation), died in 1961, Khomeini's revolutionary activities once again surfaced. His political attacks against the Shah's White Revolution became more vociferous and in 1963 when the people of Iran erupted against the Shah, Khomeini was at the centre of the revolt. He was arrested by the SAVAK but released later after an assurance that he would not take part in politics. But he was in custody again after ordering his followers to boycott the 1964 Parliamentary elections. He was arrested and released again on an understanding that he would refrain from politics. However, when a bill was passed by the Iranian Parliament giving diplomatic immunity to the American military personnel stationed in Iran, Khomeini attacked the regime's policy once more. This time he was sent into exile to Turkey but later settled at Najaf in Iraq from 1965 to 1978.

During this period he remained active politically by writing pamphlets against the Shah, criticizing his celebration of the 2500 years of Persian monarchy and boycotting of the single party system in 1975. He regularly met his followers at Najaf and gave tape recorded sermons which were circulated widely in Iran. As his attacks on the regime increased, it retaliated by murdering his son Mustafa in Kerbala (Iraq). This did not deter Khomeini from his single minded determination to destroy the Pahlavi dynasty. Political agitation increased and Khomeini was entrusted by the people to lead them. Iraq was embarrassed by his presence so he had to leave for Paris and began to direct his campaign from there. Millions of Iranians responded to his call and the Islamic revolutionary struggle against the forces of the Shah continued until the latter had to leave the country in January 1979. Khomeini returned triumphantly in February and immediately set about the task of establishing an Islamic government. He did not accept any position in the Islamic republic but as a father figure worked for the Islamic revolution and constantly urged them to beware of their enemies within and without and to always keep themselves united under the banner of Islam.

Khomeini's Political Thought:

It is not intended here to give a very detailed exposition of Khomeini's ideas, but a brief account of some of the salient features of his thoughts should give the reader a general introduction to his study and interpretation of Islam.

Khomeini raises a question of fundamental importance on the role and functions of governments in Muslim countries. In his opinion it has four important functions:

1 To enforce the laws of the Sharia justice.
2 To combat oppression of the rights of ordinary individuals and to eradicate corruption.
3 To fight heresies and errors that are legislated by false parliaments.
4 To prevent the intervention of foreigners in the affairs of the Muslims.[1]

In order to implement these, the government may use constitutional measures but for Khomeini the meaning of this term differs from that used in the Westernized sense. According to Khomeini

It is not constitutional in the popular sense of the word which means representation in the parliamentary system or in the peoples councils. It is constitutional in the sense that those in charge of the affairs observe a number of conditions and rules outlined in the Koran and Sunnah ... That is why the Islamic government is the government of the Divine Law.[2]

Who then will operationalize the Divine Law? This will be done by the Velayat-e-Faqih (Islamic Jurists). These jurists must have two credentials for the leadership of the community; first, they should have a thorough knowledge of Islamic law and secondly, they should be just. It is these persons who should be elected to parliament. The latter's role should be to act as a forum for the conflict management if it arises in the implementation of doctrinal issues in society. The jurists then

must work separately or collectively to set up a legitimate government that establishes the structures, protects the border and establishes order. If competence for this task is confined to one person, then this would be his duty to do so corporally, otherwise the duty is shared equally. In case of difficulty in forming that government the (attribution) to rule does not disappear. The jurists must act as much as possible in accordance with their assignment ... The temporary inability to form a strong and complete government does not at all mean that we should retreat. Dealing with the needs of the Muslims and implementing among them whatever laws are possible to implement is a duty as much as possible.[3]

The work of the government, however, can be carried out by the civil servants. These persons need not be jurists for:

It is not the duty of any civil servant whatever his task to know all the laws and to study them deeply. It is enough for such a person to familiarise himself with laws relevant to his functions or to the task entrusted to him.[4]

But the task of the judiciary was to be conducted by the jurist whose knowledge of law was essential to 'dispense justice among the people'.[5] The judiciary's role also extended to oversee the work of the legislative and the executive.

The government must therefore aim to establish a society based on justice according to laws of Islam. Governments should not be an end in themselves but through the implementation of Islamic Sharia meet the needs of the people. The linkage between economic and political power often leads to greed and corruption. The jurists must therefore ensure that wealth does not become concentrated in the hands of those who govern by exploiting the people and their resources for themselves. In order to check this the holders of political offices must not enjoy any special privileges or favour. Such leaders must live a simple life such as that led by Prophet Mohammad, Ali and other Imams.

Furthermore, through the implementation of the Islamic tax system an economic balance should be created in which there will be no concentration of wealth or extremes of poverty in society. Such a balance could only be restored through the proper distribution of wealth and prevention of economic exploitation.

The jurist should maintain control over the parliament and judiciary to make sure that the Executive is efficiently carrying out its responsibilities and not exceeding its powers. If the government does not like any check on its powers then the mission of the jurists is to 'revolt and fight against despotic regimes'.[6] But when despotic regimes are strong and use every means at their disposal then the Islamic struggle should be heightened to overthrow such a government. If the army resorts to kill the people, people must not fear it. It is 'a proof that things are going badly' and that in time 'it will be absorbed by the people'.[7]

Such a regime must be resisted by all means. The Ulama must use the mosques to mobilize the people. Religious occasions like the Hajj, Juma prayers and Islamic festivals must also be used. There must be unity between the people and the leaders and the people must be made aware of the legal, political-economic solutions that Islam offers for their problems. Propaganda must be widespread and reach the university students because they are the 'staunchest opponents of repression, despotism, treachery, agents of imperialism and the plunderers of national wealth'.[8] Organization, planning and political action have to be taken both on a short term and long term basis.

The struggle can be violent or non-violent. The former is essential because 'life is a lesson and struggle ... death is better than a life of humiliation, no other way out but continuation of the war by every means ... to achieve honour and glory'.[9] Passive resistance, on the other hand, must be continued through boycott and non-cooperation with government institutions, avoidance of any activity which may help such a government and establishing alternatives through judicial, financial, economic, cultural and political institutions.[10]

Khomeini's fight against imperialism is just as strong a concern as that to reconstruct an Islamic society. Imperialism is like Pharaonic structure which corrupts society and the choice for the Muslim in this regard is clear. He writes that:

Under the canopy of a pharaonic rule that dominates and corrupts society rather than reforms it, no faithful and pious person can live abiding by and preserving his faith and piety. Such a person has before him two paths, and no third to them: either be forced to commit sinful acts or rebel against and fight the rule of false gods, try to wipe out or at least reduce the impact of such a rule. We only have the second path open to us. We have no alternative but to work for destroying the corrupt and corrupting system and to destroy the symbol of treason and the unjust among the rulers of peoples. This is a duty that all Muslims wherever they may be are entrusted—a duty to create a victorious and triumphant Islamic political revolution.[11]

While he advocates a political revolution on the part of individual Muslims in Muslim countries, he is very critical of the Muslim rulers who by abandoning Islam cannot be united for 'had the current Muslim rulers tried to implement the laws of Islam, abandoning all their differences, putting aside their disputes and their divisions and uniting in one hand in the face of others, the hands of Jews and the puppets of Americans and Britain would not have been able to reach what they have reached ...'[12] for the 'only means that we possess to unite the Muslim nation, to liberate its land from the grip of the colonialists and to topple the agent governments of colonialism is to seek to establish our Islamic government'.[13]

If Muslim individuals and Muslim rulers do not become Islamically conscious of the state of their condition, Khomeini then asserts:

How can we stand nowadays to keep silent on a handful of exploiters and foreigners who dominate with the force of arms when these people have denied hundreds of millions of others the joy of enjoying the smallest degree of life's pleasures and blessings? The duty of the Ulema and of all the Muslims is to put an end to this injustice and to seek to bring happiness to millions of peoples through destroying and elimi-nating the unjust governments and through establishing a sincere and active government.[14]

Khomeini's message therefore advocates nothing short of a total revolu-tion in Muslim society.

The Movement

The Islamic movement in Iran has a long history (and it is not intended here to give a full history) since the inception of Islam. The line of Imamate started with Ali, the fourth Caliph of Islam (A.D. 656–661) who became the first Imam for the Shii. It continued in a linear pattern until the twelfth Imam, Muhammad al-Mahdi and culminated with his occultation in A.D. 874, but this Imamate provided Shii Islam with strong and bold Islamic leadership. The martyrdom of the third Imam Hussain on the battlefield of Kerbala in A.D. 680 fighting his Jihad against Yazid—an unjust ruler who did not enjoy Islamic legitimacy to rule over the centuries—provided not only a powerful inspiration but has established a strong tradition of rebelling against a tyrannous un-Islamic ruler. The Safavid dynasty (1500–1736) contained this threat by com-bining spiritual and political leadership. Other rulers who followed and the Qajars dynasty (1795–1924) could not perpetuate this style of leadership.

A debate developed during the latter's rule in which the Ulama belonging to the *Usuli* school of thought gained an upper hand over others who subscribed to the *Akbari* school of thought. The latter believed that the Shii Imam in the absence of the occult twelfth Imam could not exercise his judgement but had to follow the tradition of Islam. Members of the *Usuli* school, on the other hand, believed that the Mujtahid had the right to exercise his judgement based on his knowledge of the Islamic law and on the exigency of the situation. The Imams of the *Usuli* school started to take an active political role and established a tradition of Islamic political leadership as an alternative to secular political leader-ship.[15] This was particularly highlighted during the Qajar period by the Tobacco rebellion of 1892 and the Constitutional revolution from 1905–1911. During the Pahlavi rule such religious leadership was provided by the Ayatollahs of Qom and Khomeini belonged to this line of tradition. The establishment of such a tradition was very important for the Islamic movement in Iran.

After the uprising of 1963 Khomeini's leadership was accepted by the

Iranian masses despite his being in exile. No other leader had enjoyed greater political legitimacy and political sway with the masses to lead a revolution. From his place of exile, Khomeini's tape recorded sermons mobilized the people against the Shah's regime. With a great deal of patience and perseverance he built a strong network of followers both inside Iran and abroad. In spite of the SAVAK's reprisals and purges this group secretly and diligently kept up the work of the Islamic movement. This mass base of the Islamic movement not only provided financial support but were ready to come out in the open and sacrifice their lives. Apart from Khomeini, the second tier of leadership consisting of men such as Rajai, Bahonar, Taleghani, Mottahari, Beheshti, and many others showed a solidarity that could not be destroyed by the Shah. They all worked towards bringing about an Islamic revolution and not for personal gain. Many have been assassinated in the post-revolutionary period. Khomeini's leadership provided both horizontal and vertical linkages. Horizontally, he was held in high esteem by other Ayatollahs and leaders within the folds of Islam. Vertically, he held direct control over the masses where his word could stand up against the Shah's promises, rules and regulations, and means of coercion. Neither the Shah nor his superpower allies nor his military could withstand the force of the 1978–1979 mass revolution.

The Ideologue of the Revolution

Khomeini's writings and speeches had directly influenced the masses in their political mobilization against the regime but the writings of other Iranian thinkers influenced the intelligentsia and the upper classes. In fact the task of the hero of the revolution and the ideologue of the revolution has been very clearly outlined in the following words.

> The Ideologue, the major contributor to the formation of revolutionary thought is neither appointed, nor is he elected by popular vote. People do not choose to follow the ideologue because of the office he is holding. Rather they believe in him and accept his invitation for they have faith in his truthfulness and the sincerity this message contains. But the other prominent figure within a revolutionary movement is the hero of the revolution ... it is he, following the revolutionary messages of the ideologue, who sets out to design the foundation of the revolution and to draw its blueprints. It is the leader who decides on proper revolutionary tactics; chooses the revolutionary slogans and mobilises the revolutionary forces.[16]

These words were written by Ali Shariati. Any study of the Islamic movement in Iran would be incomplete without an understanding of Shariati's message because it was he, more than anyone else who, through his radical interpretation of Islam, inspired the intelligentsia to take up arms against the Shah. Numerous martyrs who were the heroes of the Iranian revolution had been inspired by Shariati because they shared a common goal. A brief exposition of Shariati's life and work will give an idea of his role in the mobilization of the Iranian intelligentsia.

Ali Shariati (1933–1977) was born in the village of Mazinan in the Northeastern province of Khorasan. His father, Mohammad Taqi Shariati, was a teacher and a co-founder of the Centre for the Publication of Islamic Truths. He grew up in a background of poverty among his people. He attended the Ibn-Zamin elementary school and then the Ferdowsi High school in Mashad, the provincial capital. After high school he did a two year teacher training course and began teaching in a village near Mashad. While teaching, he did a graduate course at the University and obtained a bachelor's degree.

He became involved in political activities through the Centre for the Publication of Islamic Truths and its affiliated organization, the New Islamic Revolt Centre. Under the sponsorship of the latter he started on a prolific career of writing and translating political, religious, philosophical and sociological works. His first important work *A history of the evolution of philosophy* was published in 1955.

He then went abroad for higher education and completed his doctoral studies in sociology at the Sorbonne in France. This was the most important period of his life as he came into contact with renowned European intellectuals, Islamologists and sociologists and this opened his mind to a host of new creative ideas. Later he became intensely involved with the Algerian War of Independence in 1962 and even translated the works of Frantz Fanon, the Algerian revolutionary, into Persian. He was also actively involved in student politics of the Confederation of Iranian Students that opposed the Shah's regime and was one of the founders of the Iranian National Front in Europe. He was selected as the editor of the Front's newspaper the *Iran Azad (Free Iran)*.

After a five year stay abroad Shariati returned to Iran. As he crossed the border of Turkey into Iran at Bazargan he was arrested by the Shah's police for his political activities abroad and incarcerated in prison.[17] After his release from prison he had to work for many years as a teacher at various high schools and colleges. He was finally given an appointment at the University of Mashad and was so popular with his students that the authorities considered him dangerous and forced an early retirement on him.

From 1967 to 1973 he taught at the Husayniyah Irshad and his teachings had a profound influence on the younger generation. As such the SAVAK again took him to prison and subjected him to various kinds of torture. Finally, he was released on the condition that he would neither publish nor lecture in Iran. With the help of friends he obtained a visa to leave to go abroad in 1976. He first went to Paris and then came to London in 1977 en route to the USA. Here he died in mysterious circumstances in his hotel room. His death was attributed to the SAVAK agents abroad. He was buried in Damascus by the tomb of Zainab—the sister of Imam Husayn. Shariati's interpretation of Islam sought to bring out the revolutionary spirit of Islam which would be a continuation of Prophet Mohammad's mission. Shariati regarded this in two ways. On one hand Islam was a religion (man's relationship to God) and on the other hand it was an ideology for the Muslim peoples. As an ideology it was the 'Islam of Abu-Zar; the Islam of justice and leadership, the Islam of Imamat and not the Islam of Caliphate, class and aristocracy. It is the Islam of freedom, awareness and motion, and not the Islam of captivity, ignorance and stagnation, the Islam of the Mujtahid and not the Islam of official clergy.'[18]

The goal of the Ummat was not only to reach higher levels of perfection and self-awareness but also to carry out its mission of world revolution. All members of the Ummat should try to unite the world community to avoid that which is evil (wa al-nahy an al-munkar) and act on that which is good (al-amr bi al-ma'ruf). The Ummat cannot therefore be stagnant but was to be in constant motion (hijra). If every member is aware of his responsiblity then the Ummat can be in a constant state of motion. In fact, the responsibility of each member is such that the individual should be willing to sacrifice his life so that others may live; he should accept captivity so that others may be free and he should not be afraid of deprivation and hardship for the sake of a better life for the next generation. When such an Ummat is in constant motion, then it can combat imperialist forces, of zionism, colonialism, oppression, repression, class conflict, racism, Westernism, and cultural imperialism, etc.

For Shariati the most important question which a Muslim 'should ask himself today is not whether each religious concept is rational or irrational, compatible or incompatible with science but rather what is its usefulness and its worth to the society in which he lives'.[19] His books were therefore aptly entitled *What is to be Done?*, *Whence Shall He Begin?*, *Martyrdom* [item 413], *Waiting for the Religion of Protest*, etc., in which Islamic concepts such as *Umma, Imamate, Adl, Shahada, Taqiya, Taqlid, Sabr, Hijra, Shirk, Tawhid, Hajj* etc. have been radicalized to become meaningful to the common man.

The type of believer that Shariati was seeking to inspire through his message was the *Raushanfikr*. Popularly the term refers to an intellectual but Shariati was not seeking a sterile, Westernized intellectual who was alienated from his own culture. On the contrary, the Raushanfikr was a 'man endowed with an enlightened mind' and would act as the 'torch-bearer' and 'scout' and as the 'antithesis of oppression and darkness'. Like the scientist or educated man he does not only know the facts, but also discovered the truth, is close to the masses and through Islam guides them to progress with a 'sense of self awareness and responsible leadership'.[20]

Furthermore, for Shariati, the *Ummat* (the Muslim community) was a 'Human society where all individuals have gathered together to be guided by one common leader, and to move forward to a common goal.'[21] Such an Ummat 'cannot exist without Imamate'.[22] Thus while 'Ummat is a society in eternal motion ... the Imamate is a regime which leads it'.[23] Within this Ummat, a Muslim should try 'not to be, but to become, not to live well, but to lead a good life' because freedom is 'not an ideal, but a necessary means to attain the ideal'.[24]

Shariati's sociological analysis of Muslim societies is perhaps one of the most brilliant pieces of work written in this century. He sees conflict raging within these societies but this conflict is not between modern and traditional forces (modernization theory) nor between the bourgeoisie and the proletariat (Marxian theory). For Shariati, this conflict is between the forces of *Tawhid* and those of *Shirk*.

The framework of *Tawhid* generates harmony between God, man, nature and existence. There are no contradictions in it. In addition, Tawhid does not accept legal, class, social, political, racial, national, territorial, genetic or economic contradictions. Consequently, when contradictions enter this world as between

> nature and meta-nature, matter and meaning, this world and hereafter, intellect and illumination, science and religion, metaphysics and nature, working for men and working for God, politics and religion, logic and love, bread and worship, piety and commitment, life and eternity, landlord and peasant, ruler and ruled, black and white, noble and vile, clergy and laity, Eastern and Western, blessed and wretched, light and darkness, inherent virtue and inherent evil, Greek and barbarian, Arab and non-Arab, Persian and non-Persian, capitalist and proletarian, elite and mass, learned and illiterate[25]

these form the world view of *Shirk*. It is the duty of those who believe in the contradictions of *Tawhid* to struggle for and destroy the world view of *Shirk* until it is in harmony.

This can be accomplished through various processsess, the most important of which are people, personalities and norms. The people are the most important factor because the Qur'an addresses itself to the people and they are instrumental in changing the world of *Shirk* into that of *Tawhid*. Thus individually and collectively Muslims are vested with responsibility to change their destinies. But such changes can only be brought about through a normative design which leads to the straight path derived from Islam and the Qur'an. Personalities have to understand these divine norms if they want to lead their societies to the *Tawhid* structure. While there are no accidents in *Tawhidian* structures of society, life and nature, they do happen in human societies due to the failure of people, personalities and the *Shirkian* norms they try to pursue. Thus the 'proportional influence of each of these ... factors on a given society depends on the circumstances of that society'.[26] At any one time, one or the other factor may emerge as the dominant force. In some it may be the people, in others the personality. In early Islam 'the personality of the Prophet had a fundamental and constructive role in bringing about change, development and progress, in building a future civilization and in changing the course of history'.[27] In the struggle for a *Tawhidian* world the quality of a man's belief in *Tawhid* should be such that 'man fears only one power and is answerable before only one judge. He turns to only one Qibla, and directs his hopes and desires to only one source. And the corollary is that all else is false and pointless—all the diverse and variegated tendencies, strivings, fears, desires and hopes of men are in vain and fruitless'.[28] It is then that no accidents will happen and success will be guaranteed for man.

The Present Status of the Movement ✓

The Islamic revolution in Iran had set out to achieve two objectives. First, its immediate objective was to remove the Shah and his supporters from their positions of power. Secondly, to begin the transformation of Iran into an Islamic state.

The first objective was achieved and the credit for that goes to the men who led the movement and the thousands of martyrs who sacrificed their lives for its success. The cemetery (Beheste Zahra) outside Tehran stands as a monument to the sacrifice made by the people in achieving their goal. Their were many other groups who were against the Shah's régime but they had neither the leadership nor the resources and the support of the masses to lead such a revolution. They therefore joined the Islamic movement for the achievement of the first objective, that is, the removal of the Shah from his throne, but not for the second.

Regarding the attainment of the second objective, that is, the transformation of Iran into an Islamic state the progress made by the authorities in power is slow. The progress is slow not because of the internal structural deficiencies of the movement's membership and organization but because of overwhelming external problems.

At the outset it must be remembered that Iran, unlike Egypt and Pakistan, is one of the major oil producers in the Middle East. As such the interests of the superpowers (USA and USSR) are focused in the country for the control and exploitation of this resource. Secondly, its borders are connected with the USSR which brings the USA into the region of the Persian Gulf for ideological control in Southwest Asia. It is therefore not surprising to find that pro-Russian and pro-American forces exist within the country. Both do not approve of the Islamic government until it declares its subservience with one or the other of them. In addition there are the leftists' forces which are aiming for a socialist society and the Shah's forces which are striving to bring the monarchy back to Iran. Apart from these, there are the Muslim Arab countries who are striving to bring about the downfall of the regime for various reasons. Some like Iraq are striving to increase their territorial acquisitions and become the dominant power in the region. Others like the neighbouring Gulf states and the countries of the Middle East would like to see political chaos in Iran to avoid the occurrence of a similar revolution in their countries. Thus Iraq has killed its Shii Imams, Egypt is purging its Islamic groups and Saudi Arabia has strengthened relations with the USA, in order to prevent the repetition of a Khomeini type revolution. Arms, money and secularized ideologies are not in scarcity and as such not only some prominent clergymen but also the Prime Minister, President, Head of the Islamic Republican Party as well as more than 60 members of the Majlis have been assassinated through bomb attacks by various guerilla groups.

A political revolution is a serious occurrence in any country and those which took place in Russia in 1917 and in China in 1949 have been consolidated over the years, with steady leadership and a thorough purging of the anti-revolution forces from the country. Iran's revolution is only three years old and its fight against anti-Islamic forces has only just begun. These forces have started to emerge after the euphoria of the revolution has settled down and the bidding for power and the control of the government is beginning.

The greatest danger, as stated earlier, that the Islamic regime faces is from the *munafiqun* (hypocrites) forces that are acting in the interests of the superpowers within Iran. The task of identifying the extent to which such forces have penetrated the regime's organization is a difficult one. In order to combat such agents and international intrigues the regime has paid particular attention to the socio-political organization of Islamic forces and cultivated a strong support base within Iranian society. Thus the *Pasdaran-e-Inqualab* (The Islamic Revolutionary Guards) are being thoroughly trained to forestall such dangers, combat intrigues and conspiracies within the country and special *Komitehs* (committees) have been set up to unearth such plots. Most important of all, the regime is strengthening its support bases among the *mostazafeens* (the oppressed), the masses whose lot was the worst off in the Pahlavi times. The *munafiqeens* are waiting for a crucial turning point—the death of Ayatollah Khomeini—which they think will lead to a civil war and chaos will plague the regime. Should such a situation arise, and some pro-USA or pro-USSR forces take over, the force of Islam will not be annihilated, but will suffer a temporary setback. The future of Iran forebodes conflict but the new leadership being trained at Qom is not afraid of *Kerbala* or *Shahadat* (martyrdom).

References

1. Quoted in J. S. Ismail, et al, 'Social change in Islamic society: the political thought of Ayatollah Khomeini'. *Social Problems*, Vol. 27, No. 5, June 1980, p. 613.
2. Ibid., p. 613.
3. Ibid., p. 614.
4. Ibid., p. 614.
5. Ibid., p. 614.
6. Ibid., p. 614.
7. Kotabi, M., and Leon J., 'The march toward the Islamic Republic of Iran:

society and religion according to Imam Khomeini'. *Le Monde Diplomatique* (Paris), April 6–7, 1979, p. 83.

8. Ismail, J. S., op. cit., p. 613.
9. Ibid., p. 613.
10. Ibid., p. 614.
11. Ayatollah Khomeini, *Islamic government* (translated by Joint Publications Research Service). New York: Manor Books Inc., 1979, pp. 25–26.
12. Ibid., p. 24.
13. Ibid., p. 26.
14. Ibid., p. 28.
15. For a full discussion of this debate see Algar, H., *The Islamic Revolution in Iran*, London: The Muslim Institute, 1980.
16. Shariati, Ali, Ummat va Imamat, quoted in Amini, S., 'A critical assessment of Ali Shariati's theory of revolution', in Jabbari, A., and Olsen, R. (ed.), *Iran: essays on a revolution in the making.* Lexington, Kentucky: Mazda Publishers, 1981, p. 77.
17. Algar, H., *On the sociology of Islam* (translated lectures by Ali Shariati). Berkeley, Calif.: Mizan Press, 1979, pp. 26–27.
18. Amini, S., op. cit., p. 90.
19. Bayat-Phillips, M., 'Shiism in contemporary Iranian politics: the case of Ali Shariati', in Kedourie, E., and Haim, S. (eds), *Towards a modern Iran.* London: Frank Cass and Co. Ltd., 1980, p. 156.
20. Ibid., pp. 158–59.
21. Ibid., p. 160.
22. Ibid., p. 160.
23. Ibid., p. 160.
24. Ibid., p. 160.
25. Shariati, A., 'The world view of Tawhid', in Algar, H., *The sociology of Islam*, op. cit., p. 86.
26. Shariati, A., 'Approaches to the understanding of Islam', in Algar, H., *The sociology of Islam*, Ibid., p. 54.
27. Ibid., p. 54.
28. Shariati, A., 'The world view of Tawhid', op. cit., p. 87.

207 ABIDI, A. H. H., 'The Iranian revolution: its origins and dimensions'. *International Studies*, Vol. 18, No. 2, April–June 1979. Pp. 129–161.

An intensive analysis of the Iranian revolution, tracing various aspects of the Shah's rule which led to his downfall. The Shah's carrot and stick policy could not win the support of opponents who have been divided into three distinct groups: the Islamic group, the secular-liberal group and the Marxist group. These diverse segments of the mass movements united because of the common enemy—the Shah, socio-economic problems, resentment of foreign powers, the system of government, etc. The first stage of the revolution has been reached. The next stage has yet to be reached and it is much more 'complex as it involves the intricate tasks of pacification and consolidation' (p. 161).

208 ABRAHAMIAN, E., 'The guerilla movement in Iran, 1963–1977'. Washington, DC: MERIP Reports Series, No. 86, Vol. 10, No. 3, March/April 1980. Pp. 3–21.

A good and intensive analysis of the guerilla movements who played an instrumental role in bringing about the downfall of the Shah. The author divides the guerillas into five political groupings: (1) *Sazman-i Cherik-ha-yi Feda-i Khalq-i Iran* (The Organization of the Guerilla Freedom Fighters of the Iranian People); (2) The *Sazman-i Mujahidin-i Khalq-i Iran* (The Organization of the Freedom Fighters of the Iranian people); (3) The *Sazman-i Paykar dar Rah-i Azad-i Tabaqeh-i Kargar* (The Fighting Organization on the Road for Liberating the Working Class). This is an off-shoot of the *Mujahidin-i Khalq*; (4) Small Islamic organizations limited to various towns such as the *Gorueh-i Abu Zahr* (The Abu Zahr Group) in Nahavand. *Gorueh-i Shiiyan-i Rastin* (The Group of True Shias) in Hamadan. *Gorueh-i Allah Akbar* (The Allah Akbar Group) in Isfahan and the *Gorueh-i Al-Fajar* (The Al-Fajar Group) in Zahedan; (5) Small Marxist groups: The *Sazman-i Azadibakshi-i Khalq ha-yi Iran* (The Organization for the Liberation of the Iranian people). The *Gorueh-i Lurestan* (The Lurestan Group). The *Sazman-i Arman-i Khalq* (The Organization for the Peoples Ideals). The *Razmandegan-i Azad-i Tabeqeh-i Kargar* (The Fighters for the Liberation of the Worker Class). Also cells associated with various political parties such as the *Hizb-i Demokrat-i Kurdestan-i Iran* of the Kurdish Democratic Party of Iran, the *Sazman-i Inqelah-i Hizb-i Tudeh* of the Tudeh Party and the *Gorueh-i Ittehad-i Komunistha* (The Group of United Communists)—a new left styled group.

The analysis focuses mainly on the first two guerilla groups in terms of ideologies, leadership and strategies employed against the regime.

209 ABRAHAMIAN, E., 'Structural causes of the Iranian revolution'. Washington, DC: MERIP Reports Series, No. 87, Vol. 10, No. 4, May 1980. Pp. 21–26.

An analysis of the socio-economic causes of the revolution focusing on educational, agricultural and industrial aspects.

210 AFRACHTEH, Kambiz, 'Iran', in M. Ayoob, *The politics of Islamic reassertion*. London: Croom Helm, 1981. Pp. 90–119.

The author attempts to answer three questions in his paper: (1) What were the underlying reasons for the anti-Shah protest? (2) What made Shiite Islam a uniquely effective vehicle for the revolution? (3) How has the religious institution responded to political authority? After discussing these questions, he concludes by stating that 'Khomeini's sense of mission, persistence and refusal to compromise endow him with both his strengths and weaknesses. He had a decisive role in the overthrow of the monarchy, but the same qualities could conceivably become responsible for an escalation of violence leading in the extreme to civil war. By refusing to compromise Khomeini has effectively removed the political conflict from parliament and on to the streets' (p. 116).

211 AFROUZ, Ali, 'Dealing with the counter-revolutionary forces', in K. Siddiqui, ed., *The Islamic revolution: achievements, obstacles and goals*. London: The Muslim Institute, 1980. Pp. 44–48.

The paper contends that the Islamic revolution in Iran has certain characteristics which can be applied universally to every community in the world. These characteristics are as follows: (1) It was a revolution in which everybody participated, irrespective of whether he was poor or rich, man or woman, burgess of the village, etc.; (2) The fundamental cause dynamically leading the revolution was religious ideology, economics was a secondary consideration; (3) The Islamic revolution achieved its goal single-handed and did not have the support of Western or Eastern superpowers. Although Iran had many political groups and parties, they neither led the revolution nor participated in the street battles with the authorities; (4) The mosques and Islamic societies were instrumental in mobilizing the masses.

212 AGWANI, M. S., 'The varied politics of resurgent Islam'. *India International Centre Quarterly*, Vol. 7, No. 3, September 1980. Pp. 141–148.

This article discusses the resurgence of Islam in Saudi Arabia, Pakistan, Libya and Iran. The author concludes that 'Islamic revivalism is not a monolithic entity nor a world wide movement advancing towards a common goal. What is happening is that in some countries Islam is being articulated into bringing about meaningful social and political change. In other places, Islam is being harnessed to forestall such change. Secondly, the popular appeal of revivalist Islam in general owes a great deal to the failures of the modern Muslim elite, which has been so self centered that it has ignored the plight of the common people ... the result is that the common man, who cannot comprehend the intellectual niceties of the liberal secular tradition but sees that this elite is busy helping itself, is apt to turn to the traditional elite for solace and even political guidance. Finally, I believe it is quite natural for Muslim societies to invoke the norms of Islam, particularly in moments of crises. But this should not lead us to the conclusion that the traditional Muslim elite has a panacea for the social and political maladies that afflict contemporary societies—whether Muslim or non-Muslim. The fact is that the traditional elite has neither the capability nor the will to come to grips with the challenge of our time. Moreover, the Muslim countries today stand at the periphery of the global power structure rather than at its centre; they cannot afford to opt out of the modern world' (pp. 147–148).

213 AHMAD, Bashir, *Iranian revolution: its genisis, force of regeneration or regression?* Rawalpindi: National Defence College, Individual Research Paper, 1979.

An analytical study based upon an extensive survey of materials from books, journals, magazines and newspapers. The author believes that 'for the first time in modern history, Islam has been operationalised politically to bring about revolutionary change instead of remaining on the side of a status quo ... the Iranian revolution is an ongoing process ... it has a very bright future internationally' (p. iii).

214 AHMAD, Eqbal, 'The Iranian revolution: a landmark for the future'. *Race and Class*, XXI (1), 1979. Pp. 3–11.

An analysis by a Marxist who considers that the Iranian revolution was the outcome of the 'contradictions and vulnerability of the repressive and militarist neo-colonial state' (p. 7). It was genuine revolution in 'agitational politics' and 'mass organisation' led by urban-based middle and working classes (the Bazaaris, Muslim clerics, workers, intellectuals and students). The author forecasts that the revolution will affect regional politics in South Asia and the Middle East and also US interests and Pakistan's importance in US policy.

215 AHMAD, Eqbal, ed., *The Islamic revolution in Iran*, Lahore: Vanguard Books, 1980.

The book contains reprints of seven articles that had previously appeared in the journal *Race and Class* (London). The articles are entitled:

(1) Ahmad, E., 'The Iranian revolution: a landmark for the future'.
(2) Keddie, N. R., 'Oil, economic policy and social conflict in Iran'.
(3) Farhang, M., 'Resisting the Pharaohs: Ali Shariati on oppression'.
(4) Falk, R., 'Iran and American geopolitics in the Gulf'.
(5) Dorman, W. A., 'Iranian people vs U.S. media: a case of libel'.
(6) Schaar, S., 'Orientalism at the service of imperialism'.
(7) Halliday, F., 'Thesis on the Iranian revolution'.

216 AKHAVI, Shahrough, *Religion and politics in contemporary Iran*. Albany, NY: State University of New York Press, 1980.

An important work analysing clergy-state relations in Iran. These relationships are divided into three periods, the first covering the period before 1941, the second 1941–1958 and the third 1959–1963. The Shah's rule created a bureaucratic state which existed only to execute the policies of the monarch. The two clergy movements which dismantled this state were the movement from Qum led by Khomeini and that started by Shariati at the Husayniyah Irshad. The analysis of the latter gives a good exposition of Shariati's thought.

217 ALBERT, David H., ed., *Tell the American people: perspectives on the Iranian revolution*. Philadelphia, Pa: Movement for a New Society, 1980.

Various scholars, policy researchers, human rights activists, etc., have been brought together to discuss some of the issues asked by Americans about the US-Iran relations. Thus Falk discusses the question of 'Human rights and international law' (*see* 285), Edward Said comments on 'Iran and the US press', M. T. Klare on 'Arms and the Shah', Albert gives a chronology of 'Twentieth century Iranian history' etc. A photographic essay has been presented by R. Goodman and the work concludes with excerpts from the writings of Shariati, Bani-Sadr, Ayatollah Motahheri and Khomeini.

218 ALGAR, Hamid, tr., *Draft constitution of the Islamic Republic of Iran*. London: The Muslim Institute, 1979.

This draft constitution has been translated by Algar and has a foreword by K. Siddiqui.

219 ALGAR, Hamid, *Imam Khomeini, Islam and revolution*. Berkeley, Calif.: Mizan Press, 1981.

This book is intended to serve as an anthology of the speeches of Ayatollah Khomeini. It also contains extracts from lectures delivered at Najaf in 1970 and a series of lectures given in 1979 and early 1980 on the opening chapter of the Qur'an 'Surat al-Fatiha'. The book has been written as an addition to a detailed biography which the author is currently preparing. It is an excellent reference work.

220 ALGAR, Hamid, *The Islamic revolution in Iran*. London: The Muslim Institute, 1980.

Algar's work is a transcript of four lectures given at the Muslim Institute. The first three lectures deal mainly with Shiism, Khomeini and Shariati. The fourth is a narrative of the events which took place in the year of the revolution. Although the treatment of each is not exhaustive the book provides sufficient insight into the role of Islamic leadership and ideology which led the Islamic movement in Iran to mobilize the masses and elites and remove the Pahlavis. After each lecture there follows a discussion by the participants which further clarifies certain points raised in the lectures.

221 ALGAR, Hamid, 'The oppositional role of the Ulama in twentieth century Iran', in N. R. Keddie, ed., *Scholars, saints and sufis: Muslim religious institutions since 1500*. Berkeley, Calif.: University of California Press, 1972. Pp. 231–255.

An extremely important article on the opposition of the Ulama towards the Shah's regime. The author's deep insight into the Islamic movement in Iran enabled him to predict the oncoming revolution in the following words: 'Yet it would be rash to predict the progressive disintegration of the political role of the Ulama. Despite all the inroads of the modern age, the Iranian national consciousness still remains wedded to Shii Islam, and when the integrity of the nation is held to be threatened by internal autocracy and foreign hegemony, protests in religious terms will continue to be voiced, and the appeals of men such as Ayatollah Khumayi to be widely heeded' (p. 255).

222 ALGAR, Hamid, *Religion and state in Iran: the role of the Ulama in the Qajar period*. Berkeley, Calif.: University of California Press, 1969.

For any study of the historical rise of the Iranian Ulama, Algar's study is the finest available in the field. Its special focus is on the Qajar period.

223 ALGAR, Hamid, 'Shiism and Iran in the eighteenth century', in T. Naff and R. Owen, eds, *Studies in eighteenth century Islamic history*. Carbondale, Ill.: Southern Illinois University Press, 1977. Pp. 288–302.

An important paper in which the author shows how Shiism has historically preserved vitality and predominance in spite of the conflicts which arose between Nadir Shah's Iran and the Ottoman empire.

224 ALI, *Imam, Nahjul Balagha.* Qum: Centre of Islamic Studies, 1975.

For any understanding of the Islamic movement in Iran, the Nahjul Balagha is second to the Qur'an. The above edition contains a good introduction to Shiism and the life of Imam Ali–the first Imam of Shiism. The rest of the book contains sermons, letters and sayings of Imam Ali on almost every aspect of mankind.

225 AMINI, Soheyl, 'A critical assessment of Ali Shariati's theory of revolution', in A. Jabbari, *et al, Iran: essays on a revolution in the making.* Lexington, Kentucky: Mazda Publishers, 1981. Pp. 77–104.

This paper is a good exposition of Shariati's interpretation of Islam within a revolutionary framework. It also critically assesses it by pointing out some of its weaknesses. On the whole it is an important article for understanding Shariati [*see also* 330].

226 AMNESTY INTERNATIONAL, *Law and human rights in the Islamic Republic of Iran.* London: Amnesty International, 1980.

A report compiled by Amnesty International on the Islamic Revolutionary Tribunals and a study of the 899 cases tried by these courts has been presented. The study raises a number of objections which are listed. These objections oppose the death sentence and flogging of political prisoners and call for fair trial procedures which are in compliance with the Universal Declaration of Human Rights and other declarations of the United Nations on related issues.

227 [ANONYMOUS], 'American hostages in Iran'. *The Universal Message*, Vol. I, No. 10, March 1980. Pp. 5–6.

A brief exposition defending the Iranian position in taking American hostages in Iran. The writer, a Muslim Law Professor, has not given his name, but states that the 'Iranian position does not constitute a breach of international law particularly because those actions which might prime facie be endowed with illegality have become legal under the acceptable rules and principles of International Law' (p. 6).

228 [ANONYMOUS], 22 Bahman Special Islamic Republic Party Weekly Bulletin, Tehran: Islamic Republic Party, February 1982.

This special issue celebrates the Third Anniversary of the Islamic Republic of Iran. It contains a 'Life Sketch of Imam Khomeini' and a rather brief but useful article on the roots of the Islamic movement in Iran. The present movement is considered to be a continuation of the following previous ones:

(1) The movement of al-Afghani against British colonialism.
(2) The movement of Mirza Mohammad Hassan Shirazi against the colonialistic Regia agreement.
(3) The movement of the Iranian Ulama against the colonialist Reuter agreement.
(4) The movement of the Shii Ulama for the establishment of law in the Constitutional revolution of 1905.
(5) The movement of Sheikh Fazel-ullah Nuri to rectify the course of the Constitutional Revolution which had been deviated.
(6) The movement of Mirza Mohammad Taki Shirazi against British domination in Iraq.
(7) The movement of Sheikh Mohammad Khiabai to overthrow despotism in Iran.
(8) The movement of the Ulama of Isfahan and Khorasan again Reza Shah.
(9) The movement of Ayatollah Sayyed Hassan Modarres against the Pahlavi dynasty.
(10) The movement of Sayyed Abol-Hassan Isfahani, Mirza Mohammad Hussein Naini, Shaikh Mehdi Khalessi and Sayyed Mohammad Firuzabadi against British policies in Iraq.
(11) The movement of Ayatollah Borujardi to take part in the sit-in in the Abdol-Azim Mosque of Tehran against the Pahlavis.
(12) The movement of Navvab Safavi against the Pahlavi dynasty.
(13) The movement of the Iranian Ulama to nationalize the oil and assist Dr. Mossadeq.
(14) The Freedom Movement of Iran founded by Ayatollah Taleghani. Other individuals who made significant contributions to the struggle were: Ayatollah Montazerri, Ayatollah Motahhari, Dr. Ali Shariati, Ayatollah Dastgheib, Ayatollah Taheiri (now the Friday prayer leader in Isfahan), Hojjatoleslam Hashemi Rafsanjani (presently the Majlis speaker), the late Dr. Moffatteh (head of Tehran's Theology School), Hojjatoleslam Bahonar (the late Prime Minister) and Ayatollah Beheshti.
(15) The movement led by Ayatollah Khomeini.

229 [ANONYMOUS], 'An introduction to cultural revolution', *Message of Revolution*, No. 2, June 1981. Pp. 6–9.

This journal is a publication of the Islamic Revolution Guard Corps. The article referred to discusses the relationship of culture to the Islamic Revolution. It posits the idea that the 'Cultural revolution prepares the ground for materialization of other aspects of the Islamic Revolution; it guarantees the continuation and survival of the Revolution because it is the necessary and principal condition for realization of political, social and economic transformations' (p. 8). On the other hand, the 'best way to deprive a nation of its existence and paralyse it is to take away its culture' (p. 8). The article thus examines the cultural revolution in the light of Westernization and dependence of Iran on the superpowers in the West.

230 [ANONYMOUS], 'The Islamic personality: Ayatollah Taleghani', *Echo of Islam*. Vol. I, No. 6, September 1981. Pp. 11–19.

A brief biography of Taleghani, one of the stalwarts of the Islamic movement in Iran and the most influential person after Khomeini until his death on 10 September 1979.

231 [ANONYMOUS], 'Our intellectuals are all socialists', *The Iranian*, Vol. I, No. 12, September 19, 1979. Pp. 8–11.

This article is an interview with Reza Baraheni who, while praising the Islamic revolution on one hand, believes that it will not succeed unless it abides by the principles of socialism.

232 [ANONYMOUS], 'The return of the Ummat of Iran to the source of power: Islam'. *Mahjubah*, Vol. I, No. 9, November–December 1981. Pp. 13–20.

The article analyses the historical experience of Iranians with colonialism and imperialism which led the people to move towards Western culture, ancient Persian culture and to 'accept a static Islam' and how all this was changed with the revolution within the Mosques in which 'a spirit came into being within every Mosque whereby the necessary plans were made to continue the movement and under the leadership of the Imam of that particular Mosque who was in contact with the marjaie. In this way all of the internal affairs of the movement were carried out through a widespread organizational network under the leadership of Imam Khomeini' (pp. 15–16).

233 [ANONYMOUS], 'The Revolution was Islamic'. *Mahjubah: The Magazine for Muslim Women*, Vol. I, Nos 11 and 12, February–March 1982. Pp. 5–30.

This is a special issue of the magazine to celebrate the Third Anniversary of the Islamic Revolution in Iran. The article gives a description of the events leading to the victory of the revolution from 1977 to 1979 and then lists the important events during the first, second and third years of the revolution.

234 [ANONYMOUS], 'The role of the Masjid'. *Echo of Islam*, Vol. I, No. 7, October 1981, pp. 32–33, 64; Vol. I, No. 8, November 1981. Pp. 30–33.

This two part article briefly describes the role of the Masjid (mosque) in an Islamic revolution. Part I describes the role of the Masjid in Islam during the time of the Holy Prophet as follows:
(1) A base for establishing closer ties to God.
(2) A place for scientific and theological sessions.
(3) As a court for resolving peoples' differences.
(4) As a base for military training.
(5) As a place for concluding of contracts and political treaties.
(6) A weekly meeting place for rulers to deliver their addresses to the people.
(7) A place for bringing up current political issues.
(8) A place for marriage.
(9) A place for refugees and helpless people.
(10) A gathering place for Muslim combatants before going to battle.
(11) A sanctuary for Muslims as a political means to exert pressure on their tyrant rulers.

Part II discusses the role of the mosques during the Islamic revolution in Iran. The Masjids became centres for training in martial arts, collecting financial aid for martyrs, solving peoples' family and legal problems, distributing heating oil in the winter, acting as centres of Islamic arts (films and theatre performances), collecting medicines, mattresses, sheets and equipment for hospitals, places for discussing the difficulties and problems of the Muslim peoples, resting places for crusaders in the 'way of God', delivering revolutionary speeches, etc.

235 [ANONYMOUS], 'Taleghani: The Abu Zar of our Time'. *Islamic Revolution*, Vol. 3, No. 8, September 1981, Pp. 5–7.

This version of the biography of Taleghani shows his links with the Sazeman-e-Mojaheddin-e-Khalq (The Organization of the Combatants of the People of Iran), for which he was imprisoned and tortured on several occasions. On his death Khomeini said that 'he was for Islam a Muslim of the status of Hazrat Abu Zar'.

236 ARNSON, Cynthia, *et al, Background Information on the Crisis in Iran*. Washington, DC: Institute for Policy Studies, 1979.

Gives a background to the Islamic revolution in terms of the opposition forces which resisted the Shah's regime. These were the National Front, the Iran Freedom Party led by Professor Mahdi Bazaragan, the Tudeh Party and the guerilla groups, the Fayadeen and the Mujahideen. Most important was the religious opposition in which the 'clergy in Iran has never served as a judical or educational arm of the ruling party as the Ulama did in many other Islamic countries' (p. 5), but has fiercely asserted its independence and fought for redress of the socio-economic injustices in Iran.

There is a good discussion of the Shah's trampling of 'Human Rights', his 'liberalisation' programmes and the US military involvement through arms aid. The account covers the period up to December, 1978.

237 ASARIA, I., 'Iran—a case study in Muslim political awakening', in K. Siddiqui, ed., *The Islamic revolution: achievements, obstacles and goals*. London: The Muslim Institute, 1980. Pp. 23–36.

This paper gives a background of how the Iranian Ulama had to struggle against tyranny and foreign domination. Such a struggle could only be led through their alliance with the masses.

238 ASKARI, Hasan, 'Khomeini and non-Muslims'. *Encounter* (Rome: Pontificio Instituto di Studi Arabi), No. 7, January 1981.

The article focuses mainly on Khomeini's approach to men of other faiths, but also raises many interesting issues which in the last paragraph is well expressed by pointing out that 'What is left ambiguous in Khomeini's formulation of the clergy as an agent of revolution is the question of how the clergy are themselves to be corrected if they in turn become oppressors. To be honest to Khomeini one should again recall how careful he is in setting the clergy in context with the people, and here he is very close to Shariati's formulations when he trusts the people as the ultimate vehicle of the consciousness of the oppression and its diverse forms. The people as such are not a crowd but the hand and the instrument of revolutionary consciousness which, nurtured by the religious sentiment, transcends the fear of death, and frees them to become martyrs. It is this fervour, lit up by the knowledge that there is life beyond death, which motivates a people, file after file, to declare war upon the oppressors. The clergy impart this knowledge, hand it down from generation to generation, and hence, they are the ultimate trustee of the religious revolutionary consciousness. The message of Khomeini to the Jews and the Christians of Iran is therefore clear: would you join with us in our fight against those who are the oppressors, or remain spectators, or serve the interests of those who are determined to keep the Muslim masses under mental and material subjugation?' (p. 9).

239 AYATOLLAHI, S. M. T., 'Reflections of the Islamic revolution of Iran in the Caribbean'. *Islamic Revolution*, Vol. I, No. 10, January 1980. Pp. 8–11.

The author's appreciation of the Islamic revolution in Iran for the Muslims living in the Caribbean.

240 AYOOB, Mohammad, 'Oil, Arabism and Islam: the Persian Gulf in world politics'. The Australian Institute of International Affairs

Eighth National Conference, Canberra, March 28–30, 1980. Pp. 1–28.

The paper discusses oil, Arabism and Islam which form a unique nexus of the Gulf region. The use of oil as a political weapon and the perception of Arabism as a force for Arabic countries is discussed. But Islam has also proved its revolutionary force by restricting internal order and rejecting foreign domination in countries like Iran. It has also had its impact upon problems in the Middle East. The Shah's un-Islamic rule showed indifference to the plight of the Palestinians by supplying aid to the Israelis. Islamic rule in Iran, on the other hand, has supported the Palestinians and declared Israel to be the enemy of Muslims. The interaction of these three forces mentioned above are therefore crucial factors in understanding the role of the Persian Gulf in world politics.

241 AYOOB, Mohammad, 'The Politics of Resurgent Islam'. Working Paper 21. Canberra: The Australian National University, The Strategic and Defence Studies Centre, 1980. Pp. 1–12.

The paper examines two objectives. First, to assert that Islam has been used as a political tool by various leaders, groups and parties to further its aims in varying contexts. Secondly, Islamic response in its encounter with Western intervention into Muslim lands during the last 200 years. The political strategies of various Muslim leaders are analysed. Ataturk wanted to transform Turkey into a Western country, whereas Nasser confronted the West to achieve Egypt's independence. With this as a backdrop, Ayatollah Khomeini has emerged as another Muslim leader with goals totally different from the above two. In all of this, Islam's anti-colonial and anti-hegemonial role has become evident. But Ataturk and Nasser were understood by the West and as such presented no difficulties for the latter. But 'if Khomeini cannot be understood, he cannot be controlled and that is the main danger that the Ayatollah poses to the international system as it is presently constituted ... that is the challenge that Khomeini poses to the West and that is what has made the West aware of his politics and of his religion—which together have been termed the politics of resurgent Islam' (p. 7).

242 AYOOB, Mohammad, 'The revolutionary thrust of Islamic political tradition'. *Third World Quarterly*, Vol. 3, No. 2, April 1981. Pp. 269–276.

The author discusses the rise of the revolutionary tradition in Islam from early times through to the pan-Islamic movement of al-Afghani and the insightful poems of Iqbal (like the Khizr-i-Rah) to the radical Islamic ideology of Ali Shariati.

Shariati's central concept in the exposition of Islam, the author contends, was al-Nas (the people). The Qur'an addresses itself not to a particular segment of society but to the people. In human societies there were two structures, the structure of Cain and the structure of Abel. In the structure of Cain 'individuals are owners, and masters of their own destinies, and the destiny of society', in that of Abel 'society is the lord and master of its own destiny and all men work for it and its benefit' (p. 275). Thus, according to Shariati, when it is said that 'rule belongs to God' it means that it belongs to the people as a whole; if it is said that 'property belongs to God' it means that capital belongs to the people; if it is said that 'religion belongs to God' it means that it belongs to the people and is not the monopoly of those who claim to represent it. Such 'radical Islamic populism' of Ali Shariati was responsible for mobilizing both the Islamic and Marxist groups into revolutionary activity in Iran.

243 AYOOB, Mohammad, 'Two faces of political Islam: Iran and Pakistan compared'. *Asian Survey*, Vol. XIX, No. 6, June 1979. Pp. 535–456.

A comparison is made between the Islamization of Pakistan and the Islamic revolution in Iran. The author considers that Islam has been used in Pakistan to 'legitimise a socially conservative economically unjust and politically unpopular order' (p. 537), while in Iran the Shia clergy have historically been 'catalysts for political change and as leaders of political dissent' (p. 540). The role of the mosque in opposition to the State is considered as a 'facet peculiar to Shia Islam in Iran' (p. 541). In conclusion, the 'revolutionary strand of Islam' is defined, which 'can provide both the legitimacy for relentless opposition to an established but tyrannical order, and the appropriate channel to mobilise the usually silent majority into active participation in a revolutionary process' (p. 543).

244 AYOUB, Mahmoud, *Redemptive suffering in Islam: a study of the devotional aspects of Ashura in Twelver Shiism*. The Hague: Mouton Publishers, 1978.

Much has been written about the martyrdom of Imam Husayn as the inner dynamics of the Islamic revolution. This work deals with the Shiite celebrations of Muharram. The author contends that the Shii response is unique, profound and has a cosmic dimension in which he becomes 'salvation' history by participating in the sufferings of Imam Hussain and his family.

245 AYYUBI, Mohiuddin, *Khumeini speaks revolution*. Karachi: International Islamic Publishers, 1981. 52 pp.

The booklet gives a brief introduction to Khomeini's life and six sermons delivered by him. These are: (1) Caliphate essential for the enforcement of Islamic laws: evil designs of the Western powers; (2) the nature of the Islamic State and the qualifications of the Head of the State; (3) The main aim of Islam is to create a just, welfare state; (4) The so-called scholars are the tools of the wicked. Disunity is the main cause of the disgrace of Muslims; (5) An important sermon of the Ameer; (6) O Scholars of Islam: rise and prepare for another Karbala: the defence of Islam is a greater duty than prayers.

Also included is an interview with Khomeini by the weekly *Impact International* (London).

246 AZ, *pseud.*, 'The women's struggle in Iran'. *Monthly Review*, Vol. 32, No. 10, March 1981. Pp. 22–30.

The author, using a pseudonym, is an Iranian woman residing in Iran. She contends the Khomeini's regime was a reaction from the Pahlavi's regime which on the one hand had sought to create a modern centralized state determined by the needs and demands of the world capitalist system and, on the other, reproduced important aspects of monarchist absolutism of pro-capitalist Iran. Khomeini reacted to this but in this reversion the role of women will suffer very much due to oppression by the Islamic regime. Iran women must therefore brace themselves for a struggle 'moving from a sex-in-itself to a sex for itself'. The paper puts forward a Marxist perspective on these issues.

247 BAKHASH, S., 'Who lost Iran?', *The New York Review*, Vol. XXVIII, No. 8, May 14, 1981. Pp. 18–22.

The author, in reviewing a book by Michael Leedeen [item 355] argues that the 'Shah ultimately lost his throne not because he failed to get support in Washington but because he lost the support of his own people' (p. 22).

248 BANI-SADR, Abdul Hasan, 'The twelve meanings of martyrdom'. *Islamic Revolution*, Vol. II, No. 4, July 1980. Pp. 8–12.

An exposition of the various meanings of migration and martyrdom and their implications for an Islamic society.

249 BANI-SADR, Abul Hasan, *Work and the worker in Islam*, trans. by Hasan Mashadi. Tehran, Iran: The Hamdani Foundation, n.d.

The work contains lectures delivered by Bani-Sadr at the workers' conference at the Sorbonne University during the first month following the victory of the Islamic Revolution in Iran. It attempts to answer the following questions: How does Islam value human labour? What is the dignity accorded a worker in Islam? What are the rights of the capitalists in Islam vis-à-vis those of the workers?

What does Islam offer to the workers beyond what is offered to them by materialistic ideologies such as Marxism?

250 BARAHENI, Reza, *The crowned cannibals: writings on repression in Iran.* New York: Vintage Books, 1977.

Much has been written on the repression in Iran which was one of the causes for the Islamic revolution. In this book, the author, an Iranian professor of English language, has given a lucid account of what used to happen in SAVAK prisons. The author was himself in one such prison and his brief meeting with Shariati in one of the cells is also described.

251 BATRA, R., *Muslim civilization and the crisis in Iran.* Dallas, Texas: Venus Books, 1980. Pp. 171–185.

In Chapter 7 entitled 'Crisis in Iran' the author has specifically discussed the rise of Khomeini according to the Hindu framework of caste analysis by dividing people into Khatris, Vipras, Vashyas and Shudras.

252 BAYAT-PHILIPP, M., 'Islam in Pahlavi and post-Pahlavi Iran: a cultural revolution?', in J. L. Esposito, ed., *Islam and development: religion and socio-political change.* New York: Syracuse University Press, 1980. Pp. 87–106.

The author discusses the role of Shiism from pre-modern to modern Iran. The Pahlavi's anti-Islamic attitude alienated the lay professionals and their influence apart from the Ulama's cannot be underrated. Such lay professionals were Mehdi Bazargan, an engineer, and Shariati, a sociologist. They commanded a following among the educated strata of society which also helped the revolution.

253 BAYAT-PHILIPP, M., 'Shiism in contemporary Iranian politics: The case of Ali Shariati', in E. Kedourie and S. Haim, eds, *Towards a modern Iran.* London: Frank Cass, 1980. Pp. 155–168.

The author considers Ali Shariati's problem as the crisis of identity of the Iranian intellectuals. Such intellectuals belong to a new breed in the Muslim world who are not secularized or Westernized. Shariati therefore did not question the Islamic faith but how to understand that faith within the modern context. Shariati was against believing in Islam without thinking as much as against those who were preoccupied with attempting to prove its scientific validity. In Shariati's opinion, the most 'relevant question a Muslim should ask himself today was not whether each religious concept is rational or irrational, compatible or incompatible with science; but rather what is its usefulness and its worth to the society in which he lives' (p. 156). Shariati then explores the radical notions ensconsed within Islamic concepts. The author has not examined all the works of Shariati but materials for the paper have been drawn from five of Shariati's works. These are *Az Kuja Aghaz Kunim; Intizar, Mazhabii i'tiraz; Masuliyat-i Shiah Budan; Ummat va imamat; Pidar, madar ... ma muttahimim.*

254 BAYAT-PHILIPP, M., 'Tradition and change in Iranian socio-religious thought', in M. E. Bonine & N. R. Keddie, eds, *Modern Iran: the dialectics of continuity and change*. Albany, NY: State University of New York Press, 1980. Pp. 37–58.

The paper argues that 'the so-called modernist thought of the turn of the century despite its loud call for Westernisation was in spirit and in form, if not in content, deep-rooted in tradition, bearing as much the mark of the Irano-Islamic heritage outwardly rejected by some of its spokesmen, as of the European systems it strongly wished to emulate' (p. 37). The author then discusses the religious reforms of the nineteenth century and the political activism of the twentieth century which have influenced Shii socio-religious thought in Iran.

255 BAZARGAN, Mehdi, *The inevitable victory*, trans. by M. Yusefi. Bedford, Ohio: Free Islamic Literature Inc., 1978.

Medhi Bazargan was the first Prime Minister of the Islamic Republic of Iran. He has been the author of many books and in this little booklet he explains some of the doctrines of Shiism such as Mahdism and Occultation.

256 BEHESHTI, *Ayatollah*, 'Autobiography', *Echo of Islam*, Vol. 1, No. 6, September 1981. Pp. 11–14.

An extract from an autobiographical interview of Dr. Beheshti which focuses on a very crucial period from 1962 to 1979. In this he mentions how he and a group of other Ulama secretly formed the Ruhaniyat-e-Mobarez (Revolutionary Clergy) in 1977 and how after a meeting with Khomeini in Paris the nucleus of the Revolutionary Council was formed. Among its earliest members were men like Mutahari, Hashemi Rafsanjani, Musavi Ardabili and Bahonar. Later others like Khamenei, Taleghani, and Sahabi joined the Council until Khomeini's return to Iran.

257 BEHN, W., *The Iranian opposition in exile*. Berlin: Rosenheimer Strasse No. 5, 1000 Berlin 30, 1979.

An annotated bibliography of publications from 1962 to 1979.

258 BEHN, W., *Islamic revolution or revolutionary Islam in Iran*. Berlin: Rosenheimer Strasse No. 5, 1000 Berlin 30, 1980.

A selected and annotated bibliography of political literature from the overthrow of the Shah until his death. Lists books and articles in Persian and European languages.

259 BEHN, W., 'The revolution of the pen: Iranian underground publications, 1963–1978', in B. C. Bloomfield, ed., *Middle East studies and libraries*. London: Mansell Publishing, 1980. Pp. 13–22.

The author surveys a vast range of literature produced during the period 1963 to 1978. This came from the leftist, rightist and nationalist groups and was written for mobilization of the masses against Muhammad Reza Shah's regime. The libraries where such literature can be located are also mentioned, this being of considerable help to the researcher.

260 BENAB, Younes D., 'Political organisations in Iran: a historical review'. *The review of Iranian Political Economy and History*, Vol. 3, No. 1, Spring 1979. Pp. 13–18.

The author traces the advent of the popular supervision forces during the period 1945–1979. The account traces the forces which arose before 1941, the second period in which political parties arose, 1941–1953, and the third period, 1953–1977. An analysis of all these forces is then categorized and in the author's opinion fall into three distinct categories: religious, nationalist and leftist.

261 BILL, J. A., 'Iran and the crisis of 1978'. *Foreign Affairs*, Vol. 57, No. 2, Winter 1978–79. Pp. 323–342.

This analysis is restricted to the deterioration of the Shah's rule up to 1978 and the policy alternatives open to the US in dealing with the situation. The Shah, it is considered, ruled like the lion and the fox by being 'wedded to no set of ideological principles, he has sought to overcome challenges to his person or his programs by shrewd political manoeuvre and calculated manipulation. Weaving, dodging, feinting, retreating and attacking, he has emphasised survival by wit' (p. 326). But in spite of the animal talents of the Shah and other Iranian rulers of the past, they have not been able to surpass Islam and since 1501 'secular Shahs have ruled partially in the shadow of the Mujtahids' (p. 332).

The latter, on the other hand, are 'men of great learning, integrity and popularity. They are renowned for the simplicity of their standard of living and are among the most democratically chosen grassroots leaders' (p. 332). The Shah's rule alienated him from the people and ultimately reduced him to rule from 'behind bayonets' for he could not control 'his sophisticated population by brute force indefinitely' (p. 335). With political affairs in such a mess, the writer considers four national policy alternatives for the US. First, it could encourage the Shah to open his system to accommodate his opponents. Secondly, the US could remain neutral and allow the Iranians to sort out their own affairs. Thirdly, it could rethink its policy of unprecedented arms sales to Iran, and fourthly, American diplomats in Iran could acquaint themselves with knowledge of Iranian politics not only from the Shah's people but also from the religious leaders, members of the middle class, journalists, poets, lawyers, students, teachers, provincial leaders, etc.

262 BINDER, L., 'The proofs of Islam: religion and politics in Iran', in G. Makdisi, ed., *Arabic and Islamic studies: in honour of Hamilton A. F. Gibb*. Leiden: E. J. Brill, 1965. Pp. 118–140.

The question is posed: how can Islam and politics be meaningfully studied? The author, therefore, puts forward various hypotheses. First, that Shiite Islam grants greater religious authority to the Ulama than does Sunni Islam. Secondly, certain historical events and other situational factors have determined that the Shiite clergy are not so strongly challenged in their authority as the Sunni Ulama. Thirdly, the Iranian Ulama are more centralized in terms of formal institutional status-roles than are the Sunni Ulama. Fourthly, the Iranian Ulama have maintained grassroot influence and also maintained their independence of government control 'in eliminating and weakening competitors and in satisfying their own demands as individuals' (p. 121).

263 BINDER, L., 'Revolution in Iran: red, white, blue or black', *Bulletin of the Atomic Scientists*, No. 53, January 1979. Pp. 48–54.

The author considers that the revolutionary confrontation in Iran was a mixture of 'conflicts of culture, developmental strategy, foreign policy orientation and religious doctrine'. Furthermore the author believes that 'even if the Islamic opposition means to change things in Iran they will have to retain solidarity even if Khomeini turns against the left' (p. 53).

264 CARLSEN, R. W., *Crises in Iran: a microcosm of the cosmic play*. Victoria, B.C.: The Snow Man Press, 1979, 56 p.

The author carries out a multi-disciplinary analysis from the moral, political, psychological, spiritual and aesthetic points of view. His analysis unfolds by taking into consideration the seizure of diplomatic hostages in November 1979 by Iranian students.

265 CARLSEN, R. W., *Seventeen days in Tehran: revolution, evolution and ignorance*. Victoria B.C.: The Snow Man Press, 1980.

An account of a personal journey into revolutionary Iran with in depth interviews with officials, students and scholars. It attempts to assess the Islamic revolution in relation to western civilization

266   CHAMRAN, Mustafa, *The Islamic Revolution and the imposed war.* Tehran: The Ministry of Islamic Guidance, 1982.

A brief exposition of the thoughts of one of the important revolutionary figures who died in the Iran–Iraq war.

267   CHEEMA, Pervaiz I., *Conflict and cooperation in the Indian Ocean: Pakistan's interests and choices.* Canberra, Australia: Australian National University, Canberra. Papers on Strategy and Defence, No. 23, 1980.

The political, military, economic and cultural factors as well as super-power involvement in the Pakistan–Iran relationship has been discussed. Islam is considered as the cultural bond between Iranians and Pakistanis although 'the Islam practised in Pakistan is much closer in its operational form to that practised in most Arab countries than is Iranian Islam' (p. 53). Furthermore, Iran and Pakistan need each other and the 'new regime can hardly afford to ignore the useful role Pakistan can play, especially in view of Pakistan's cordial relations with most Arab states. Hostility between the Persians and the Arabs is long standing, and the clandestine preaching of the Shia revolution by some of Khomeini's lieutenants is causing further tension between Iran and some of the neighboring Arab states' (p. 50).

268   CHUBIN, S., *Soviet policy towards Iran and the Gulf.* London: International Institute for Strategic Studies, 1980.

The author discusses the Soviet foreign policy towards Iran and its strategic implications. He contends that Soviet policy has played down its atheistic communism to gain favour with the Muslim world. But it has been reluctant to respond wholeheartedly to Iran since Khomeini showed lack of enthusiasm for the USSR when he was in exile in Paris. The Soviet hope is that after Khomeini Iran may take a secular turn and thus become more vulnerable to Soviet influence.

269   COTTAM, R., 'Goodbye to America's Shah'. *Foreign Policy*, Vol. 34, Spring 1979. Pp. 3–14.

The author believes that the Iranian revolution was a popular revolution of the masses. This view is supported by evidence of considerable support for Khomeini and a lack of loyalty for the Shah before the revolution. Furthermore, the Shah was considered a traitor to his people because he was seen by the masses as a 'creation of American and British imperialism' (p. 3). The author therefore poses the questions: What was the basis for this perception of American control? Why has so little been done to counter that perception? How has it affected the Carter administration's ability to deal with the crisis in Iran? These questions are discussed in the light of the failure of American diplomacy and the ignorance of Iranian history. The author is of the opinion that the Iranian revolutionary movement did not emerge spontaneously, but that its roots were buried deep in Iran's ancient past. Furthermore, America's total support of the Shah and the latter's total identification with America reinforced the perception of the Iranian people that the Shah was the creation of American imperialism. In such a milieu three schools of opinion emerged in Iran during the period 1963–1977. First were the security forces, and the newly rich, the technocrats, etc., who believed in the Shah's dream of a great Iranian civilization and alliance with America was considered instrumental in achieving it. Second, there was the large segment of the population who disagreed with the Shah's policies and the corruption of his regime and foreign domination of the country but did not see any other alternative for survival within the system. Thirdly, there was the opposition group who held the deep conviction that the Shah was no more than 'a faithful servant of America and Western capitalist interest and a man who tyrannized and brutalized his own people, willingly replacing Iran's own rich national and Islamic culture with the Hilton-style Western import' (p. 10). The Carter administration has also been blamed for its failure to correct the perception pointed out earlier. When Carter travelled to Tehran he ignored the statement of 29 opposition leaders and instead praised the Shah for maintaining stability. After his departure most of these opposition leaders were arrested and jailed and many demonstrations in the streets of Iran were suppressed by American-equipped soldiers. Carter even telephoned a message of support to the Shah. This, the author considers, further destroyed any lingering faith that the Iranians might have had in the impartiality of the Carter administration. The article then draws the lessons for America. It considers that 'any regime considered by the attentive public to be an American creation, or at least dependency, will be fundamentally fragile' (p. 14).

270 DATAJEE, A. M., Khomeini-ism. *The Task Force on Christian-Muslim Relations Newsletter* (Conn.: Hartford Seminary Foundation). No. 12, March 1980. Pp. 3–5.

The author who is from the Islamic Society of Greater Harrisberg in Pennsylvania describes Khomeini-ism as an idea which is 'reactionary in content, but revolutionary in form' (p. 4). It stands for emphasis on local interests rather than foreign and mobilization of natural resources. In conclusion, the author advises the West to co-exist with Khomeini until he dies and then 'to look round for to find a suitable person or persons who could look after Western interests in that part of the world' (p. 5).

271 DEKMEJIAN, R. H., 'The anatomy of Islamic revival: legitimacy crises, ethnic conflict and the search for Islamic alternatives'. *The Middle East Journal*, Vol. 34, No. 1, Winter 1980. Pp. 1–12.

The writer focuses on Islamic revival in the Muslim world in general with particular reference to Egypt, Iran and Pakistan. He finds that revival has three basic attributes; its pervasiveness in the Muslim world; its polycentrism in that it erupts in various Muslim countries rather than being inspired from one centre; and its persistence to reoccur again and again. Such revival emanates from three sources, political, economic and military. The failure to provide political legitimation of the regimes in Muslim countries has brought Islam into the political arena. Where this legitimation has been done through various ideologies, social inequalities have been created which has again brought in Islam to provide social justice for the people. Thirdly, the failure of Muslim countries to win any victories at the battlefronts has again brought Islam to their rescue. Thus, 'with respect to the West, the Islamic rebirth movement could constitute a clear political and economic challenge' (p. 12) and within Muslim countries, Islam 'constitutes a fall back ideology to capture the alienated, the disorientated and the angry; in this sense it constitutes a powerful check on mass alienation and social mobilization. Islam can accommodate the political activist as well as provide an escape from politics in the ascetic milieu of the mosque' (p. 11).

272 DORMAN, W. A., 'Iranian people versus US news media: a case of libel'. *Race and Class*, Vol. XXI, No. 1, 1979. Pp. 57–66.

Before 1978, few Americans would have been able to answer the simplest quiz about Iran. But after the Islamic revolution in Iran, most Americans have become aware of it. But the author shows how the news media's reportage has completely distorted Iran's image for the American people which at best seems to have 'been guilty of ethnocentrism and, at worst, have been guilty of racism' (p. 57).

273 DORMAN, W. A. and FARHANG, M., 'Uncovering a revolution: the Iranian experience'. *The Universal Message*, Vol. II, No. 10, March 1981. Pp. 23–25.

These two academics, after a survey of the media reportage of the Islamic revolution in Iran have come to the conclusion that 'the news media have covered Iran from a narrow, highly ethnocentric perspective, whose boundaries were first established in Washington and not in the news rooms. It seems clear from the Iranian experience that the American press, if it is to conform to its own professed values, and if it is truly interested in serving the legitimate interests of the U.S. in the region must come to recognize the subtle interplay between ethnocentrism and ideology. Similarly, it must abandon the notion that worthwhile coverage can result from parachuting unsophisticated generalists into foreign cultures, a lesson that anthropologists learned long ago' (p. 24).

274 DREFUSS, R., *Hostage to Khomeini*. New York: Benjamin Franklin House Publishing Co., 1981.

The author discusses the following questions: how British intelligence projected the Mullah's revolution, how Billigate was just one part of the Carter administration's secret alliance with the Khomeini regime, why Carter let 60 Americans be taken hostage, why the April rescue by the Americans failed, etc.

275 ELIASH, Joseph, 'The Ithna Ashari-Shii juristic theory of political and legal authority'. *Studia Islamica*, Vol. 29, 1969. Pp. 2–30.

The author discusses the doctrine of the authority of the Imam in Shiism.

276 ELWELL-SUTTON, L. P., 'The Iranian revolution'. *International Journal*, Vol. 34, No. 3, Summer 1979. Pp. 391–407.

The author starts by positing that the role of Islam in bringing about political change in Iran is not in question, but what is not clear is the nature and significance of the part it has played during the revolution. He then traces the development of the Shia religious organization through Safavids, Qajars and Pahlavis. The Shii hierarchy have always maintained their independence and hence have been opposed to any temporal authority within Iran. Their opposition to the regime, the author believes, has not been consistent and after 1941 with the rise of leftist groups associated with the Tudeh party on the one hand and rightist groups associated with the Navab Safavi and Kashani, the religious hierarchy again attempted to assert itself.

The religious hierarchy have always retained their hold on the Iranian masses through their bazaaris rouze-khane which described the martyrdom of Imam Hussain at Karbala. This event was symbolic of how a tiny minority was crushed by an oppressive tyrant. This was therefore helpful in whipping-up opposition against the Shah and his secular rule. What ignited the revolution, according to the author, is that the leftist guerilla group must have made overtures to the religious heirarchy for their support—and the 'bait held out to them was the possibility of re-establishing their power so seriously undermined by the Shah; at the same time the left must have hoped to be able to lead and direct the movement once it got under way' (p. 405). The opposition was therefore an ill-assorted but powerful group which successfully attained their goal but instead of the left the religious hierarchy led the movement.

Having nothing in common after the revolution they have now fallen apart and the religious leadership have not been able to solve the country's social and economic problems. Iran, the author asserts, has acquired a regime which is 'Islamic in name only, whose foundations are extremely unsteady and whose policies are likely to be determined by practical considerations of survival' (p. 407). As such the possibility of a civil war, communist takeover, military coup d'etat and even the return of monarchy cannot be dismissed.

277   ELWELL-SUTTON, L. P., 'The Iranian revolution: triumph or tragedy?', in H. Amirsadeghi (ed.) *The security of the Persian Gulf.* London: Croom Helm, 1981. Pp. 231–254.

In this paper the author analyses the causes of the revolution as being due to many factors. Some of these are the Shah's autocratic rule, his economic reforms which created a new industrial proletariat through the influx of landless peasants to urban areas, the growth of big business due to the oil boom which weakened the small merchants. The latter were the main pillars of financial support of the Ulama and their weakened position eroded the economic base of the Ulama leading to hostility against the Shah and the role of Shiism which does not compromise with the temporal authorities and becomes the protector of the oppressed.

278   ENTESSAR, Nader, 'Arab factions in post-revolutionary Iranian politics'. *Middle East Review*, Vol. 12, No. 3, 1980. Pp. 52–54.

The article describes the role of arab groups in Iran, particularly the PLO and AMAL (Afwag al-Moghavemah al-Lobnanieh).

279   EZZATI, Abul-Fazl, *The concept of leadership in Islam.* London: The Muslim Institute for Research and Planning, 1979.

The author is an Iranian scholar who belongs to the Iranian Islamic movement. In his seminar published as a paper later he distinguishes the special features of leadership in Islam. According to him, leadership in Islam does not mean political power but it is a 'social responsibility to provide security and peace for the Muslim society to enable it to fulfil its divine purpose and goal' (p. 8). It is in fact based on the doctrine of *Amr bi al-Mauroof va al-Nahy An al-Munkar* (bidding the doing of good and forbidding the abominable) and social responsibility (*Wajib al-Kifai*) which belongs 'to the community as a whole and the government and leaders simply represent the community. Government responsibility does not release the community from its own responsibility but it simply becomes a double responsibility of the community and government' (p. 8).

280 EZZATI, Abul-Fazl, 'Legitimation of the Islamic revolutionary movements'. *Al-Serat*, Vol. 6, Nos. 3–4, 1980. Pp. 36–41.

The author investigates the sources of legitimation of Islamic movements.

281 EZZATI, Abul-Fazl *The revolutionary Islam and the Islamic revolution.* Tehran: The Ministry of Islamic Guidance, 1981.

This book has been written by an Iranian Muslim scholar and diplomat and attempts to explain the dynamics of the Islamic revolution from within. In Part I it covers The revolutionary Islam, and in part II it explains the outlines of Shiite Islamic politics and revolutionary traditions. Part III focuses on the impact of the Islamic revolution. Although the book was published by the Ministry of Islamic Guidance, it is made clear in the Foreword that 'it does not regard the author's views as the official views of the government of Iran'. The author, on the other hand, contends that the book portrays the revolution 'the way the Iranian people would like it explained'. The book is an important addition towards understanding the Islamic revolution.

282 EZZATI, Abul-Fazl, 'The spirit of Islamic revolution: government and constitution.' *Islamic Defence Review*, Vol. 5, No. 3, 1980. Pp. 26–31.

The author at the outset makes it clear that the Islamic revolution is based on the ideology of Islam and which has its own identities, features and characteristics which differentiates this revolution from any other. After this, he articulates the principles and objectives of the Islamic revolution, government and constitution. The objectives of the revolution, governments and constitution is to spread the message of Islam, emancipation of mankind from all forms of oppression and the creation of conditions for the maximum development of human potential. All these must be based on the principles of Tawhid (oneness of Allah), the responsibilities of Muslims, as individuals and as a community towards Allah, to each other, to themselves, to humanity and the universe.

283 FALK, Richard, 'Comments on international law and the United States' response to the Iranian revolution in international conflicts, law and a just world order: the 1980 David Stoffer Lectures.' Reprint from the *Rutgers Law Review*, Vol. 33, No. 2, Winter, 1981. Pp. 399–409.

An important article which discusses how international law can be unfair when used in international conflicts. In this article the author shows how it has favoured the US when the Iranians held American hostages. The author contends that if international law has to be objective then individuals have to free themselves from state and class identities. Since the US had no military option to free hostages it resorted to international law which was quite helpful to it. The law only condemned the holding of hostages but did not look at the Shah's crimes against the Iranian people, or of the United States complicity in subverting the constitutional order of Iran in 1953. The author concludes that 'Dean Acheson said that the United States can cast laws aside because its sovereignty is at stake; why can't Ayatollah Khomeini say and do the same thing? After all, who sets the rule of the game? Always, the dominant actors do. And once those rules are set, why can't the other side play by them as well? To me, the essential challenge is to adopt international law to the basic rhythm of change going on in the world today, especially as associated with the resurgence of non-Western peoples in exerting control over the political, economic and cultural domains of their national existence' (p. 409).

284   FALK, Richard, 'Iran and American geopolitics in the Gulf'. *Race and Class*, XXI, No. 1, 1979. Pp. 41–55.

The US is shown as the enemy of nationalism in non-Western countries. The article exposes US political intervention in Iranian politics, from the CIA involvement in 1953 to the Nixon doctrine and Carter's interference. In conclusion the objectives of US policy and tensions emanating from it are discussed.

285   FALK, Richard, 'Iran: human rights and international law', in D. H. Albert, (ed.), *Tell the American people: perspectives on the Iranian revolution*, Philadelphia, PA: Movement for a New Society, 1980. Pp. 81–91.

The paper makes some interesting comments on human rights in a revolutionary situation. It notes that the success of the revolution has demonstrated 'once and for all that the relation of forces in a Third World society has not decisively shifted from the people to the state. Iran is such an important case because the populist possibility seemed so remote until it succeeded into success' (p. 82). Furthermore, it is acknowledged that the success of the revolution 'resulted from the mobilization of the Iranian people on the basis of leadership and beliefs that had intense mass appeal and deep domestic roots. In that sense, the activation of the Shiia perspective by Ayatollah Khomeini, and its ideological expression in the influencial work of Ali Shariati, were crucial catalysts' (p. 82).

Falk then makes observations on various controversial issues which have received world wide publicity such as women, ethnic minorities, religious minorities, the role of the Left, etc. He points out that the Khomeini movement has been criticized because popular assessments of the Islamic Republic were made by simple 'yes/no' answers to the questions on the referendum rather than by asking more subtly whether a monarchy, a constitutional monarchy, a non-religious republic or an Islamic Republic was preferred by the people. Falk then argues 'it should be noted that the Khomeini movement made it clear throughout the revolution that an Islamic Republic was its objective. This political outcome was promised to the followers of Khomeini, and, in a sense, the extent of popular support for that promise is the only relevant question with regard to the reorganization of the Iranian state. The argument that a range of other options should have been presented to the Iranian people is both an academic insistence given the level of support for an Islamic Republic and probably overstates the political sophistication of the Iranian people so long victimized by a monochromatic tyranny' (p. 86).

The author concludes that patience should be exercised in appraising Iran for the problems of post-revolutionary adjustment present a host of difficulties but Khomeini seems 'dedicated to evolving a form of governance for the people of Iran that includes a central commitment to social justice for the poor' (p. 91). The question of human rights and international law should not be taken for granted because they went against the 'immunity claims of the American diplomatic personnel, but, failing to uphold either extradition claims directed at the Shah or charges that the American Embassy in Tehran has been used to encroach upon the political and personal human rights of the Iranian people' (p. 81).

286 FARHANG, Mansour, 'I witnessed the most incredible celebrations in the streets of Tehran'. *The Review of Iranian Political Economy and History*, Vol. 3, No. 1, Spring 1979. Pp. 91–116.

This is an account of an interview with Professor Farhang by Tom Ricks and it proceeds to analyse the various aspects of the Iranian revolution.

287 FARHANG, Mansour, 'Resisting the Pharaohs: Ali Shariati on oppression.' *Race and Class*, Vol. XXI, No. 1, 1979. Pp. 31–40.

The article gives a brief introduction to Shariati's life and thought. It is contended that Shariati believed that the pre-requisite of a truly Islamic society depended upon an equitable system of production and distribution. But his conception of equity did not only stress the importance of the material realm but also interrelated it with the moral dimension without which any society could degenerate into 'dictatorial and fraudulent practices' (p. 32). After this brief introduction an excerpt from Shariati's writing on the 'Reflections of a concerned Muslim: on the plight of oppressed peoples' is given.

288 AL-FARUQI, I. R., 'Islam and the Tehran hostages'. *The Universal Message*, Vol. I, No. 8, January 1980. Pp. 12–13.

The author is a professor at a university in the USA and holds the opinion that 'seizure of U.S. embassy employees in Tehran, is illegitimate and unacceptable' because 'Islamic Law recognizes that foreign envoys in the Islamic state enjoy full personal immunity and may not be treated except as envoys. They cannot be incarcerated or executed; they only be expelled. However, if their conduct brings material damages to the Islamic state or its citizens, they will have to compensate for the damage inflicted' (p. 13).

289 FATEMI, Faramarz S., *The USSR in Iran*. New York: A. S. Barnes & Co., 1980.

A study of Irano-Soviet politics during the 1941–47 period. Attention is focused on the Azerbaijan revolution and Premier Qavam's political skill. In the epilogue, a few pages are devoted to the Islamic revolution in Iran. The book ends with a hope that the revolutionary leadership should 'commence the task of building a new Iran and satisfying the long-desired needs of the people' (p. 191).

290 FATEMI, K., 'The Iranian revolution: its impact on economic relations with the United States'. *International Journal of Middle East Studies*, Vol. 12, 1980. Pp. 303–317.

This paper focuses on the American influence and influx into the Iranian military, the oil industry, the banking system, the capital goods market and consumer products before and after the revolution.

291 FERDOWS, Adele, 'Religion in Iranian nationalism: the study of the Fadayan-i-Islam'. Indiana: Indiana University, 1967. Unpublished Ph.D. dissertation.

The dissertation focuses mainly on Nawab Safavi and his movement the Fadayin-i-Islam which was started in 1945 and rose to power during the 1950s.

292 FESHARAKI, F. 'Revolution and energy policy in Iran: international and domestic implications', in H. Amirsadeghi (ed.), *The security of the Persian Gulf*. London: Croom Helm, 1981. Pp. 255–280.

The author contends that ever since its discovery in Masjid-e-Soleiman in 1908, oil has been the most important factor in Iranian politics. The US backed coup in 1953 which brought the Shah back to power was motivated by Western oil interests. The 1978 oil strikes also proved itself to be the most important factor in bringing the Shah's downfall.

After proving the importance of the oil factor, the author then analyses the oil policy of the Islamic regime and its impact from four different perspectives: world petroleum supplies, international trade, oil prices, inflation and balance of payment problems.

293 FISCHER, M. M. J., *Iran: from religious dispute to revolution*. Cambridge, Mass.: Harvard University Press, 1980.

The book is based on the author's fieldwork carried out in Iran particularly in the city of Qum. The focus is therefore mainly on the Madrassas of Qum and the styles of teaching students and its effectiveness. Appendices are also attached of the courses of study. The last chapter concentrates on 'the revolutionary movement of 1977–79' and narrates the events as they took place. The author observes two 'ideological shifts . . . in the course of the revolution. First, it became practical to stress that the Karbala paradigm is not a passive weeping for Husayn but rather an active fighting for Husayn's ideals and it is not merely a personal and individual commitment but a social one. Second, after the removal of the Shah there was a shift from Husayn as the symbol of protest against tyranny to Ali as the symbol of constructive government and Muhammad as the symbol of universalism' (p. 213).

294 FISHER, C. B., 'The Shah's white revolution'. *The Muslim World*, Vol. XIV, No. 2, April 1964. Pp. 98–103.

A brief account of the religious opposition to the Shah's white revolution which occurred in Iran in June 1963.

295 FLOOR, W. M., 'The revolutionary character of the Iranian Ulama: wishful thinking or reality?'. *International Journal of Middle Eastern Studies*, Vol. 12, No. 4, 1980. Pp. 501–524.

The author contests the contention that opposition to tyranny is a fundamental and pervasive characteristic of Shii Islam. Instead he holds the thesis that the Ulama's perception of the socio-economic and political structure of Iranian society does not basically differ from that held by the secular power elite.

296 GALLAGHER, C. F., *Contemporary Islam: the plateau of particularism, problems of religion and nationalism in Iran*. New York: American Universities Field Staff Reports, 1966.

Problems of religion and nationalism in Iran are discussed.

297 GAROUSSIAN, Vida, 'Ulema and secularisation in contemporary Iran'. Illinois: Southern Illinois University, 1974. Unpublished Ph.D. dissertation.

The dissertation analyses the relationship between Islam and politics in Iranian society. It focuses on the Ulama in their confrontation with the modernizing elite. After tracing the roots of Ulama power in Iranian society during the Reza Shah regime it shows their change of political status during Muhammad Reza Shah's time specially during period 1951–53. The activities of the two religious movements, the *Fadaiyan-e-Islam* (Devotees of Islam) and *Mojahedin-e-Islam* (Warriors of Islam) has also been discussed and the conflict of the Ulama with the modernization of the country which helped to reduce their power has also been analysed.

298 GASTIL, Raymond D., *Freedom in the world: 1980. Political rights and civil liberties*. New York: Freedom House, 1980.

One section of Part III is devoted to the Islamic revolution in Iran. According to the author Islam has always maintained power over the middle and lower middle classes—specially the bazaar merchants. Since they 'poured their millions into Muslim welfare funds giving the clergy for the first time ample funds for political action and strikes' (p. 132). The clergy led the revolution but it was backed by the bazaar merchants. The Pahlavi dynasty could not justify its right to rule for it did not have an old family background. On the other hand, the clergy had established a strong credibility and had grassroot influence but above all from the 'history of Islamic countries Islam appears to have laid a foundation for tyranny and authoritarianism. But looked at from the vantage point of Islamic history and theology, Islam appears to have played a freeing and democratic role' (p. 135) and safeguarding the rights of the people by placing them all as equal before the law. This was the type of Islam taught to generations of Iranian theology students and which lent its dynamic force of the revolution.

299 GILANI, *Ayatollah* Mohammadi, 'Judgement in Islam'. *Message of Revolution*, No. 6, n.d. Pp. 31–33.

A brief discussion of Islamic justice by the President of the Islamic Revolutionary Courts of Tehran.

300 GOODEY, C., 'Workers Council in Iranian Factories.' Washington, DC: MERIP Reports Series, No. 88, Vol. 10, No. 5, June 1980. Pp. 5–14.

The writer makes observations about the workers council in Iranian factories. He finds that the experience has been unique for the workers and useful for mobilization during the revolution. But no attempt has been made to institutionalize it, generalize from it or co-ordinate the activities of various councils in different factories.

301 GRAHAM, R., *Iran: the illusion of power*. London: Croom Helm, 1978.

The author looks at the various factors that led to the Islamic revolution in Iran. He contends that Mohammad Reza Shah was the prime cause of it for he weakened all individuals and institutions that might challenge him and strengthened his own power. Money was considered the panacea for Iran's problems but in reality it only disguised them. Many groups were responsible for causing the upheaval, such as the Bazaar traders, students, guerilla groups, women and 'the Khomeini phenomenon'. The author however has not been able to dissect a spring-head of the Khomeini phenomenon in terms of Islam but lists the causes of the grievances of the clergy such as corruption in society, the uncertain nature of state financial support and the rise of Bahaiism, etc. (p. 221). In one of the Appendices the author gives a brief biographical note on Khomeini.

302 GREIG, I., 'Iran and the lengthening Soviet shadow'. *Atlantic Community Quarterly*, Vol. 17, No. 1, 1979. Pp. 66–72.

This paper makes the observation that Iran has become the hot-bed of Soviet activities. For example, Robert Moss's publication from the Institute for the Study of Conflict, *The campaign to destabilize Iran*, gives details of the strategies of Soviet intelligence agents in recruiting Iranians. Another publication surveyed is the weekly journal, *Navid*—issued by the Tudeh Party in Iran. In one of its issues, entitled 'The Tudeh Party and the Muslim Movement' it suggested that there was a close cooperation between the Islamic and the Communist forces to fight their enemies. These publications take a pro-Soviet line and have been appearing weekly in the streets of Tehran. The author concludes 'The fact that the West nowadays seems to be so often in the position of merely attempting to catch up with events, instead of trying to shape them, is probably due in part to the damage done to Western intelligence services by the witch hunt against them by sections of the media. It is clearly damage that must be repaired at once if there is to be any hope for the emergence of a constructive Western strategy to meet the dangers of a steadily worsening international situation, now centered in the Persian Gulf region' (p. 70).

303 GRIFFITH, W. E., 'The revival of Islamic fundamentalism: the case of Iran'. *The Universal Message*, Vol. 1, No. 6, November 1979. Pp. 16–20.

The author considers that the Western model of modernization has had successes in the Sinic Confucian cultural area of Japan, South Korea, Hong Kong and Singapore, but encounters difficulty in the Muslim world because 'Islam is an all-embracing system of social and political order, embodied in the code of law and contained in the Qur'an and the Sharia' (p. 16). Within this framework the author analyses the case of Iran which he maintains contains two

political traditions, antique Persian kinship and Shia Islam. Shia
Islam more than Sunni Islam has a potential for revolt dating from
the seventh century battle of Karbala. As such he discusses Shia
doctrines to show their tradition of revolt. In the case of the revolution in Iran the role of the Ulama as well as intellectuals was
important. Ali Shariati, the sociologist, criticized the Ulama for
preaching a passive, contemplative version of Shia Islam which
limited Islam to ritual and law when 'in fact it should be a revolutionary social creed' (p. 19). Thus Shariah bridged the gap between
the Ulama and the intellectuals by giving a revolutionary interpretation of Islam and so activating the revolution.

304 HAAS, R., 'Saudi Arabia and Iran: the twin pillars in revolutionary times', in H. Amirsadeghi (ed.), *The security of the Persian
Gulf*. London: Croom Helm, 1981. Pp. 151–169.

Four major areas of Saudi-Iranian interaction have been examined. These are, oil, arms, regional security and Israel's existence.
The differences between the contexts of the two countries have also
been examined and their implications for revolutionary change
that has occured in Iran and its potential in Saudi Arabia. The
influence of US foreign policy on the two countries has also been
effected by the revolution in one of the pillars and this leads the
author to conclude that 'what is most significant about Iran is not
so much what it is as what it is no longer. As a result, and as any
architect would point out, the stress on the remaining pillar is much
greater, and stability all the more difficult to maintain' (p. 168).

305 HAIRI, Abdul-Hadi, *Shiism and constitutionalism in Iran*. Leiden: E.
J. Brill, 1977.

The work focuses on the career and writings of Mirza Muhammad
Husayn Naini (1860–1936) and his role in the constitutional revo-
lution. An important work in understanding the Ulama's role in
Iranian politics.

306 HALLIDAY, Fred, *After the Shah*. Washington, DC: Institute for
Policy Studies (Issue Paper series), 1980. 13 pp.

The paper focuses on the seven main opposition groups who were
responsible for the downfall of the Pahlavi regime. These were (1)
the religious opposition; (2) the National Front and other middle-
class political groups; (3) the professional organizations; (4) the
Tudeh Party and its off-shoots; (5) the guerilla groups; (6) the
groups representing different nationalities and (7) the student community. In conclusion, the author states that 'Iran will have to
build a new order in which the demands of those ignored and
repressed under the Shah's regime will have to be reckoned with'
(p. 13).

307   HALLIDAY, Fred, 'Iran's revolution: the first year'. Washington, DC: MERIP Reports Series, No. 88, Vol. 10, No. 5, June 1980. Pp. 3–5.

An analysis of the first year of the revolution pointing out that: (1) the revolution was a major defeat for US imperialism; (2) the collapse of the old regime has opened up new political initiatives; (3) more rhetoric has taken place than actual socio-economic transformation; (4) the nationalities issue remains to be assessed; (5) the economy remains in a precarious condition; (6) the forces of the left remain weaker than Islam; (7) international ramifications contain hidden dangers.

308   HALLIDAY, Fred, 'Theses on the Iranian revolution'. *Race and Class*, Vol. XXI, No. 1, 1979. Pp. 81–90.

The author looks at the revolution in Iran from the Marxist point of view. For him the revolution was neither a socialist, social, nor Islamic revolution but a class and nationalist revolution. Although he concedes that 'Islam as an ideology played a major role in the opposition, both because of the ideological-political vacuum prevailing under the royal dictatorship and because of the key organizational part played by the Mollahs and their associates'—yet the 'term "Islamic" serves as an ideological mask to conceal the multi-class character of the opposition movement and in particular to legitimate the substantial role of the petty bourgeoisie within it, since their social power is expressed in the first instance via their influence over the Mollahs' (p. 85). The opposition forces were comprised of intellectuals, urban workers, professional middle class, students and the traditional petty-bourgeoisie. These forces proved too strong for the army because the latter had shallow roots not going further back than the 1920s. Further, since the revolution was nationalist, it was also anti-imperialist. Finally the analysis suggests what the loss of influence in Iran will mean for the West.

309   HAMIDI, *Sheikh* Khalil, 'Khomeini's views on the rule of Shariah'. *Rabitat al Alam al Islami*, Vol. 6, No. 8, June 1979. Pp. 54–55.

An excerpt from an Urdu translation of Khomeini's book *Hukumat-e-Islamia*.

310   HANIFFA, M. H., *Iran under the Islamic revolution*. Hong Kong: Muslim Herald Publication, n.d.

In this booklet, a journalist based in Hong Kong and editor-in-chief of the *Muslim Herald* gives his impressions of his visit to Iran, his interview with Bani-Sadr and how Iranians perceive Khomeini.

311   HARNEY, D., 'Some explanations for the Iranian revolution'. *Asian Affairs*, Vol. II, Part 2, July 1980. Pp. 134–143.

The situation in Iran before the Islamic revolution resembled a barrel of gunpowder. The clergy had pent up feelings against the Pahlavi dynasty for 'fifty years of modernization and secularization which was to, and was intended to, undermine the traditional hold of the Mosque on Iranian society' (p. 135). In this sense it was not a revolution but a convulsion which was conservative and populist and used modern methods like the strike weapon and the masses. The immediate consequence of such a revolution was that 'the clergy, operating like militant worker priests—were catapulted into control at all levels, heady with excitement and possessing power they had never dreamed of in their most ambitious moments; and employing in their service that Mosque-network and mass discipline which throughout all the years of the Pahlavis had remained— as we know now—the silent opposition, a hidden parallel society sufficient to itself' (p. 138). The long term consequences, the author asserts, are just beginning to emerge. First, modern economic development has been retarded. Secondly, national unity has become weak. Thirdly, the entrepreneurial-professional and technocratic middle classes have been half destroyed and demoralized and have fled to London, Paris, Cannes and California. Fourthly, all social and cultural movements have been blighted. The author further poses the question whether Khomeini's revolution will survive him? He goes on to observe 'does he himself understand what forces and indeed who, put him there? Could he afterall been a dupe, used as the only battering ram of sufficient force to bring down the Pahlavis, himself later to be cast away having served his turn? ... Did he see this and yet was prepared to use what help was to hand to achieve his overriding goal? Or was he blind to everything but this: the destruction of the Pahlavis and all they stood for? I think one should not be too sure of the constancy of mass support that he enjoys and the high emotions he has generated. The Iranian masses can be fickle, can be malleable, can be bought. Among other than the simple people, there is much cynicism about Islam—and of the Mullahs in particular—and certainly a contempt for Islam and its exponents among many of the secular intellectual youth' (pp. 138–139).

The author believes that the hidden force behind the revolution was that of the Left. The Soviets must have known more about the political situation in Iran than did the West. The advantage to the Soviets was obvious 'in the destruction of an entrenched and seemingly powerful Western position. The revolution has upset the entire regional, political and economic status quo, and this has been achieved not by force of Soviet arms or direct subversion, but by the unleashing of the old traditional forces of Islam ... to use Islam to dislodge the Shah was thus a two-edged weapon' (p. 140).

312 HIRSCHFELD, Y. P., 'Moscow and Khomeini: Soviet-Iranian relations in historical perspective.' *Orbis*, Vol. 24, No. 2, Summer 1980. Pp. 219–240.

The author analyses Soviet-Iranian relations since 1941, focusing on the Iranian Left in Soviet-Iranian relations. He concludes by observing that although the Soviets dislike Khomeini's policies they do not want the restoration of the monarchy. Also, as long as they do not have complete control over the leftist forces in Iran they will avoid a confrontation between the latter and Khomeini.

313 HODGKIN, T., 'The revolutionary tradition in Islam'. *Race and Class*, Vol. XXI, No. 3, Winter 1980. Pp. 221–238.

The author attempts to find out how far Muslims and Marxists can work together 'from the standpoint of both theory and practice, in the continuing struggle against the institutions of capitalism and imperialism?' (p. 121). Although a Marxist, he believes that this question deserves attention because of its 'intrinsic seriousness'. He analyses the work of Afghani who investigated the causes of 'the poverty, indigence, helplessness and distress of the Muslims' and the work of Sultan Galiyiev through 'all the Muslim colonial peoples are proletarian peoples'. He arrives at the main points on the revolutionary tradition of Islam through the following formulations: (1) The idea that the individual is responsible for his/her own actions is 'a principle of great importance for a revolutionary movement seeking to detach people from habits of obedience and deference to established authorities' (p. 233); (2) The idea of activism generated by the Qur'anic verse that 'God does not change the state of a people until they change themselves inwardly' which allows men to make their own history; (3) The egalitarian-democratic idea in Islam which insists on the equality of all believers irrespective of wealth, social status, sex, lineage and ethnic origin; (4) The idea of austerity (Zuhd) with ideas of puritanism and abstinence from alcohol, tobacco, gambling, etc.; (5) The idea of universality in which Islam seeks to establish a model Islamic community; (6) The idea of history in which the model Islamic community is seen as the future perfect Islamic community. All these ideas can therefore find common ground with the Marxist.

314 HOOGLUND, E., 'Rural participation in the revolution'. Washington, DC: MERIP Reports Series, No. 87, Vol. 10, No. 4, May 1980. Pp. 3–6.

A good analysis of the politicization and participation of rural youth in the revolution in Iran. This youth, working mostly in cities, identified themselves as workers (Kargars) rather than peasants. Their orientations towards materialism in terms of rising expectations, positive attitude towards education and Islam, mobilized and politicized them against the unequal structures of society.

315 HOOGLUND, M., 'One village in the revolution'. Washington, DC: MERIP Reports Series, No. 87, Vol. 10, No. 4, May 1980, Pp. 7–13.

An analysis of the political behaviour of the villagers of Aliabad after the downfall of the Shah. During the latter's rule they were suppressed because the regime identified with landlords. This resentment, coupled with the new government's support of the downtrodden and infused with the slogans and symbols of the revolution, has led to general local revolutionary activity to redress their grievances.

316 HOVEYDA, Fereydoun, *The fall of the Shah*. London: Weidenfeld and Nicolson, 1980.

The author is the brother of Amir Abbas Hoveyda who was Prime Minister of Iran for more than a decade and who was hanged by the Islamic regime for the crimes he directly or indirectly committed during his tenure of office. The whole account is directed to legitimize the political actions of his brother and prove that his execution was unjustified.

317 HUREWITZ, J. C., *The Persian Gulf: after Iran's revolution*. New York: Foreign Policy Association Headline Series 244, 1979.

The author analyses the political situation in Iran from the American point of view. America raised two pillars of support in Iran and Saudi Arabia to ensure its oil supply and to maintain its interests in the region. Both these powers converted their oil wealth into political power and military hardware and, 'as Washington was to help them do so, thus recycling petro-dollars back into the US economy and also laying the foundations of a new security structure in the Gulf. From this set of facts unfolded the so-called twin-pillars policy, in which the flow of modern military equipment and training in its use was combined with US diplomatic support within the region and beyond' (p. 56). The Shah's programme of modernization, however, led to the creation of new pockets of dissidents against his rule as economic inequality spread among the people. The Shah's answer to this rising unpopularity was built on his own personality cult, loyalty from the new economic classes and the use of SAVAK against those failing to give such loyalty. The Ulama therefore led the revolt as the Shah's secular rule threatened their authority, and thus with the support of 'disoriented peasants in the towns and cities, the estimated 180,000 men of religion became the mobilizers of protest and ultimately of revolution' (p. 47). The other dissident groups supported them due to reasons mentioned earlier. Consequently, as a result of this revolution, the military posture of the US has become more active in Saudi Arabia to prevent the Soviet Union and its allies from extending their sphere of influence in this region. The US will also 'have to do what it can to uphold, when challenged, the Saudi monarchy and the quasi monarchies of the mini-states, to protect the struggle for the succession in Iran against external meddling' (p. 62).

318 HUSSAIN, Asaf, 'A select bibliography of recent literature on the Islamic revolution'. *The Muslim World Book Review*, Vol. 1, No. 2, Winter 1981. Pp. 21–24.

This bibliography lists 36 books and 48 references to articles on literature relevant to the Islamic revolution. Also included is a small paragraph giving additional references to source materials such as the Mizan Press in California, and the journals *The Message of Peace* (Qum), *Review of the Iranian Political Economy and History* and the MERIP series from the USA.

319 HUSSAIN, J. M., 'The role of tradition in the occultation of the Twelfth Imam'. *Al-Serat*, Vol. 6, Nos. 3–4, 1980. Pp. 42–52.

The occultation of the Twelfth Imam in Shiism has important implications for the Shiite Imamate. The author discusses the Imamite traditions as distinguished from the Sunnite traditions.

320 HUSSAIN, Mushahid, 'How Western media didn't report Iran'. *Asiaweek*, August 15, 1980. Pp. 26–27.

In this brief article the author discusses how Western media gave a distorted view of the Third World by its reportage. The question is not what they cover but how they cover it. The case of Iran was significant for according to its 'largely unchallenged and generally accepted assumptions' Iran was 'to blame for the hostage crisis, Carter's actions were correct, the Shah was not all that bad, Ayatollah Khomeini is returning Iran to medieval times, only Iran has violated international law, corruption and repression are part of people's lives in Muslim and Third World countries etc.' (p. 27). Such reportage takes place because US government policy and media perceptions, although not under each others control, seem to run along similar lines particularly with regard to the Muslim world.

321 HUSSAIN, Mushahid, 'Iran, setting the record straight'. *Islamic Defence Review*, Vol. 5, No. 2, 1980. Pp. 8–10.

The analysis focuses on how US imperialism exploited Iran from 1953–1978. In conclusion the author observes that the US 'in its rhetoric, manifests a holier-than-thou morality on democracy and human rights in the Third World. However, her practices and professions pertaining to Iran reflect a yawning chasm: a gross incapacity to relate to Ayatollah Khomeini; the popular leader of Iran or its government elected through universal suffrage. Perhaps the reason for this collusion of American policy with the yearnings of sovereignty with corrupt self-serving cliques who are sustained in power through her magnificence ... the US must endeavour to relate to revolutionary change sweeping much of the Third World (Iran, Nicaragua, Zimbabwe etc.) which is a legitimate expression of an oppressed people's quest for a more equitable order ... Given these aspirations, it is not surprising that the assertion of Iranian independence and self-respect has coincided with the destruction of all neo-colonial influence in Iran' (p. 10).

322 INTERNATIONAL INSTITUTE FOR STRATEGIC STUDIES. 'Iran after the revolution'. *Strategic Survey*, Spring 1980. Pp. 41–47.

A political analysis of the constitutional changes, internal dissent, relations with the US and the USSR, and the impact of the Islamic revolution in the region.

323 INTERNATIONAL INSTITUTE FOR STRATEGIC STUDIES, 'Iran and the Middle East'. *Strategic Survey*, 1978. Pp. 50–57.

The article discusses the causes of unrest in Iran which led to the revolution, the attitude of the US and the USSR towards the crises and the future prospects of the revolution.

324 IOANNIDES, C. P., 'The hostages of Iran: a discussion with the militants'. *The Washington Quarterly*, Vol. 3, No. 3, Summer 1980. Pp. 12–35.

The author conducted interviews with a couple of students holding the American hostages in Tehran and gives their views on various aspects of the Iranian revolution: ideology; the role of Imam Khomeini; the qualities of a Muslim Revolutionary; International Law and the United Nations; Christian values and revolutionary Christianity; Islam versus socialism; Communist ideology and Che Guevera; the Soviet Union; relations with the Arab World; the occupation of the United States Embassy, etc.

325 IRANI, R. G., *Changes in Soviet policy towards Iran*. Penn.: Strategic Studies Institute, 1980. Strategic Studies Research Memorandum No. ACN 80016.

This paper traces the course of Soviet policy towards Iran starting from 1941 with the reign of Mohammad Reza Shah Pahlavi. It points out that withdrawal of Iran from the Western orbit must please the Soviets because it upsets the 'pro-Western balance in the Persian Gulf and the Arabian Peninsula' (pp. 14–15).

326 IRVING, T. B., 'The looming Crescent: Carter's Canossa'. *Islamic Revolution*, Vol. II, No. 5, August 1980. Pp. 3–8.

The article critically evaluates the failure of Carter's misguided foreign policy in the Muslim world. This was because Carter's experts were trained in French and British schools of Orientalism whose 'aim was to contain or destroy Islam by occupying the Middle East . . . such tactics might have worked in the past century, but they have brought disaster to American policy' (p. 3).

In the Muslim world, all political leaders have feared the rise of fundamentalist Islam and 'Khomeini's ardor has contributed to the spread of Islamic awareness which reaches out from Iran to other parts of the Islamic world' (p. 6). Consequently, Carter's adversary 'on the world stage has become Islam personified in the figure of the Ayatollah Khomeini' (p. 3).

327 IRVING, T. B., 'The stricken lion'. *Islamic Order*, Vol. 2, No. IV, 1980. Pp. 18–31.

The author believes that Iran is like a 'sorely stricken beast, wounded in many places, the victim of some cruel accident or plot' (p. 18). He focuses on the 'grave crisis' in Iranian leadership between Bani-Sadr and Rajai and questions 'what moreover is to be the relationship between the Presidency and Parliament? Nobody knows, a full year after the presidential elections and two years following the Shah's departure' (p. 30). The author also believes that the Islamic Revolutionary Party who already dominate the Judiciary, now hold the legislature and have 'forced a Prime Minister on President Bani-Sadr' are now taking on the executive wing of the state as well. In this way it is slowly and steadily making Iran into a one-party state.

328 ISMAEL, J. S., *et al*, 'Social change in Islamic society. The political thought of Ayatollah Khomeini'. *Social Problems*, Vol. 27, No. 5, June 1980. Pp. 601–619.

After a brief analysis of the three schools of Islamic political thought, *viz.* the Sunni, Kharijites and the Shiiah schools, the paper gives a good exposition of the Shiiah political theory, in which various aspects of the political thoughts of Naini, Shariati and Khomeini are presented.

329 ISRAELI, R., 'The new wave of Islam'. *International Journal*, Vol. 34, No. 3, Summer 1979. Pp. 369–390.

The paper discusses the potential of Islam as a political force in the contemporary world. The Islamic upsurge in various countries such as Iran, Pakistan, Malaysia, Cyprus, Turkey, Indonesia, etc., is discussed with particular emphasis on Egypt and the Israeli-Arab war. The author discerns two particular developments in this Islamic upsurge. The first is the emergence of a renascent sense of international Islamic identity as an alternative to other blocs (capitalist and communist) throughout the world. The second is the revival of Islam within Muslim countries, which has begun to influence national policies. These trends and the efforts made to achieve them are discussed within the political context of each country. Furthermore, the author believes that it is a fallacy to assume that Islam is practised only by the illiterate and ignorant masses of the Muslim world while the urban intelligentsia, the state bureaucracy and the business community have been disassociating themselves from the Islamic heritage as the focus of their sense of identity. On the contrary, the author argues that Islam, considered in the broader sense as a culture, a way of life and a spiritual identity, is deeply ingrained in all sections of society including the middle and upper middle classes, the urban and rural population and the university communities. This has been supported by findings in the Egyptian case. The resurgence of Islamic tendencies in Egypt has also been manifested through overt behaviour such as changes in dress, abstention from tobacco, growing beards and a keen interest in study and research in the Islamic heritage. Furthermore, this is also reinforced through the refutation of modernization, technology and Westernization in general with the demand that Shariah law be restored. The author wonders how long Sadat will be able to maintain a balance between religion and technology. He fears that if Sadat fails to maintain this balance and the rising tide of Islam dominates Egypt, then the Jews and Zionism will be blamed for it.

330 JABBARI, Ahmad and R. Olsen (eds), *Iran: essays on a revolution in the making.* Lexington, Kentucky: Mazda Publishers, 1981.

This book contains seven articles and analysing the historical, political, economic, religious and social conditions which in various ways led to the culmination of the Islamic revolution in Iran. The various articles are entitled:

1 Background to the Iranian revolution: imperialism, dictatorship and nationalism 1872–1979, by Thomas Ricks [*see also* 392].

2 Development of political institutions in Iran and scenarios for the future, by G. Hossein Razi [*see also* 390].

3 A critical assessment of Ali Shariati's theory of revolution, by Soheyl Amini [*see also* 225].

4 Women in Islam, by Shanin E. Tabatabai.

5 Revolution, Islam and contemporary Persian literature, by Michael Hillman.

6 Revolutionary struggle over economy: some experienced benchmarks, by Allan N. Williams.

7 Economic factors in Iran's revolution: property, inequality and inflation, by Ahmad Jabbari. Lists the economic factors which directly or indirectly led to the revolution.

Some of these articles are important for the study of the Iranian Islamic movement and are annotated separately.

331 JAMEII, M. M., *The revolution which Islam created*. Tehran, Iran, The Hamdami Foundation, n.d.

An evaluation of the Islamic revolution in Iran and its implications for the Third World—for this revolution is neither the first nor the last but 'the value and importance of this Revolution is not only in its amazing and unexpected victory but it is more in fact in this that it brought about a new method and way of thinking' (p. 64), which could direct the deprived and oppressed people of the Third World towards independence and freedom.

332 JANSEN, G. H., 'International Islam: Muslims and the modern world'. *The Economist*, January 3–9, 1981. Pp. 21–26.

The author considers that Islam and the Muslim world not only pose a challenge to each other in the present context but have been in disaccord with each other for the last 1,500 years. This is not only due to oil wealth or geographical contiguity but because religion and politics are integrated in Islam. Hence, when any forces of change contradict the Koran, it creates an inescapable dilemma which in turn gives rise to various types of Islamic responses. In the Iranian case, there can be 'no discussion about the nature of the Koranic state, only acceptance or rejection' (p. 22). According to a second group 'Islam must indeed adapt itself to the twentieth century but that, at the same time, the divine immunity of the Koran cannot be questioned' (p. 22). The Jamaat-i-Islami represents this view. The third group argues that to 'a certain extent Islam must adapt to the twentieth century but in many very important respects the twentieth century must also adapt itself to Islam' (p. 22). This view is held by the younger generation of the Jamaat-i-Islami and the followers of Bani Sadr. The fourth group argues 'why shouldn't the twentieth century adapt itself to Islam? The Koran is a complete guide in all its points, but it can be given a modern interpretation' (p. 22). This group is represented by the Islamic Mujaheddin and the Movement of Militant Muslims led by Habibullah Peyman and other thinkers in Indonesia such as H. M. Rasjidi and Saifuddin Anshari.

333 JAVADI, Ali Asghar Hadj-Syed, *Letters from the great prison: an eyewitness account of the human and social conditions in Iran*, trans. by the Committee for Human Rights in Iran. Washington, DC: Committee for Human Rights in Iran, 1978.

Javadi is a well known Iranian writer and this booklet contains his observations and the letter written by himself to the Prime Minister of Iran as well as a letter written by 32 prominent Iranians to the Prime Minister about the condition of human rights in Iran.

334 JAZANI, Bizhan, *Capitalism and revolution in Iran*. London: Zed Publications, 1980. 51 pp.

Jizani was a founder member of a Marxist group in Iran, popularly known as the Fidaiyan-i-Khalq (FID). The book therefore offers an introduction to FID thinking about Iran in a Marxist framework. In short, the theme is that Iran, through the penetration of capitalist ideologies and the collaboration of the native bourgeoisie with the capitalist forces had become a US dependent. Hence the message is that to bring about change class struggle must continue.

335 KEDDIE, N. R., 'Iran: change in Islam: Islam and change'. *International Journal of Middle Eastern Studies*, Vol. II No. 4, 1980. Pp. 527–542.

The case of Iran is based within a general framework of why Islamic revival is taking place in the Muslim world. These factors are (1) unequal distribution of wealth; (2) uprooting of people from rural to urban slums; (3) Western influence; (4) support of Israel by Western governments; (5) Western style governments who have only encouraged oligarchies or dictatorships. Iran was no exception to these factors and given Khomeini's charismatic leadership and uncompromising stand against the Shah towards which both secular and non-secular forces had turned against, it was easy for the Islamic revolution to take place.

The Islamic revival in Iran however was not solely attributed to Khomeini but to the writings of many 'lay Islamic progressive authors' such as Shariati (1933–1977), Al-e-Ahmad (d. 1969), Abul Hassan Bani Sadr as well as Ulama like Mahmud Talegani (1910–1979) and Ayatollah Kazen Shariatmadari. The above factors and the ideas of these men in projecting Shii ideology were therefore instrumental in igniting the revolution.

336 KEDDIE, N. R., 'The Iranian power structure and social change 1800–1969: an overview'. *International Journal of Middle Eastern Studies*, Vol 2, 1971. Pp. 3–20.

The author discusses the power structure in Iran and as regards the Ulama observes that 'the position of the Ulama seems bound to continue in general to decline as literacy, secular schools and scientific education spreads' (p. 17).

337 KEDDIE, N. R., 'Oil, economic policy and social conflict in Iran'. *Race and Class*, Vol. XXI, No. 1, 1979. Pp. 13–29.

Keddie shows the importance of oil in the transformation of Iran. It was the prominent feature of Pahlavi rule, who monopolized it and decided the policy for the allocation of its resources. It helped finance Iran's development plans and influenced industrial expansion by giving tax holidays and encouraged foreign investors, while reform in the organism area was not comparable to it. The outcome of such policies was that the rich became richer while the urban migrants, bazaar classes, students and the Ulamas were ignored. The potential of this was felt in the cities, because while 'growing numbers of urban-educated Iranians were Westernized and secularized, their place was in a sense taken by religious rural migrants into the towns and by the students, who increasingly came from petty bourgeoisie religious classes—hence the total number of religious believers in the towns must have increased, even apart from the modernists who turned to the radical religion of men like Dr. Ali Shariati' (p. 27).

338 KEDDIE, N. R., 'Religion and irreligion in early Iranian nationalism'. *Comparative Studies in Society and History*, Vol. II, 1961–62. Pp. 265–295.

The author discusses the intellectual background of the Constitutional revolution (1905–1911) of Iran and the role of religion.

339 KEDDIE, N. R., *Religion and rebellion in Iran: the Iranian Tobacco Protest of 1891–1892*. London: Frank Cass, 1966.

The Tobacco revolution of 1891 was a precursor of the Iranian Constitutional revolution of 1905–1911. The role played in it by the leading Shii Mojtahed is important to the understanding of the role of the Ulama in Iran.

340 KEDDIE, N. R., 'Religion, society and revolution in modern Iran', in M. E. Bonine and N. R. Keddie, eds, *Modern Iran: the dialectics of continuity and change*. Albany, NY: State University of New York Press, 1981. Pp. 21–36.

The author traces the dynamic traditions which have been prominent in Shiism throughout the centuries. She contends that in the earlier centuries the dominant tradition in Shiism was of quietism, which turned to the parliamentary constitutional monarchist in the later centuries. But in the 1980 it has negated such traditions. Radical thinkers such as Mahmud Talegani and Ali Shariati have interpreted 'Islam in ways that would accommodate revolt, change, political engagement and activism' (p. 34).

341 KEDDIE, N. R., *Roots of revolution: an interpretive history of modern Iran*. New Haven: Yale University Press, 1981.

The author shows that the revolution in Iran was characterized by a religious-radical alliance in which bazaar merchants, artisans and secular intellectuals united with religious leaders. The analysis proceeds historically from the Tobacco rebellion in 1891 to the Constitutional (1905–11) and Islamic revolution of 1979. It is updated to the mid-1981 period.

342 KEDDIE, N. R., 'The roots of the Ulama power in modern Iran', in N. R. Keddie, ed. *Scholars, saints and sufis: Muslim religious institutions since 1500.* Berkeley, Calif.: University of California Press, 1972. Pp. 211–229.

Keddie explains why the Iranian Ulama have retained and exercised much more political power than the Ulama of other Middle Eastern countries.

343 KEDDIE, N. R., 'Understanding the Iranian revolution'. *The Center Magazine* (The Hutchins Center for the Study of Democratic Institutions, Santa Barbara, California), Vol. 13, No. 3, 1980. Pp. 38–46.

The author considers that in Iran the Ulama had become economically and politically independent, unlike their counterparts in other Muslim countries. Also, their top leadership, having been outside Iran, living in Iraq, had considerable freedom in political activities. They also had family, economic and other ties with the 'bazaar classes' who had proved instrumental in other revolutions in Iran. Lastly, the Ulama role in Iran has been different from other Muslim countries because of Shiism. All these factors are considered relevant to the revolution in Iran.

344 KEDOURIE, E., 'Islam and nationalism: a recipe for tension'. *The Times Higher Educational Supplement*, November 14, 1980. P. 9.

Islamic movements such as those led by Mawdudi, Hassan al-Banna and Khomeini are reactions to the divorce of Islam from the dominant political doctrines and institutions in Muslim countries. Also 'to guard against the insidious intellectual and spiritual danger posed by the west—just as serious as its political and military domination—these thinkers argued, Muslims had to go back to the original Islam of the Prophet and set up an Islamic polity regulated by the Koranic prescriptions and Prophetic traditions' (p. 9). But 'western civilization still provides the yardstick and the organizing ideas . . . by which all other civilizations are judged and understood . . . the restless centre of political and economic innovation. In the second place, is it really feasible that a modern society of any complexity or sophistication should be governed and organized according to principles which Muslim societies in all their variety from the Umayyad Caliphate up to the present have found it impracticable to follow? To ask this question is to appreciate the spiritual tension which modernity has created for Islam—a tension which is very uncomfortable to live with but for which no resolution is in sight' (p. 9).

345 KEDOURIE, E., 'Islamic revolution'. (London: The Salisbury Group) *Salisbury Paper* 6, November 1979. Pp. 1–5.

The author considers that the revolution occurred as a result of imperialism and the moral decay of the West and its desire to exploit the world. He considers the revolution as a kind of Islamic radicalism and close comparisons are made with Marxist-Leninist ideology.

346 KHAN, M. A. Saleem, 'Religion and the state in Iran'. *Islam and the Modern Age*, Vol. II, No. 3, August 1971. Pp. 67–88.

The author gives a history of 'Shiism and the State' and the rise of the power of Ulama in Iran. The 1963 uprising led by Imam Khomeini is also discussed.

347 KHOMEINI, *Ayatollah* Ruhallah, *Islamic government*. New York: Manor Books Inc., 1979.

This is a translation of an important work written by Ayatollah Khomeini. The translation, carried out by the Joint Publications Research Service in Arlington, Virginia, is good, but both the publisher and an analysis of the contents, added as an introduction, show the biases persisting among Americans. At the beginning of the book the publishers have stated their objective that 'understanding the intentions and tactics of an enemy is the first defense against him. In that spirit we offer this volume'. In the analysis by George Carpozi Jr., the opening paragraph sets the tone of the article by stating that 'like Adolf Hitler in another time, Ayatollah Ruhallah Khomeini is a tyrant, a hater, a baiter, a threat to world order and peace. The principal difference between the author of *Mein Kampf* and the compiler of the vapid *Islamic government* is that one was an atheist while the other pretends to be a man of God' (p. 123). One does not have to read the polemical article any further.

The book, however, is an important addition in the English language to the thoughts of the great Islamic revolutionary. Its central message is clearly stated in the chapter on the 'Need for Political Revolution' in the words 'Under the canopy of a pharonic rule that dominates and corrupts society rather than reforms it no faithful and pious person can live alluding by and preserving his faith and piety. Such a person has before him two paths, and no third to them; either be forced to commit sinful acts or rebel against and fight the rule of false gods, try to wipe out or at least reduce the impact of such a rule. We only have the second path open to us. We have no alternative but to work for destroying the corrupt and corrupting systems and to destroy the symbol of treason and the unjust among the rulers of peoples. This is a duty that all Moslems wherever they may be are entrusted—a duty to create a victorious and triumphant Islamic political revolution' (p. 26).

348 KHOMEINI, *Ayatollah* Ruhallah, *Sayings of the Ayatollah Khomeini*, translated by Jean-Marie Xaviere. New York: Bantam Books, 1980.

These political, philosophical, social and religious sayings are extracted from three major works of Khomeini: (1) *Valayate-Faghih* (*The kingdom of the learned*); (2) *Kashfal-Asrar* (*The key to mysteries*); (3) *Towzihal-Masael* (*The explanation of problems*). These sayings have been selected out of context and tend to give the impression that this edition was printed just to put a book on the American market and to give a negative picture of Khomeini's ideas, for as the book states on the cover, these are 'the astonishing beliefs of the man who has shaken the Western world'. One however does not gain any idea of Khomeini's thoughts after reading this book.

349 KHOMEINI, *Ayatollah* Ruhallah, *Selected messages and speeches of Imam Khomeini*. Tehran: The Hamdani Foundation Publishers, n.d.

A collection of selected speeches of Imam Khomeini given on various occasions between April 1979 and January 1980.

350 KRAMER, Martin, *Political Islam*. Beverly Hills, Calif.: Sage Publications, 1980.

Islampolitik is discussed on an idealistic and realistic level. In the latter, case studies of Iran, Afghanistan, Turkey, Pakistan, Egypt, Syria, Iraq, Saudi Arabia and Libya are discussed. Excerpts from Ayatollah Khomeini's writings are interspersed throughout the book to explain the idealistic levels.

351 LAMBTON, Ann K. S., 'Quis Custodiet Custodes: some reflections on the Persian theory of government. I'. *Studia Islamica*, Vol. 5, 1956. Pp. 125–148.

Discussion of political power in the Islamic theory of government. *See also* item 352.

352 LAMBTON, Ann K. S., 'Quis Custodiet Custodes: some reflections on the Persian theory of government. II'. *Studia Islamica*, Vol. 6, 1956. Pp. 125–146.

The author's discussion continues from Part I (item 351) and the focus is on temporal rulership.

353 LAMBTON, Ann K. S., 'A reconsideration of the position of the Marja Al-Taqlid and the religious institution'. *Studia Islamica*, Vol. 20, 1964. Pp. 115–135.

The *Marja al-Taqlid* is the highest position in the Shii religious hierarchy and the paper discusses its implications in Shiite religious thought.

354 LAQUEUR, W., 'Why the Shah fell'. *Commentary*, Vol. 67, No. 3, March 1978. Pp. 47–55.

An apologistic account of the Shah, attributing the downfall of his regime to the corruption of the people surrounding him because 'the Shah himself was a very wealthy man, and was not out for personal gain' (p. 48). Also it is considered that another factor was that the Shah stayed for too long on his throne, during the course of which Egypt was ruled by Farouk, Neguib, Nasser and Sadat, Syria by a dozen colonels and generals and America by seven Presidents, and so 'all the frustrations were directed at him' (p. 49). The clergy, it is considered, revolted because of the Shah's policy on agriculture, women, religious courts, etc., and fundamental Islam and was 'xenophobic and intolerant towards infidels, thus by a stretch of imagination it could pass off as anti-imperialist' (p. 51). The Shah's system was replaced by another 'autocracy' which envisaged a state dominated by the clergy and Sharia and which was 'a little inconvenient for their Western sympathisers' (p. 52). The Ayatollah himself, it is contended, was surrounded by some 'curious advisors whose prime loyalty is certainly not to Allah and his prophets and this inevitably raises the question who has been manipulated by whom and what foreign power (or powers) have supported the Khomeini operation' (p. 52).

355 LEEDEEN, M. and W. Lewis, *Debacle: the American failure in Iran*. New York: Alfred Knopf, 1980.

The book covers the period from the second half of 1978 to early 1979 when the Islamic revolution succeeded in Iran. It focuses on the faults of American foreign policy and the Carter administration's attempts to salvage their disaster in Iran. (*See also* 247).

356 LOIS, B., 'Revolutionary Iran and its tribal peoples'. Washington, DC: MERIP Reports Series, No. 87, Vol. 10, No. 4, May 1980. Pp. 14–20.

An account of the political behaviour of the tribal people during the revolution and afterwards.

357 McGEEHAN, R., 'Carter's crises: Iran, Afghanistan and Presidential politics'. *World Today*, Vol. 36, Part 5, May 1980. Pp. 163–171.

This paper discusses Carter's politics with Iran and Afghanistan. It is argued that Carter's prime concern for the release of the American hostages took on a secondary importance when the Russian's invaded Afghanistan. This shift in American policy occurred because the Russian invasion posed a greater threat to the resources in the Gulf.

358 MANSUR, Abul Kasim, 'The crisis in Iran: why the US ignored a quarter century of warning'. *Armed Forces Journal International*, January 1979. Pp. 26–33.

A perceptive article warning the US to take an 'intelligent approach to intelligence' surveillance in developing nations. The case of Iran is discussed to prove the failure of US policy and a note of caution is added so that a revolution may not occur in countries where the US has vested interests like Saudi Arabia, Indonesia, Korea and the Philippines. The US must rethink five critical aspects of its relationship with Iran and other countries and these are: (1) The US must accept the risk involved in its contact with pro-Western countries and the unpredictability inherent in these countries; (2) It must adopt a new realism in providing military aid to such countries; (3) It must improve its approach in analysing the economic development of these countries; (4) It must rethink its policy for the education of the youth of these countries; (5) It must rethink its approach to intelligence networks in these countries and its reporting about it.

The article then proceeds to point out that there were many long- and short-term indicators which could have warned the US of the impending crisis in Iran. Some of these long-term indicators were the exploding population growth, resentment of youth, urbanization, the time-bomb of urban workers, students as a political force, bureaucratization, unstable military and policies such as the 'white revolution' which failed to work. Some of the short-term indicators were the Shah's authoritarianism, creation of a police state, oil wealth, corruption and growth without progress, etc. Misreporting and ignorance of all these factors led to the revolution.

359 MILLWARD, W. G., 'Aspects of modernism in Shia Islam'. *Studia Islamica*, Vol. 137–138, 1973. Pp. 111–128.

The influence of modernism in Shii Islam is surveyed by the author through the writings of influential Shii thinkers. He concludes that 'this increased literary activity has obviously not assumed such proportions where it constitutes a total re-examination or reformulation of the structure of religious thought in Shia Islam. It may be fairly said however that it represents evidence of increasing awareness on the part of greater numbers of clerics and committed laymen to the need for general scrutiny of religious norms and beliefs with a view to a reconstitution and restatement thereof in terms more meaningful in a modern context' (p. 128).

360 MINISTRY OF ISLAMIC GUIDANCE, A biography of Imam Khomeini. Tehran: the Ministry, 1982. 24p.

Booklet published by the Ministry to mark the Celebrations of Third Anniversary of the Victory of the Islamic Revolution in Iran. It focuses mainly on Imam Khomeini's political struggles.

361 MINISTRY OF ISLAMIC GUIDANCE, *A biography of Martyr Ayatollah Beheshti.* Tehran, the Ministry, 1982. 12p.

Booklet published under the auspices of the Council for the Celebrations of the Third Anniversary of the Victory of the Islamic Revolution in Iran. It is a biography of one of the most important figures of the Islamic Revolution, who was assassinated.

362 MINISTRY OF ISLAMIC GUIDANCE, *A biography of President Martyr Rajai.* Tehran, the Ministry, 1982. 26p.

Booklet published under the auspices of the Council for the Celebrations of the Third Anniversary of the Victory of the Islamic Revolution in Iran. It is the biography of one of the most important political figures of the Islamic Revolution, who was assassinated.

363 MINISTRY OF ISLAMIC GUIDANCE, *The Imam and the Ommat.* Tehran, the Ministry, n.d.

This publication contains the messages of Ayatollah Khomeini on the American hostages in Iran.

364 MINISTRY OF ISLAMIC GUIDANCE, *Imam Khomeini's message for April 1st.* Tehran: the Ministry, 1982. 15p.

Booklet containing Khomeini's message to the nation on 1 April 1979 declaring the establishment of the Islamic Republic after the referendum had voted in its favour.

365 MINISTRY OF ISLAMIC GUIDANCE, *Imam Khomeini's message for Black Friday,* Tehran: the Ministry, 1982. 17p.

Booklet containing the text of Imam Khomeini's message to the nation on Black Friday (8 September 1978) when thousands of people were killed in the Martyr's Square by the Shah's troops.

366 MINISTRY OF ISLAMIC GUIDANCE, *Imam Khomeini's message for February 11th.* Tehran: the Ministry, 1982. 27p.

Booklet containing Khomeini's message to the nation on 11 February, 1980, marking the First Anniversary of the Victory of the Islamic Revolution in Iran.

367 MINISTRY OF ISLAMIC GUIDANCE, *Imam Khomeini's views and particularities of Divine Religions.* Tehran: the Ministry, 1982. 31p.

Booklet containing brief excerpts from Khomeini's speeches under the following titles 'Imam Khomeini's views on faith and reliance upon God'; 'The characteristics of Islam as viewed by Imam Khomeini'; and 'Imam Khomeini's views on the relationship between religion and politics'.

368 MINISTRY OF ISLAMIC GUIDANCE, *Imam Khomeini*'s *views on the Superpowers*. Tehran: the Ministry, 1982. 27p.

Booklet containing brief excerpts of Imam Khomeini's speeches on the superpowers as well as statements in support of liberation movements throughout the world.

369 MINISTRY OF ISLAMIC GUIDANCE, *The messages of the Imam of the Ummat*. Tehran: the Ministry, 1981.

A collection of Ayatollah Khomeini's speeches during the June 1963 uprising in Iran.

370 MOAZZAM, Anwar, 'Resurgence of Islam: the role of the state and the peoples.' *The Bulletin of Christian Institutes of Islamic Studies*, Vol. II, No. 4, October–December 1979. Pp. 14–24.

The author begins by discussing what is the meaning of Islamic resurgence. The ideology of Khomeini and Ali Shariati, he contends, ignited the Islamic revolution in Iran but the resurgence still requires answers to many questions which he poses without answering. These questions are: (1) Is the present phenomena really an Islamic resurgence or is Islam being used as an ideological weapon by various groups to serve their own interests in certain countries?; (2) Can Islamization be effected through state-authority? If so, is it in tune with the Qur'anic spirit? How does it compare with Islamization of the Arabs by the Prophet prior to the emergence of a Muslim State? Would it not be more valid to assume that Islamization depends on the success of movements among the people, as such?; (3) Can the traditional religious elite—the Ulama—run a state in the modern world? At least the Muslim history does not affirm it; (4) Can an Islamic state survive on the basis of the political and economic theories formulated by the medieval Muslim jurists? In case a revaluation of these theories is essential, in what way can the possible conflicts between areas of cultural necessity and cultural identity be resolved?; (5) What is the status and strength of the modernist point of view (as represented in Jamaluddin Afghani, Sir Syed and Iqbal) in the shaping of a workable Islamic system? (pp. 23–24).

371 MONTAZERI, *Ayatollah* Hussein Ali, 'Surely the frailest of all dwellings is that of the spider'. *Message of Revolution*, No. 6, n.d. Pp. 6–7.

Montazeri is Khomeini's successor and in this message to the Iraqis he analyses the 'extraordinary role of Ashura and the martyrdom of the Vanguard of Martyrs and the freedom lovers of the world' (p. 6), as the root of the Islamic movement.

372 MUTAHERY, M., *Islamic movements in twentieth century.* Tehran: Great Islamic Library, 1979.

The author starts by describing the movements led by Sayyid Jamal-ud-Din, Sheikh Mohammad Abdoh and Abdur Rehman Kawakebee and Iqbal. The focus then shifts to the Iranian Islamic Movement in which the author discusses its nature, objectives and the perils involved. The Iranian Islamic movement was not restricted to a particular class or group but the rich and the poor, the man and the woman, the school boy and the scholar, the warehouse man and the factory labourer, the artisan and the peasant, the clergy and the teacher, the literate and the illiterate—all fell into its gambit. Once the man achieves 'divine awakening in himself and higher human values become to him his objectives ... he becomes the upholder of justice ... and searches for "Islamic values"' (p. 58).

But the roots of the movement have to be traced during the last half century which was acting contrary to the Islamic values in Iran. Some of these were the barbaric despotism, denial of freedom of every kind, maintaining distance between religion and politics, violation of Islamic laws, severing relations with Islamic countries, etc.

373 MUTAHERY, M., *The martyr.* Tehran: Great Islamic Library, 1980.

An exposition of martyrdom in Islam which was a very important aspect of the Islamic revolution in Iran.

374 NASH, M., 'Islam in Iran: turmoil, transformation or transcendence?' *World Development,* Vol. 8, Nos. 7-8, 1980. Pp. 555-561.

Shiite Islam is considered to express itself through popular religious dramas and expressions which are expressions of the meanings of the Shiism. The clergy therefore are a powerful force of social change and through turmoil keep change in Iran from moving too precipitously away from the Shiite world view.

375 NASR, S. H., 'Ithna Ashari Shiism and Iranian Islam', in A. J. Arberry, ed., *Religion in the Middle East.* Cambridge: Cambridge University Press, 1976. Pp. 96-118.

The author discusses the role, ritual and doctrines of Ithna Ashari Shiism in Iran.

376 NOBARI, Ali Reza, *Iran erupts*. Stanford: InterAmerican Documentation Group, 1978. 237pp.

This book contains a collection of articles by various writers such as Bani Sadr, Helmut Richards, Eric Rouleau, and the message of Khomeini. The main focus is on the repression and torture inflicted by the Pahlavi regime on the people. Other areas relevant to the study of the Islamic revolution are also covered, such as Carter's Human Rights policy, the tragedy of Abadan, etc.

377 NOORI, *Ayatollah* Yahya, 'The Islamic concept of the state'. *Hamdard Islamica*, Vol. III, No. 3, Autumn 1980. Pp. 71–92.

An illuminating discussion of what the nature of an Islamic State should be. The objective of an Islamic government should be to eradicate inequality and the lack of social justice. It should aim to 'raise the standard of living of its citizens, seeing that all material and immaterial needs of the citizens are duly fulfilled' (p. 82). The distinctive features of an Islamic government are listed as: (a) it must have an ideological base in which the geographical, ethnic, national or linguistic background of the individuals does not play any part. (b) It should be unequivocally opposed to burdensome bureaucracies, ceremonies, pomp and splendour. (c) It should be run on a modest budget by eliminating ceremonies and the bureaucratic machinery. (d) Its concern with economics should not divorce the development of the individuals' human and moral potentialities. (e) It should emphasise the character and moral qualities of its officials. (f) It should be free of trickery, deception, duplicity etc., which are elements of international politics today.

378 NOURAIE, F. M., 'The constitutional ideas of a Shiite Mujtahid: Muhammad Husayn Na'ini'. *Iranian Studies*, Vol. VIII, No. 4, Autumn 1975. Pp. 234–247.

The constitutional ideas of Na'ini are discussed in this paper.

379 PIPES, D., 'This world is political: the Islamic revival of the seventies'. *Orbis*, Vol. 24, No. 1, Spring 1980. Pp. 9–41.

The author contends that the Islamic revival has emerged mainly in the 1970s and that it is due to the oil boom. The rise of Islamic political activities falls into three categories: (1) To project Islam to facilitate policies which the author labels 'governmental Islam'; (2) To project Islam as a way of life which has been labelled as 'neo-orthodox movements'; (3) To free Muslim action of non-Muslim control labelled as 'autonomist movements'.

  Each of these is discussed with particular reference to Saudi Arabia, Libya and Iran. In the latter case Khomeini's example has inspired Muslims all over the world because his 'modest personal habits, evident piety, utter determination, honesty, high religious stature and advanced age all contribute to make him a paragon of Islamic neo-orthodoxy' (p. 34).

380 POVEY, T., *et al*, 'From Moguls to Mullahs', by T. Povey, C. Montague, J. Perera and R. Joseph. *The Middle East*, March 1979. Pp. 25–32.

The article is divided into various sections taken up by each of the contributing authors. Povey looks at the various forces in Iran and how the situation will develop in their interaction. Montague and Perera look at how Khomeini's Islamic republic is put into action, and Joseph examines the views of Shariat Madhari.

381 PRYER, Melvyn, *A view from the Rimland: an appraisal of Soviet interest and involvement in the Gulf*. Durham: Centre for Middle Eastern and Islamic Studies, University of Durham, 1981. Occasional Papers Series No. 8.

In his assessment of Soviet interests in the Gulf region, the author refers to the attitude of the Soviet regime towards the Islamic revolution in Iran. According to the author the Soviets have been very cautious towards Iran and did not involve themselves in the revolution through the Tudeh party, etc. Indirectly they have supported Iran's thrust against Western imperialism. Some of Iran's actions also, such as the oil boycott of South Africa, severing of relations with Israel and Egypt as well as Iran's support of PLO, have all been in line with Soviet policy. But the Soviets, the author contends, are concerned with the internal instability of the Islamic regime.

382 PULLAPILLY, C. K., (ed.), *Islam in the contemporary world*. South Bond: Ind: Crossroads Press, 1980.

One chapter of the book surveys various trends in Iranian Islamic thinking.

383 RAHIMI, A. R., 'Hostage crisis: the central Islamic issue'. *Islamic Revolution*, Vol. I, No. 10, 1980. Pp. 19–21.

The author discusses some of the main issues involved in the taking of the American hostages in Iran.

384 RAJ, C. S., 'U.S.–Iran relations: post hostage phase'. *Strategic Analysis*, Vol. IV, No. 11, February 1981. Pp. 537–542.

The article discusses the American attitude towards Iran after the release of the 52 American hostages.

385 RAMAZANI, Nesta, 'Behind the veil: status of women in revolutionary Iran'. *Journal of South Asian and Middle Eastern Studies*, Vol. IV, No. 2, Winter 1980. Pp. 27–36.

The author contends that Iranian women under the Family Protection Law of 1967 had acquired some rights which they are in danger of losing under the Islamic regime. They had wholeheartedly participated in the revolution and Khomeini is reported to have said that they could work as well as travel so long as they were properly clothed. But the ascendancy of other clerical leaders will endanger the rights gained by the women.

386 RAMAZANI, R. K., '"Church" and state in modernising society: The Case of Iran'. *The American Behavioral Scientist*, Vol. 7, January 1964. Pp. 26–28.

The author discusses the conflicts between the Ulama and the successive Iranian governments. He contends that these conflicts have resulted in leaving a number of unresolved problems which calls for policy research.

387 RAMAZANI, R. K., 'Constitution of the Islamic Republic of Iran'. *Middle East Journal*, Vol. 34, No. 2, Spring 1980. Pp. 181–204.

The author's translation of the Constitution is published in this journal and his introduction is important because it critically analyses the controversial issues which arose when it was being framed.

388 RAZA, S. M., 'Iran after the revolution'. *The Universal Message*, Vol. I, No. 4, September 1979. Pp. 32–33.

A brief assessment of the revolution, which according to the writer was led by the dissatisfied ideological and religious groups of Iranian society.

389 RAZI, G. H., 'The background and emerging structure of the Islamic Republic in Iran'. *Review of Iranian Political Economy and History*, Vol. III, No. 2, 1979. Pp. 1–19.

The article focuses mainly on various aspects of the Draft Constitution of 1979.

390 RAZI, G. H., 'Development of political institutions in Iran and scenarios for the future', in A. Jabbari and R. Olsen, eds, *Iran: essays on a revolution in the making*. Lexington, Kentucky: Mazda Publishers, 1981. Pp. 55–76.

This paper points out that in spite of the modernization which preceded the Islamic revolution during the Pahlavi regime, it failed to gain legitimacy which on the contrary was provided by Islam. It further contends that the scenarios for the future are not very optimistic for they could result in chaos, dictatorship of a theocratic or military nature or in the formation of a constitutional-representative government. (*See also* item 330).

391 REZA, M., *Answer to history*. New York: Stein and Day, 1980.

The Shah finished this book in exile in Mexico. It is a narrative of his illness, his disappointment with his influential friends in the West, his dynasty, his innocence and the future of Iran. He argues that there was a conspiracy between The Black (clergy) and Red (Communist) forces in Iran to oust him. He believes that Iran is under the rule of an Iranian Torquemada and that the regime through its 'hatred, vengeance and massacre can never serve the cause of Islam' (p. 189) and is convinced that Khomeini's 'reign of terror ... can only lead to communism' (p. 188).

392 RICKS, T. M., 'Background to the Iranian revolution: imperialism, dictatorship and nationalism, 1872–1979', in A. Jabbari and R. Olsen, eds, *Iran: essays on a revolution in the making*. Lexington, Kentucky: Mazda Publishers, 1981. Pp. 15–54.

The paper spans a large period starting from 1872 when the Reuter concession was granted by the Qajars which opened the door for the penetration of imperialist forces into the country. Such forces collaborated with the indigenous ones such as the monarchy, landlords, industrialists and the military to combat nationalism, which led to the revolution in 1979. [*see also* 330].

393 RICKS, T. M., 'Islamic republic and Iran today'. *Review of Iranian Political Economy and History*, Vol. 3, Spring 1979. Pp. 1–16.

The author analyses the Iranian revolution and relates it to the martyrdom of Husayn. In Husayn's martyrdom, the author finds the essential dynamism of the Iranian National movement. Four important aspects of the Husayn tradition begin to appear in the Iranian movement: (1) Husayn demonstrated the need for the community to protect their principles and leaders against oppression; (2) The martyrdom of Husayn also showed the Iranians the high price to be paid for the ideals of social justice; (3) The annual re-enactment of Husayn's martyrdom also signified the continuity of problems and suggested the methods of solution through the Islamic and cultural medium of Middle Eastern life for all classes and strata; (4) The tenth day of mourning (day of Ashura) during Muharram identified for all Iranians the enemies of the body politic (the Pahlavis, the foreign advisors and Iranian supporters).

394 RIZVI, Hasan-Askari, *Islamic reassertion: a socio-political study*. Lahore: Progressive Publishers, 1981. Progressive Series No. 46.

Emphasizing the multi-dimentional nature of the current reassertion of fundamentalist Islam in Muslim countries, the monograph focuses on its three aspects. First, the reactions of the west as well as of the ruling elite of the Muslim states to Islamic revivalism.

Secondly, the major features of the transnational wave of Islamic upsurge. Thirdly, it identifies three clusters of factors contributing to the rise of fundamentalist Islam. It also includes a select bibliography on Islam.

395 RIZVI, *Moulana* Syed S., *Commandments of Islam*. Qum, Iran: Dar al-Tabligh al-Islami, 1976.

These commandments of Islam are according to the decree of Ayatollah Sayyed Mohammed Kazin Shariatmadari. The commandments relate mainly to the rituals prescribed for personal and social areas of human life.

396 RIZVI, S. A. A., *Iran: royalty, religion and revolution*. Canberra, Australia: Marifat Publishing House, 1980.

The author, a historian, has produced a comprehensive historical work covering the period from the pre-Islamic dynasties to the present. Various aspects are highlighted such as religion and philosophy, art and architecture, etc. In the last three chapters, the focus is on the landmarks of Islamic revolution pertaining mainly to the Qajar period and the Pahlavi period. The Shah's Machiavellian rule, his measures to perpetuate his dynasty and remove Islam from Iran led to the rise of political leadership under Khomeini and Shariati's revolutionary Islamic ideology which led to the success of the Islamic revolution in Iran.

397 ROBITAILLE, G., 'Iran-U.S.: a conflict of values'. *Islamic Revolution*, Vol. II, No. 4, July 1980. Pp. 3–7.

The differences in the value systems of Iran and the U.S.—the former, spiritual and the latter materialistic—has been the root cause of the conflict in Iran. The Americans 'have personified power and money and bow down to whoever possesses these qualities—be it a government, a nation or an individual. The relationship of man to God and man to man have lost their importance for the modernized man' (p. 3). On the other hand, Iran 'in order to provide nourishment for the soul, is attempting to reinforce the values and sacred traditions that were established 1400 years ago by the Prophet Mohammad' (p. 4).

398 RODINSON, M., 'Khomeini and the primacy of spirit'. *New Outlook*, Vol. 22, No. 4, May–July 1979. Pp. 23–25.

The author believes that religion or philosophies are not important because they do not play a major role in the movements they legitimize. What is important about revolutions is that 'revolt is primal and seems up to now eternal as seems the wish to establish (i.e. to inhabit) a stable social order even if that order is inegalitarian. Similarly the need to justify both urges is constant' (p. 23). So the important thing about Islam 'whether Sunnite or Shia' is that it 'is prone to be used as a doctrinal springboard for those hoping to interpret (traduce or betray) widely spread aspirations after the patent downfall of other ideological currents' (p. 24). Shiism 'founding myths exalt resistance to oppression and to the reason of statehood'. Finally, the author compares Khomeini and considers that he cannot be a Robespierre or a Lenin. And he hopes that Khomeini will not be a Dupanloup 'a nineteenth century French Catholic Liberal' with the inclinations of Torquemada (the grand inquisitor of fifteenth century Spain).

399 ROSS, Lester, 'Khomeini's Iran and Mao's China: crises of char-ismatic authority'. *Asian Thought and Society*, Vol. V, No. 14, September 1980. Pp. 150–159.

A comparison is made between Mao and Khomeini, using the charismatic model. It is concluded that both the aging leaders imposed their personal ideological imprint upon their countries. Charismatic authority was enhanced through the use of the media and their followers carried their messages to excess, bringing about disorder in the country. Charismatic authority, it is pointed out, 'is too unstable when the charismatic entertains profound doubts about the wisdom of modernisation' (p. 159).

400 ROULEAU, E., 'Khomeini's Iran'. *Foreign Affairs*, Vol. 59, No. 1, Fall 1980. Pp. 1–20.

An analytical article focusing on the Islamic revolution in Iran. It considers that the revolution 'is like no other. It is *sui generis*. Hence, the difficulty of understanding its day-to-day evolution' (p. 2). The favourite theme of the clergy are foreign domination, despotism and injustice. But the death of Khomeini can create a very unstable political situation in Iran which cannot be predicted except in the sense of evaluating 'the balance of forces such as it exists today' (p. 19).

401 ROYANIAN, Simin, 'A history of Iranian women's struggle'. *Review of Iranian Political Economy and History*, Vol. 3, No. 1, Spring 1979. Pp. 17–29.

An account of the Iranian women's contribution to the struggle against imperialism, from the constitutional revolution (1905–1911) to the Islamic revolution of 1979.

402 RUBIN, Barry, *Paved with good intentions: the American experience and Iran*. New York: Oxford University Press, 1980.

The author analyses US-Iranian relations focusing particularly on the Pahlavi dynasty through to the Islamic revolution and the post-revolutionary periods. The main thesis of this work, which the author claims to be objective, is to justify US policies which were 'paved with good intentions'.

403 SABRI-TABRIZI, Gholam-Reza, 'The acceptable face of the Ayatollah's Iran'. *The Times Higher Educational Supplement*, 28 March, 1980. P. 10.

The author traces how academic freedom was crushed by the Pahlavi dynasty. Professors and lecturers in Iran's academic institutions were recruited or promoted only on the basis of their loyalty to the Shah and not on the basis of intellectual brilliance or merit. Those who objected to this were imprisoned, tortured or murdered by the SAVAK who took over the complete supervision and control of academic institutions. Even those intellectuals who attempted to stay neutral were forced to abandon their position and take a political stand since they were 'paid by the government, they should support the government' (p. 10).

Iran under Khomeini, in the opinion of the writer, has been given full academic freedom, for in the Islamic republic of Iran there was full freedom of speech and thought which took Iran a step forward rather than backwards.

404 SABRI-TABRIZI, Gholam-Reza, 'Why the West fails to understand Iran'. *The Scotsman*, 21 December, 1979. P. 13.

The article deals with conditions prevailing in post-revolutionary Iran which have brought greater freedom and put an end to exploitation of the people with the departure of the ruling elite. The revolution has raised the status of one group in particular, that is women. Those who were liberated in the Shah's time were the wealthy upper class women—for the 'majority still stayed at home and were economically dependent'. The new status gained by women is due to the fact that they took an active part alongside their men to bring about the revolution. Iran's revolution has been a success for it is on the way to 'return Iran to its cultural origins, find its own identity and solve its many problems without domination by East or West' (p. 13).

405 SAID, Edward W., *Covering Islam: how the media and the experts determine how to see the rest of the world.* New York: Pantheon Books, 1981.

An interesting case study of the media and how the media cover reportage on Muslim countries. The author shows how distorted views of Islam and hatred of it reflects itself in the biased reporting of Muslim countries in general. Chapter two is devoted to the reportage on Iran after the Islamic revolution in 1979. Such reportage made 'much of the most dramatic news of the past decade, including not only Iran but the Arab-Israeli conflict, oil and

Afghanistan, has been news of Islam. Nowhere was this more evident than in the long Iranian crisis during which the American consumer of news was given a sustained diet of information about a people, a culture and a religion—really no more than a poorly defined and badly misunderstood abstraction—always, in the case of Iran, represented as militant, dangerous and anti-American' (p. 77).

406 SAIKAL, Amin, *The rise and fall of the Shah*. Princeton, NJ: Princeton University Press, 1980.

The author focuses mainly on the economical, political and military policies of the Shah which may have made Iran a regional power in the Persian Gulf but left him open to internal opposition. The failure of these policies created this opposition which was spearheaded by Khomeini. The role of Islam in bringing about the revolution is not given much importance and the book therefore fails to give an insight into the Islamic revolution.

407 SHANKAR, M., 'Iran: continuing Turmoil'. *Strategic Analysis*, Vol. IV, No. 12, March 1981. Pp. 567–575.

The author identifies the polarization of political factions in Iran. The Islamic faction is headed by the Islamic Republican Party (IRP) while the moderates are led by Bani-Sadr. Other forces have had to take sides. For example, the pro-Moscow Tudeh Party supports the IRP while the Fedayeen-e-Khalq and other leftists support Bani-Sadr.

408 SHANKAR, M., 'Iran: internal struggle becomes sharper'. *Strategic Analysis*, Vol. IV, No. 11, February 1981. Pp. 525–533.

This article focuses upon the internal political conflicts raging within Iran. The conflict between the secular and Islamic forces has widened. According to the former, Iran should be transformed into a modern nation state and they are willing 'emphasize the Islamic character of the Iranian nation, but are in no way prepared to concede the primacy of Islam—in other words their vision of modern Iran does not envisage a theocratic state' (p. 529). The Islamic forces, on the other hand, insist that there can be no separation of religion from politics.

409 SHARIATI, Ali, *Art awaiting the saviour*; translated by H. Fordjadi. Tehran: The Shariati Foundation, 1979.

In this booklet Shariati expounds the view that art has a responsibility to fulfil and can be a saviour of humanity. Art in Shariati's words 'is the expression of the human being's creativity and through the continuation of this being, it becomes an expression of the creativity of God' (p. 22). On the other hand art today takes the form of a bourgeoisie philosophy of entertainment as its mission and thus to 'consider art as a pleasure, a pastime activity, a relief from the rigid industrial life, is to give this lowest of tasks to the most sacred of activities' (p. 30).

410 SHARIATI, Ali, *Civilisation and modernisation*. London: Islamic Students Association, n.d.

In this booklet Shariati analyzes the concept of modernization. It was created by the Westerners but used to exploit the non-Europeans to divest them in whatever form and mould of thought they were. It placed the temptation of modernization before them so that they could break off from their culture, history and religion. For Shariati modernized means modernized in consumption, that is, he consumes new and modern products.

411 SHARIATI, Ali, *Fatima is Fatima*; trans. by Laleh Bakhtiar. Tehran: The Shariati Foundation, 1980.

Through the life of Fatima, the Prophet's daughter and Imam Ali's wife, Shariati brings out a model of femininity which should be operationalized for all Muslim women.

412 SHARIATI, Ali, *Islamic view of man* and *Reflections of a concerned Muslim*. Houston, Texas: Book Distribution Center, n.d.

This booklet contains two of Shariati's articles. The second piece is written in the passionate style of Shariati on the plight of the oppressed peoples.

413 SHARIATI, Ali, *Martyrdom: arise and bear witness*; trans. Ali Asghar Ghassemy. Tehran: The Ministry of Islamic Guidance, 1981.

Shariati's exposition of the concept of martyrdom in Islam which is interpreted in a revolutionary manner.

414 SHARIATI, Ali, *Marxism and other Western fallacies: an Islamic critique*; trans. by R. Campbell. Berkeley, Calif.: Mizan Press, 1980.

Shariati's critique of Marxism is the major thrust of the book.

415 SHARIATI, Ali, *On the sociology of Islam*; trans. by Hamid Algar. Berkeley, Calif.: Mizan Press, 1979.

An important translation of some of Shariati's works by Hamid Algar. The selections give a fairly good idea of Shariati's world view within the framework of his Islamic sociology. Among the translated pieces are 'Approaches to the Understanding of Islam', 'Man and Islam', 'The World View of Tawhid', 'The Ideal Society—the Umma', 'The Ideal Man—The Vicegerent of God', etc. Until all of Shariati's works are translated this book is recommended for reading.

416 SHARIATI, Ali, *One followed by an eternity of zeros*. Tehran: The Shariati Foundation, 1979.

A unique exposition of unity which resides in one, for that, according to Shariati, is the only real unit, the rest being zeros which is nothing.

417 SHARIATI, Ali, *Red Shiism*; trans. by Habib Shirazi. Tehran: The Shariati Foundation, 1979.

Shariati further develops the concept of Alavite Shiism as different from Safavid Shiism. The latter developed a kind of Islam which was contrary to the original teachings of Islam. Alavite Shiism, on the other hand, did not press upon forms as much as upon content which called for a return to Islam brought by the Prophet.

418 SHARIATI, Ali, *Selection and/or election*; trans. by Ali Asghar Ghassemy. Tehran: The Shariati Foundation, 1979.

The author discusses a controversial issue between the Shiites and Sunnis that is, should the leadership of the Islamic community, after the death of the Prophet, be someone the Prophet selected or should it be someone the people elect?

419 SHARIATI, Ali, *The visage of Mohammed;* trans. by A. A. Sachedin. Tehran: Committee for International Propagation of the Islamic Revolution, 1981.

This is the concluding part of a larger work entitled 'Islam Shanasi' written by Shariati. The above mentioned work has been quite controversial among Shia theologians in Mashad and Najaf; it distinguishes between three facets of history, that of a politician, a philosopher and a prophet.

420 SHARIATI, Ali, *Yea, Brother! That's the way it was*. Tehran: The Shariati Foundation, 1979.

This booklet contains the lecture given by Shariati at the Hoseinniyeh Ershad in May 1972. It is an impassioned analysis of civilization and how the poor have suffered at the hands of the rich, the powerful in creating history and civilization such as the Pharaohs who were known for building the pyramids but not the thousands of slaves who died while building it and were buried in mass graves on the site.

421 SHUJA, Sharif M., 'Islamic revolution in Iran and its impact on Iraq'. *Islamic Studies*, Vol. XIX, No. 3, Autumn 1980. Pp. 213–233.

The article explores the causes of the deterioration of Iran–Iraq relations during the pre- and post-Islamic regime. Attention is focused on the Kurdish and Shatt Al-Arab issues.

422 SICHERMAN, H., 'Iraq and Iran at war: the search for security'. *Orbis*, Vol. 24, No. 4, Winter 1981. Pp. 711–718.

The author believes that the war was a consequence of the Islamic revolution in Iran and the policies of its revolutionaries which coupled with the past relations of Iran with Iraq led to the ignition of the conflict. He contends that it has exposed the prevailing insecurity in the Gulf region and that 'American military force does have a useful role in the Gulf: to shore up the crucial but militarily weak Saudi Arabia, to keep the Straits of Hormuz open. But a more impressive military capability is required if the United States is to sustain the Carter doctrine and influence the complexion of future events' (p. 717).

423 SIDDIQUE, K., *Islam and revolution*, Washington DC: The American Society for Education and Religion, 1981.

This book provides an interesting discussion of the basic issues facing the Muslim world. The focus of the book is mainly on Iran and Pakistan. There is a good discussion of the socio-economic implications of the Islamic revolution in Iran. It also raises some pertinent questions about the *Jamaat-i-Islami* in Pakistan in a chapter entitled 'Is centralised organisation Islamic?'

424 SIDDIQUE, K., *Khomeini's Iran*. Falls Church, Va: Research and Publications, 1981.

This little booklet is an attempt to counteract the systematic efforts at smearing the Islamic revolution in Iran by the West. Distorted accounts of Iran by journalists such as Oriana Fallaci have been criticized and there are accounts of personal meetings with Ayatollah Khomeini and Azam Taleghani and the Islamic transformation of Iran.

425 SIDDIQUE, K., 'Revolution and the world's Muslims'. *Islamic Revolution*, Vol. I, No. 5, August 1979.

This article attempts to formulate four types of development approaches which could take place in the relationship between the Islamic revolution in Iran and other Muslim countries. These types are labelled, (1) The Government-to-Government approach; (2) The sectarian approach; (3) The Islamic Movement approach; and (4) the people-to-people approach.

426 SIDDIQUI, Kalim, 'The Islamic revolution: achievements, obstacles and goals' in K. Siddiqui, *et al*, eds. *The Islamic revolution: achievements, obstacles and goals*. London: The Muslim Institute, 1980. Pp. 9–22.

The author argues about a two civilization theory in which Islam and the West both want to dominate the world. The author then focuses on Iran where the revolution proved the 'first defeat of the Western civilization at the hands of Islam' (p. 13). Iran's case was significant also because the West's domination over it was 'imperial, total and complete' (p. 13). Imam Khomeini's achievement in leading the revolution to success was due to the following: (1) Through total opposition to the Shah; (2) Exposure of the regime as a puppet of the US; (3) Not compromising through constitutional reforms. [*See also* 6.]

427 SIDDIQUI, Kalim (ed.), *Issues in the Islam movement*. London: The Open Press Ltd., 1982.

This book brings together a collection of articles that were previously published in the *Crescent International*, a news magazine from Toronto, Canada. The articles cover a whole range of issues on Islamic movements, struggling or victorious in Muslim countries. Most articles have been inspired by the Islamic Revolution in Iran and as such are helpful in understanding various aspects of Islamic movements in general and that of Iran in particular.

428 SMOGORZEWSKI, K. M., 'Ayatollah Ruhollah Khomeini', in *1980 Britannica Book of the Year*, Chicago: Encyclopaedia Britannica Inc., 1980. Pp. 83–84.

Brief biography of Imam Khomeini and his role in the Islamic revolution.

429 SPOONER, B. J., 'The function of religion in Persian society'. *Journal of the British Institute of Persian Studies*, Vol. I, 1963. Pp. 83–95.

The author has described the religious aspects of rural life during the cause of his travels in the north, east and south of Iran during the period 1959–1962.

430 SPRINGBORG, R., 'Egypt, Syria and Iraq', in M. Ayoob, ed. *The politics of Islamic reassertion*. London: Croom Helm, 1981. Pp. 30–54.

The author discusses the rise of Muslim Brotherhood in Egypt and Syria. Nasser, he asserts, defanged the *Ikhwan* to consolidate his own power but Sadat has dealt with the movement differently. Resurgence of Islam in the region 'assisted by Sadat's nurturings in Egypt, has brought the Muslim Brotherhood back to life, but this time it is accompanied by numerous radical splinter organizations less inclined to become part of the President's balancing act' (p. 35).

431 TAHIR KHELI, S., 'Proxies and allies: The case of Iran and Pakistan'. *Orbis*, Vol. 24, No. 2, Summer 1980. Pp. 339–352.

The author analyses US interests and its policy decisions regarding its allies and proxies in South and South West Asia. It contends that one fault of this policy was to make Iran the sole pillar of American support in the Persian Gulf. It was further assumed that even if the Shah fell there would be a moderate pro-Western government in Iran. Consequently Iran's eschewing of relations not only with the US but also the USSR came as a shock to the former. US handling of the Iranian situation also undermined the confidence of other countries dependent on it for support. US foreign policy, therefore, has to be rethought in terms of such questions: Does America have interests in South and South West Asia? Does America need regional allies and proxies? Which countries might serve as US allies? What should be the US policy towards Nuclear Proliferation in the region? What about the US Human Rights policy? What about arms sales? What action might trigger a US response?

432 THAISS, Gustav, 'Religious symbolism and social change: the drama of Husain', in N. R. Keddie, ed. *Scholars, saints and sufis: Muslim religious institutions since 1500*. Berkeley, Calif.: University of California Press, 1972. Pp. 349–366.

This paper discusses the place of Imam Husain in Shia thought and how its symbolic forms can lead to social change.

433 TREVERTON, G., ed., *Crisis management and the superpowers in the Middle East*. London: International Institute for Strategic Studies, 1981. Adelphi Library series no. 5.

One of the papers in this book refers to Iran and is entitled 'Revolution in Iran'. The causes of the revolution are attributed to oil wealth and indiscriminate policies of the Shah, which aggravated the problems of modernization in the country. The renewal of Islam 'represented a traditionalist backlash against the regime' (p. 96). Under Khomeini's leadership, Islam became the rallying cry against Westernization, etc., and combined with the oil strikes made the country ungovernable. The Islamic renewal in Iran however is considered nationalistic and not pan-Islamic. Its impact on the region is considerable in terms of damaging the security of the region. It is doubtful whether Islam will be a sufficient force to bind the nations together for in none of the countries mentioned does Islam provide an alternative direction.

434 WHETTEN, Lawrence L., 'The lessons of Iran'. *The World Today*, October, Vol. 35, No. 10, 1979. Pp. 391–399.

The article analyses the failure of US policies in Iran and concludes that the 'Iranian case demonstrated graphically that in the final analysis Third World nations retain powerful leverage in determining their own destinies, their own mixture of nationalism and traditionalism and modernity' (p. 399).

435 WROBEL, B., *Human Rights in Iran: testimony on behalf of Amnesty International*. London: Amnesty International, 1978.

This is an investigation into the trial procedures of Iran's political prisoners which fell within the jurisdiction of the Iranian Military Tribunal during the Shah's regime. It was submitted before the sub-committee on International organizations of the Committee on International Relations, House of Representatives of the US Congress. The investigator concluded that no legal advice was permitted to defendants in pre-trial detention. Furthermore, the defence counsel could not freely meet clients before trial nor were they permitted to call their own witnesses. The appeal procedures were also unsatisfactory. The Shah was therefore in violation of the Universal Declaration of Human Rights to which it had voted in the General Assembly in 1948.

436 YADEGARI, Muhammad, 'Islam: a new school of thought'. *Al Ittihad*, Vol. 17, No. 4, October–December 1980. Pp. 9–18.

The new thought of Islam, it is contended, has been started by the intellectual fabric of Shariati's teachings, the economic teachings of Bani-Sadr and the politico-religious movement of Khomeini and Talegani. The author then goes on to briefly explain the thought of Shariati and Bani-Sadr.

437 YOSHITSU, M. M., 'Iran and Afghanistan in Japanese perspective'. *Asian Survey*, Vol. XXI, No. 5, May 1981. Pp. 501–514.

The author focuses on the implications of the hostage crisis through the Japanese perspective.

438 ZABIH, Sepehr, *Iran's revolutionary upheaval: an interpretive essay*. San Francisco, Calif.: Alchemy Books, 1979.

The main thesis of the book is that the Shah's policies alienated the significant political groups in Iran. The various protest movements which erupted acted as a sort of referendum against the regime and they finally united due to three reasons. First, because they all perceived the regime as the cause of their alienation; secondly, after many attempts they realized that separately they could not bring about the downfall of the Shah and thirdly, each saw that acts of civil disobedience could gain them concessions from the regime.

The role of Islam in all this was crucial for several reasons. First, it rooted these movements in the mass base. Secondly, it provided them with networks of communication and mobilization through the mosques and other religious centres. Thirdly, the Mojahedin attacks weakened the state apparatus, and fourthly, the Shia clergy by using concepts of 'Jihad', etc., swayed the armed forces from supporting the regime to side with the masses. Within this framework, Iran's revolutionary upheaval took place.

Author index